PRAISE FOR TANGO LESSONS

Adriana Díaz is North American, but she has captured perfectly the soul of Buenos Aires. *Tango Lessons* invites us into the suspense of a tango thriller infused with the unfortunate sinister days of the military dictatorship in Argentina. Her perspective, at once relentless and compassionate, recreates the uniquely porteño alchemy of sensuality, love, and death in a passionate plot that one wants to read in one sitting. Like a modern Agatha Christie, she captures the record of an unforgettable journey.

— Prof. Ana Jachimowicz, The Center for Spiritual Studies, Buenos Aires, Argentina

Tango Lessons is a stirring portrait of a passionate woman, a North American Latina, who's journey first takes us from the urbane and bustling streets of Buenos Aires into the inner sanctum of tango culture, then into the hands of a junta sympathizer from Argentina's Dirty War. Díaz writes with the assurance and grace of a dancer and the grit of a resister.

— Ellen Greenfield, author of *Come From Nowhere* and *White Roses*

TANGO LESSONS

TANGO LESSONS

A NOVEL BY

Adriana A. Díaz

Tango Lessons is a work of fiction. Names, characters, places and incidents are either the product of the author's imagination, or are used fictitiously. Any resemblance to actual persons, living or dead, events, or locales is entirely coincidental.

2017 Paperback Edition

Printed in USA
First Edition: August 2017
10 9 8 7 6 5 4 3 2 1

ISBN: 978-0692932490

Baskerville
AMBROSE
Alias Union Medium | SMALL CAPS
Wade Sans Light

Book and cover design: Alex Martin
"Dancers" and "Penitente" illustrations © Adriana Díaz

For my mother
with love & gratitude
in her centennial year

Al Tango hay que entenderlo.

Es profundo, una cosa muy seria. Enseña a vivir y a morir.

One has to understand Tango. It is profound, a very serious thing.

It teaches one how to live and how to die.

— Gerardo Portalea

CHAPTER ONE

A shroud of humidity fell over me as I left the bookstore and entered the crush of afternoon shoppers. Just three steps into the sidewalk and they pressed in on me from all sides. "Gotta get used to this," I told myself. But, jostled from side to side, my head throbbed with the cacophonous uproar of the city. When a rough shove from behind pushed me almost off my feet, I fought to maintain balance, struggled to get a breath. "Stay calm," I muttered out loud. Then another nudge to my right. Relentless chatter. A noose seemed to tighten at my throat. The curb beneath my feet became a precipice; the traffic, a growling river. Cars, buses, and a flotilla of yellow taxis jockeyed for position in the churning current of *Avenida Santa Fe*. I caught a breath and directed it deep into my chest. Returning to the bookstore was no option. I'd have to push back through the crowd to get there. So I counted my breaths, as Dr. Stern had instructed. Expanding nostrils: In slowly, one, two, three, four. Leaning on a hydrant, I considered the medication in my purse, but my spirit rebelled. "Breathe out slowly through the lips," I told myself. "You can do this!"

For three days I'd imprisoned myself in my new Buenos Aires apartment, afraid to stand my ground on this sidewalk. I'd opened the windows to watch and listen to the rhythm of the city from a safe distance. I expected dense pedestrian traffic, I just didn't know how panicked I'd feel in the midst of it. Finally, it was shame that forced me out. So there I was, desperate and determined to hold my ground. This was the day to find my strength. The day to put the past behind me. I'd had it with fainting spells and sympathy from strangers. "Just breathe," I said. "Breathe, damnit!"

Then a blaring horn stole my attention. I looked up to see a cab coming at me. God! I was standing in the street. When had I stepped off the curb? I turned back and lunged for the hydrant that had been my support.

"*¡Señora!*" yelled the cabbie through the open window. He'd stopped in front of me inciting the wrath of honking drivers behind him. "*Señora?*" he asked again, suddenly beside me. I wanted to respond, but breathing was all I could manage.

"*¿Señora, le puedo ayudar?*" he asked, taking hold of my arm.

"*Si,*" I said finally, and gestured toward the back door of the cab. He opened it and guided me onto the seat. "*Gracias.*"

"*¿Está enferma? ¿Quiere que la lleve al hospital?*"

"*No, no! Gracias,*" I said, refusing to be driven to a hospital. "*Es-*"

toy bien." Whether or not he believed I was fine, he shut the door and ran back to his driver's post.

"*¿Y entonces?*" he asked, looking at me in the rearview mirror.

"*¿Perdon?*"

"*¿A dónde vamos?*" he asked.

"Oh! Where *was* I going?" I vacillated between going back to my apartment or going on to the tango club as originally planned. I reached into my bag for the address. "*Suipacha trescientos ochenta y cuatro,*" I said, quoting the tango guide.

"*Suipacha 384,*" he repeated, checking the constant stream of traffic to his left. "*Confiteria La Ideal, palacio de tango. ¿Seguro?*" He looked at me again in the mirror.

"*Sí,*" I said with resolve.

"*Muy bien.*"

I was surprised that he knew the club just by the address, until I remembered that Carolina had said that La Ideal is very famous. Dabbing sweat from my forehead with a tissue, I closed my eyes, and rested my head back trying to normalize my breathing. On the radio a DJ announced, "*Ahora, la orquesta de Carlos Di Sarli tocando El Amanecer.*" As if I'd phoned in a request, one of my favorite tangos filled the cab. I inhaled the melody, and my heart quickly synchronized its natural pace with the even rhythm of the tango.

The air smelled unusually sweet for a cab, I thought. Opening my eyes, I noticed a no-smoking sign and a deodorizer dangling from the front passenger headrest. I'd heard Buenos Aires had a tobacco addiction rivaling European capitals, so I presumed my cabbie to be either an asthmatic or an environmentalist. Lifting my eyes from the de-odorizer I found him observing me in the rear-view mirror.

"*¿No le molesta la música?*" he asked, making sure the music didn't disturb me.

"*No, el tango me calma.*"

"*¿Como se encuentra ahora?*"

"*Mejor, gracias.*" I smiled to reassure him. "*Era un ataque de ansie-dad.*" Why did I have to explain my anxiety attack to him?

He nodded and smiled, as if it happened to him all the time. "*¿Y esta tarde, la milonga?*" He graciously changed the subject.

"*Sí. Es la primera vez bailando tango en Buenos Aires.*" Why explain myself? Did I need him to think that my first Argentine *milonga* was sufficient cause for an anxiety attack? "*¿Usted baila tango?*" I focused back on him. A photo of the tango composer Osvaldo Pugliese dan-gled from his rearview mirror, telling me that he was at least a tan-go aficionado if not a dancer.

"*No, muy poco.*" He smiled into the mirror.

At first glance I'd taken him for a scruffy character, but a clos-er look told me that his unshaven face was actually groomed as a fashion statement, not a sign of dissoluteness. He was really quite handsome. Only about thirty-five. His crisp white shirt looked new.

"*¿De dónde es Usted?*" he asked.

"*Estados Unidos.*" I confessed quickly, though being an Ameri-can can draw resentment in Latin America. I guess his consistently pleasant demeanor inspired me to risk the truth.

"*O, Americana!*" he said, nodding, "*Mirá vos. Usted habla* English, *no?*"

"Yes. Want to practice your English with me?"

"Yes. O.K." He looked at me inquisitively. "You know, you don't look *americana.*"

"You mean, I don't look <u>*norte*</u> *americana?*"

"Uh," his brow furrows deepened until suddenly they lifted. "*Ah, sí,* <u>*norte*</u> *americana!* We too are *americanos,* eh?" He nodded, repeating his realization. "*Sí, sí, somos **sur** americanos.*"

"Rock music made the world think that California girls are tall, thin, blondes. But really, many California women are *morena* like me. My parents were born here in Buenos Aires, and my grandparents were Spanish immigrants who came first to Argentina, then went to California. Although you could still say I'm a *gringa.*"

"I would not say such a thing to you, *señora.* We say we hate *gringos,* but we love the *gringo* dollars. We trust dollars more than pesos. Don't tell no one I say this, please."

"I know Argentina went through a terrible economic collapse recently. It was just a few years ago. When was it, 2002?"

"*Sí,* 2002, and longer. It was a very, very bad time. Much," he sought out the word, "humiliation, for my country, and much suffering."

"I'm sorry to say I didn't follow the events very closely. I was going through a divorce. I do remember that Argentina had a rapid succession of presidents."

"Yes. And people lined up the streets outside the banks, but the banks locked up. The money was froze." He went silent, and in the mirror I saw his expression darken. He shook his head. "It was a bad time. Still we work to get back, how do you say? On our feet?"

"Yes. But in two years there's been some recovery. That crowd of shoppers on *Avenida Santa Fe* nearly overwhelmed me." I still felt grateful for the safety of the cab.

"Yes, but not so many *porteños* take the taxicabs."

"*Porteños?*"

"It is the name for us, people of the port of Buenos Aires."

"Oh, I see. *Porteños*. Did you drive a cab during the economic crisis?"

"No, I worked for *La Nación*, the newspaper. I have a university degree in journalism. It was a good job, but many people were . . . uh, fired."

"So now you drive a cab."

"I am grateful for a job."

"Can you get rehired at the newspaper?"

He shook his head and glanced into the mirror, "Not yet."

"Sorry to hear that."

"Well, I must see the good side. This job gives me opportunities to study English, so I can read the great English writers: Dickens, Hemingway. You know, literature 'big shots'." He flashed a smile into the rear view. "*Señora*, you OK? You still, uh, what is the word? Pale?"

"I'm just a little jittery." I was sorry it showed. "Now I'm nervous about the *milonga*. Thank you for your concern, uh, what is your name?"

"Alfonso. Do not worry about the *milonga, señora*, the tango men are very smooth with ladies. The tango embrace will make you feel safe."

I nodded, smiling. I was well aware of the *tangueros'* reputation with women. That's why I was nervous.

"*Señora*, can I ask what work you do in your country?"

"It's a good question, Alfonso. My last job was in an anthropology museum. I have a Master's in Cultural Anthropology. But I went on maternity leave just before my son was born and, well, I guess I've been on maternity leave for nearly twenty years." I'd never thought of my life as a prolonged maternity leave, and the new perspective didn't please me.

"You travel alone?"

"Yes. I'm divorced. And my only child, my son David, went away to college this year, so I'm learning to do everything alone. On top of that, when I returned from taking him to college, I found my house burned down to the foundation." Suddenly, I realized that I'd just told a perfect stranger that I was alone and vulnerable.

"*Señora*," he said tenderly, "these are the reasons for your *ansiedad*, no?"

He was as perceptive as he was kind.

"Well, the divorce, the fire, the empty nest, I guess, it's not hard to see the reasons for my anxiety, Alfonso,' I said. "I confess I feel vulnerable no matter where I am, and being in a strange city just magnifies that. I don't miss my husband, you understand, but away from my son, I feel more alone than ever." Suddenly I worried that I'd made myself a perfect mark. So I quickly counteracted my stupidity with a ridiculous follow up. "Of course, I'm a very capable traveler," I said. "Before leaving California I studied self-defense. I'm very good at it. I can kick and punch my way out of any situation."

He turned and looked at me over his shoulder. "Oh, yes *Señora*, I'm sure you can."

"I may look petite," I said, "but leverage is everything, you know. In martial arts, leverage is everything." Why did I have to say that? The lie made me feel foolish, and fear reattached itself when I realized that I had no idea where I was. Even if I'd pulled out the map I'd just bought at the bookstore, I had absolutely no orientation to the city. When the radio dispatcher made the next garbled announcement, I felt strangely comforted that at least I'd followed Carolina's instructions to take only radio-dispatched cabs.

"*¿Estamos cerca?* Are we close?" I asked.

"We turn now onto *Avenida Nueve de Julio*," he said. "Don't worry, I don't cheat such a pretty lady."

I felt guilty that he'd caught onto my suspicion. He was smart, and obviously a hard working guy with an optimistic attitude despite the tumultuous economy. I wanted to trust him, but my vulnerability was obvious to us both.

"I didn't mean to distrust you, Alfonso," I said sheepishly.

"No worry, *señora*. I understand."

An uncomfortable silence settled between us.

"Do you meet friends at La Ideal?" he asked.

"No," I said, grateful for the shift in conversation, "I don't know anyone in Buenos Aires. My friend Carolina, well, she's also my tango teacher in California, she is *porteña*, so she gave me a list of people and phone numbers: her friends in tango. Today I begin to introduce myself. Hopefully, before long I won't feel quite so alone among three million strangers."

"When do you arrive?"

"I *arrived*, uh, yesterday." I lied, too embarrassed to confess that I'd been holed up in my apartment for three days.

"Oh! Now I understand how you are nervous. You are new to our city. How long do you stay?"

"I don't know. I have some family business to attend to."

"Oh, you don't come just for tango?"

"Well, tango is a big part of my visit. I've been dancing for only two years, so I still have a lot to learn. I want to be a *really good* dancer, and of course, Buenos Aires is the best place to learn tango, I mean the whole culture of it. My teacher always says dance is not something you do just with your feet. Tango is a *whole* culture, and it requires your *whole* being. *Abuelo* Carval tried to teach me when I was a teenager, but I didn't have time for tango then. Now, when I listen to tango music, it shoots like an arrow straight into my soul."

"Ah, tango has possessed you." He flashed a broad grin. "This is a beautiful thing."

"I guess I'm very spiritual about life in general. Not really religious, you understand, but spiritual. And to me, dancing tango expresses the soul and the identity. What's in your heart, that's what comes through when you dance: in your style, the way you move, and the connection you make with the partner. When you dance from your heart, it's a prayer."

"It makes me happy to see another country's person so passionate for our tango."

"Well it's part of my history, too. My *abuelos*, used to play tango records when I was a little girl. Sometimes they would dance. I always smiled when they danced because I liked to see them hug. They didn't hug very much. Dancing, they moved like one person. Later, I would stand on *Abuelo's* feet and ask him to 'dance me' like he did *Abuela*. Being in Buenos Aires is a way to touch the spirits of my grandparents. It presents many challenges, but it means so much to me."

"I see that *señora*. Any of your family is still here?"

"Maybe. That's the other business that brought me here. I hope to find my uncle, if he's still alive. I know he lived here from the nineteen fifties to the nineteen seventies. Everyone thought he'd died in the Spanish Civil War, in the1930s, but earlier this year I found letters he'd written to my father from Buenos Aires, dated 1977. He lived long past the Civil War, but we don't know what happened to him here after seventy seven."

"Ah! A family mystery! As a writer I love a story with hidden secrets."

I realized that the cab was surrounded by traffic, some cars so close I could not have opened the doors. "This street is like a sea of cars," I said, "and we're barely moving."

"Yes. *Avenida Nueve de Julio* is the broadest avenue in the world," he said, as if reading leisurely from a city tour manual.

"Even in Mexico City I never saw traffic like this." Cars covered the entire breadth of the avenue, with some divisions of parallel concrete islands dotted with pedestrians and plantings. On either side of the broad avenue tall trees reached for the tops of Victorian buildings, their deep purple flowers fluttering in the breeze. When we stopped at the traffic light, I could see no visible indication of lanes at all. It was more like a scrum of cars jockeying for position.

"Where are the lanes?" I asked in disbelief.

"The lanes are painted on the street," he said.

"But no one uses them?"

He looked around and seemed to notice it for the first time.

"In California, drivers stay in the lanes," I said.

He shrugged his shoulders. "We do what we want," he said. "*Argentinos* are *anarquistas de alma*." He pounded his chest softly.

"Yes, Alfonso, thinking of the Argentines I've known in The States, I think you're right. They too were anarchists in their souls."

"Tell me, why you search for your uncle now?"

"It looks like traffic will give me time for at least part of the reason," I said. "First, the answer to why now, is my aunt Leticia. She was the youngest and last surviving sibling, unless Mateo is still living. She's also my godmother, my *madrina*. I'd do anything for her. She is old and very ill, near death, I'm afraid. Leti never really knew Mateo because she was very young when he left home, and he became kind of a mythical figure in the family. When I discovered a stash of letters he'd written to my father, I found the only thing that made her want to keep living. She begged me to find him. So, here I am."

"What do you mean, he was a mythical figure?"

"Well, some people thought he was a wonderful person, a saint. While others saw him as a manipulative do-gooder, that's someone who does good things for hidden purposes. Mama told me Mateo's story when I was a teenager, and I never forgot it. It began right here in Buenos Aires when her oldest brother, Luciano, was seven years old and Mateo was five. Mateo adored Luciano and followed him like a shadow. One day, when Luciano thought Mateo was napping, he went to play ball with boys his own age, out in the street. When the ball got away from them, Luciano went to retrieve it and found Mateo already running for it in the middle of traffic. Whether or not Luciano saw the delivery truck coming toward them, no one will ever know, but he dove into the road to stop his little brother. The driver swerved to avoid the boys, but as his load shifted, he lost control. The truck skidded, hit a building, then ricocheted rolling over and over. In the end, the driver lay dead in the cab, four boys were dead in the street and five others were severely injured. Luciano's body was thrown far from the point of impact. They presumed he died instantly. Little Mateo and another boy were pinned beneath the wreckage."

"¡Dios!"

"Yes. Mateo lost his left arm, and was hospitalized for months with a concussion. Mama said that a deep cut in his upper lip and a disfiguring scar across his forehead stayed with him for the rest of his life."

"At five years old!" Alfonso's eyes were glassy. "I have a little son," he said, "he has four years now."

"So you can imagine how bad this was for the whole family. But worse than the amputation of Mateo's arm, was the forfeiture of his father's affection. Luciano, *Abuelo's* first-born son, was his great pride and joy, and he blamed Mateo for Luciano's death. Mateo tried everything to regain his father's affection. Despite his handicap he was constantly doing good deeds for the poor and the elderly. A lot of people loved Mateo, but not his father."

"*¡Pobrecito!*"

"Yes, but the story gets more complicated. Mateo's good deeds were apparently directed by a priest who took him under his wing, so to speak. Some people thought his alliance with the priest was Mateo's way of getting even with his father for the rejection. You see, my grandfather was an avowed atheist, so Mateo's relationship with a priest made him furious. *Abuelo* tried to forbid him from going to church, but my grandmother was grateful for the care and attention of the priest, so she encouraged Mateo's religious direction. You can imagine the constant painful conflict in that family. As he got older, Mama said some people believed that Mateo cared less about the charity work than the fury it ignited in his father. She also told me another sad side to the story: her father grew so bitter about the loss of his sons, that he rejected his daughters, as well. I'll never forget her showing me Luciano's photo. 'Raquel,' she said, 'this photo got more love from my father than all the rest of his children combined.'

"Eventually, Mateo went into the seminary, and *Abuelo* banished him from the family."

"Banished?"

"Uh, *lo desterró.*"

"*Sí, sí, entiendo.*"

"The last time they saw Mateo was the day he said goodbye to his mother before going to fight in Spain. Everyone thought *Abuelo* would be proud of his son for that, but when Mateo explained that he was going to defend the Church against the Republicans, my grandfather pulled out his rifle. Can you imagine! My grandmother wrapped her arms around her son and dared my grandfather to shoot her in the back before he touched Mateo. He didn't shoot, of course, but from that day on *Abuelo* declared Mateo dead, and never spoke of him again. My grandmother received one letter from Mateo saying that he'd arrived safely in Spain. No one ever heard from him again."

"Except you found letters?"

"Yes, letters Mateo wrote to my father, who kept them hidden. You see, Mateo and my father were altar boys together. The two families were very close, and the boys were best friends, like brothers, I guess."

As we advanced slowly a shadow fell across the cab. "Wow!" I said, looking out the window, "my first famous Argentine landmark."

"What?" Alfonso was oblivious to the shadow.

"The Obelisk!"

"Oh, yes. The Obelisk of Buenos Aires, is 67 meters high," he said in his tour guide tone. "It was designed by Alberto Prebisch, built in 1936 to mark the 400 years anniversary of the city." His sudden shift of persona made me laugh. He looked at me in the mirror. "I say something wrong?"

"Not at all, " I said, "thank you for the information."

"*Señora*," he said, "this is a soup of cars! It is not far to La Ideal. You can walk from here."

The idea of stepping outside the protection of the cab sent a jolt of adrenalin through me. I'd become comfortable with Alfonso. Yes, maybe I'd said too much, and maybe that made me vulnerable, but he wasn't going to abduct me from here, and the quiet interior of the cab, with the tango music still playing beneath our conversation, allowed me to observe the city safely. I didn't want to leave.

"*Señora*," he said again, turning to me, "you walk to the corner," he pointed to the sidewalk ahead on the left. "You cross with the lights and the other people. Go to *Suipacha*, it is only two blocks. First *Pellegrini*, then *Suipacha*. *A la derecha*, turn right at *Suipacha*, cross *Corrientes*. La Ideal is very near the corner."

I must have looked like a possum in headlights because his face softened as if he were talking to a child. He went into the glove compartment. "Here," he said, "take my card. If you want to go anywhere in Buenos Aires, you call me."

"Oh, thank you Alfonso." I cradled the card in my palm. "When I call this number do I ask for you? Is this a dispatcher's number?"

"Yes, but, you know what . . ." He took the card back and pulled a pen from his pocket. "Here is my cellular," he said, writing on the back, "You call me direct."

"Oh, thank you, Alfonso. I'll keep your card with me all the time. My name is Raquel Camer . . . uh, Carval. Raquel Carval."

"*Encantado*," he said, reaching back to shake my hand. "Soon, *señora*, you will be as comfortable in Buenos Aires as a real *porteña*. You will see."

CHAPTER TWO

I had barely left the safety of the cab when I realized I was holding my breath. So I took conscious steps on the sidewalk counting them in an even rhythm. In my head I played a tango whose title I'd never known, using it to soothe away my anxiety as I kept time to its rhythm. Before long I realized that the counting had faded away and my attention was caught up in the urban sounds of the city. *Nueve de Julio* was not crammed with pedestrians as *Avenida Santa Fe* had been. I had space to move and appreciate the people around me. It was a workday afternoon yet many *porteños* were out enjoying themselves. Some lounged on the lawn around the Obelisk, reading, kissing their sweethearts, or playing with their children. Men in business suits perched comfortably on benches chatting on cell phones. As I walked, I observed the graceful stride of the *porteños* and used them as a metronome to guide the rhythm of my hips and legs. My shoulders relaxed. My neck lengthened in order to carry my head proudly at a slight angle, *porteña*-like. Once I had the attitude, I picked up the pace and melted into the scene. That's when I had my first epiphany: I fit in here. In California I'd been mistaken for a foreigner my whole life, but here, with my dark hair and olive complexion, I looked like a real *porteña*.

By the time I arrived victoriously in front of the big display window at the *Confitería La Ideal* my heart pulsed with the aerobics of the walk, not anxiety. I watched the reflection of pedestrians passing behind me on the sidewalk, and then I saw myself. With my American passport hidden in the camouflage of genetics, I saw my original self. This was the Raquel I'd met two years ago in the tango studio mirrors. Now, after dance training and psychotherapy, after a journey of over six thousand miles, here she was on the threshold of a new chapter in her life. My grandparents would have been happy to see me standing there, I thought, honoring the past and stepping into the future.

In the foyer of the old building I watched dancers arrive, ascending the very stairway my grandparents must have climbed as a young couple. The humidity of the season inspired men to arrive in lightweight suits, or dark slacks and short-sleeved shirts. Women wore eye-catching colors, short hems, and softly draping fabrics. There would be competition for male attention apparently, and these ladies were armed with fragrances, patterned hose, and accented curves. Shoulders and bosoms were tastefully displayed, eye makeup carefully applied. I had dressed in accordance with what I called "the black rule": when in doubt choose something black with eye-catching jewelry and a colorful scarf or jacket. It made for easy packing, too. I knew that my black cotton jersey dress showed off my dancer's legs, and, as I assessed the women who would be my competition, I gave myself a 50-50 chance of attracting partners.

The vibrations of an orchestral tango recorded in the 1940's resonated seductively within the nautilus-like chamber of the curving stairwell. Ascending, my heart fluttered with that sensation I associate with lift off from an airport runway. At the top of the stairs, I smoothed my hair and straightened my dress, then approached the cashier, a young lady with a perpetual smile.

"*Hola*," I said, handing her my pesos.

"*Buenas tardes*," she said sweetly, stamping my wrist with faint ink and gesturing toward my next destination: the hostess. What the cashier had in personality was countered by the penetrating stare and stern expression of the dark-haired Middle Eastern woman whose intense gaze seemed to question my qualifications for entry. She was only about 5'4", but her authority was certain. The closer I got, the more impenetrable she appeared. I summoned my courage to ask if she was Anita. She nodded, raising one eyebrow.

"*Soy amiga de* Carolina Guzman," I said.

"*Ah! ¿Sos Raquel?*" she asked, wide-eyed.

"*Sí.*"

"*¡Bien venida!*" she said, embracing me. Suddenly the impenetrable sobriety melted into warm hospitality. She planted a little kiss on one cheek then the other. I couldn't hear what she whispered into my ear, it was inaudible beneath the orchestral tango that swelled into every crevice of the building. We waited for the music to end before she seated me, and I felt a heavy scrutiny from the men's section to our left. The new arrival, *moi*, was being assessed, it seemed, and as there was no way to determine my level of dance, I figured I was being 'graded' on other criteria. I stood tall and channeled my new inner *porteña*.

When the tango ended, the unexpected music of Glen Miller marked the *cortina*, the interval between *tandas*, or sets. I followed Anita across the marble dance floor dodging dancers returning to their seats. The captivating beauty of the old tango palace, was distracting, despite its neglected and somewhat tarnished condition. Tall marble columns on the right were reflected in vertical wood-framed Victorian mirrors on the opposite wall. Their smoky patina gave an eerie reflection, a timeless image of the setting. I imagined spirit dancers from bygone eras still dancing there within the reflection of my contemporaries. They flashed quickly from my mind as I rushed to catch up with Anita who was waiting for me at a table on the edge of the dance floor where two women sat in deep conversation.

I knew that in tango, as in real estate, location is everything, and hosts or hostesses ensure the success of their event by attracting good dancers and seating them in clear view of each other. Anita must have trusted Carolina's recommendation that I could be a front row commodity. Now I had to live up to expectations, or next Monday she would seat me behind one of the columns.

"*Hola*," I said to the women at my table. They nodded, perfunctorily.

As she left me, Anita whispered, "*No te olvides el cabeceo.*"

I winked at her. I'd done the *cabeceo* only in class when we learned some of the rituals of the Argentine *milonga*. In California, men usually came up to ask a woman to dance, I knew that would not happen here. So I fiddled with putting on my dance shoes in order to observe the actions of the women at my table, before attempting it myself. I saw one of them make eye contact with a man at the opposite side of the dance floor. I had to search a bit to find which one she'd contacted. He was in a dark blue business suit. He nodded to her – *el cabeceo* - cocking his head toward the dance floor. She nodded in acceptance, then waited until he was about halfway across the dance floor before she stood and moved just in front of our table. When he arrived, he led her out to dance without touching her. And not a word was spoken.

Once the music started, she placed her left hand on his upper right arm and her right hand into his open left palm. I kept my eyes down after that, to study the quality of the dancing. By San Francisco standards I was a good dancer, but I feared not dancing well *enough* for Argentina, so reconnaissance was important. My observations proved that, contrary to my assumption, all Argentines are not born with a tango gene. It was easy to determine the best from the worst. I knew that the best dancers would not give the *cabeceo*, that nod of the head, to an unknown dancer, but I needed to determine who they were because dancing with them was my ultimate goal. I had to stay away from poor dancers who could make me look bad, so I had to identify those who were 'good enough' and willing to take a risk on me. I knew they would begin with basic steps then slowly increase the level of difficulty as they gauged my ability to follow. Hopefully they'd eventually allow me to highlight the quality of my technique, as it was certain I would be observed by men and women alike.

By the time Glen Miller played again, I'd clasped my shoe straps into place and sat erect with an inviting smile on my face. I glanced here and there to locate the good-enough dancers I'd spotted, and to my surprise I caught the eye of a classy looking gentleman in the front row of the men's section. With gleaming white hair and cocoa colored skin, I imagined him to be in his seventies. He looked into my eyes and nodded toward the dance floor. I felt my head go up and down. I had accepted. As tango music began again, he came toward me, his lean frame graceful in a black short sleeved silk shirt and black slacks. I stood up, straightened and smoothed my dress, and stepped around the table to meet him.

"*Buenas tardes,*" he said, taking me by the hand.

"*Buenas tardes,*" I replied. My heart beat like hummingbird wings. We stepped into a tango embrace that was so close I wondered how we would move. My body was tense, my face flushed. So much for feigning sophistication.

"You can relax with me," he said, quietly, in Spanish-flavored English.

I pulled back just enough to look at his elegant face. His dark eyes assured me that I was safe. I leaned gently into his chest, took a deep breath, and exhaled the tension that had gathered in my neck and shoulders. The music surrounded us. He shifted his weight from one foot to the other, leading me to shift with him in time to the music. Weight on left foot, weight on right foot. Couples glided past us. Left foot. Right foot. It could have been an exercise for a beginning tango class, except that in his arms I was a woman embraced by a man, and this was tango. It was not an exercise, nor a sexual encounter. It was more like a meditation on the sensual essence of gravity. Suddenly I understood one of Carolina's lessons: Tango teaches that the nature of the universe is allurement.

Tension melted into an eagerness to move, yet we remained in one place, forcing me to release my impatience, too. This is a lesson in Buddhism, I thought. I had to surrender everything to the embrace. He held my entire being in his arms, and slowly our bodies melted together. Then we glided into a broad step to the side, and began the movement of our dance. I went with him confidently, without thought and without fear. We began with simple steps, then through increasingly complex combinations. I let go of thinking, filled completely with exhilaration and joy.

When the music ended, he continued to hold me. I waited for him to release me. Other couples had separated, chatting between tangos, but he never broke our connection. I felt my breathing against his chest and realized that it felt as if we were one person breathing, masculine and feminine, balanced, as in the symbol of the yin and the yang. As I sank deeper into the embrace, the chatter around us softened into a singular hum. The music began again, and I stayed in that state of bliss for three more tangos.

It was Glen Miller who came between us. The *cortina*. My partner stepped away, and we were singular entities again. Back at my table, he thanked me for the *tanda*.

"*Bailás muy bien,*" he said.

"*Gracias,*" I said.

He kissed my hand, then turned and disappeared into the crowd.

Could it get any better than this, I wondered. I felt giddy, as if I'd just been on the best ride in Disneyland. I wanted desperately to share my experience with the women at my table, but only one of them was seated and she was busy getting something from her purse. As I turned away from her I inadvertently made eye contact with a man in a blue shirt beside a column across the room. He nodded toward the floor and I read his lips, "*¿Bailás?*" I nodded in return, and he started walking toward me. I stood up full of reservations. Something very special had happened between the first gentleman and myself. Despite his age, we had bonded in some kind of miraculous way.

"*Buenas,*" said my new partner.

"*Buenas,*" I said. He was younger than the first fellow. In his fifties, I suppose, and a little, well, husky for his height. The subtle scent of his cologne quickly pulled me deep into the circle of his embrace. Pressed heart to heart, we began swiftly, and moved unimpeded about the densely populated dance floor. The tango waltz, like all waltzes, carried us in triplets of rhythm using tango steps. We moved together as one body, each moment fresh and new. When the first tango ended, as others around us were chatting, we disengaged, and stood a single step apart. We looked at each other, smiled, then looked away, maintaining the purity of our silence. This dance, I thought, transcends all the issues of physical attraction. This wasn't a handsome man, but together our bodies spoke a beautiful language. The next tango began, and though others continued chatting through the beginning bars, he lifted his left hand and I placed my right palm across his. Our fingers cupped together, and the warmth of him encircled me again. It was as though I could feel our atoms combine and the music became our universe to dance in, freer than the stars in the night sky.

As the *tanda* ended, we separated slowly. A breeze from the fans caressed my face. My partner escorted me to my table.

"*Muchas gracias,*" I said when we arrived.

"*Gracias a vos,*" he replied, then walked away.

My tablemates were seated. I glanced at them still smiling. They were beaming at me.

"*No viniste para planchar poyeras,* eh," one of them said to me. They laughed.

"*¿Planchar poyeras?*" I asked, confused at the meaning.

"*¿Vos no sos de acá?*"

"*No, no soy de acá.*" I said. They thought I was *porteña*.

"*Ah! Poyeras son faldas,*" said the one with the red blouse. You didn't come here to iron your skirt she said, using an Argentine expression I'd never heard. Anyway, they were complimenting me on getting out on the dance floor quickly and successfully. They thought I was *porteña*!

"*¿De donde sos?*" asked the one with midnight black hair.

I hated to answer truthfully, afraid that being a North American might ruin our budding friendship. "*Pues, soy de San Francisco.*" I said.

"*¿San Francisco?¿Cual San Francisco?*"

"*El San Francisco que se ubica en California.*"

"You are from California?" said the one with the red blouse, in excellent English.

"Yes. Where are you from?"

"Chicago."

"Chicago?"

"Yes, we're originally from here, but we live now in Chicago. We come home to visit family and dance tango once a year. "

The one with the black hair was Pilar, her friend in the red blouse, Fina. They quickly pointed out good dancers, and shared some *chisme* – gossip – that made me feel right at home. I was no longer afloat in a sea of anonymous strangers. Now I knew the stories of the guy who'd just lost a hundred pounds, the woman who deals dope, the bigamist, and the ex-con. I learned an important lesson, too: as in every dance community, just beneath the surface of music, laughter, and conversation, the *milonga* vibrates with relationships and gossip.

The palpable pulse of sexuality in the air, made it a strange place for my spiritual dance experiences. Nothing – maybe not even the act of sex- brings two people closer than tango. Tango puts two people into motion, heart to heart, constantly sharing the dynamics of balance and synchronization. Dancing at La Ideal filled me spiritually the way really great art fills me, with a level of satiety that is also exhausting. So after three hours of dancing I wanted to go home, to rest and savor the sensations and elation of the afternoon's experience.

"We're going to Gricel tonight," said Fina, handing me their phone number on a napkin. "Meet us there around 11:15."

"Okay," I said, "I'll see how my feet feel once I get them out of these shoes." The prospect of dancing in the evening after hours of three-inch heels on a marble floor sounded decadent and delicious, albeit painful.

"Just put them up for a while and you'll be ready to go again in a few hours," said Pilar.

I changed my shoes and tossed the heels into my SFMOMA Toulouse Lautrec bag. By the time the *cortina* ended I was on the far side of the dance floor. Then the opening refrain of one of my favorite tangos by Pugliese filled the room and like Lot's wife, I looked back one last time. The scene was mesmerizing: couples moving counterclockwise like a slow river whirlpool. The scene and its reflection in the tall smoky mirrors captured my heart and imagination again. For a split second I thought I saw those long-ago Victorian dancers and I was drawn into a flirtation with the past. Unfortunately, I must have continued walking because the next thing I felt was the impact of my body crashing into someone else's.

"AY!" A yelp escaped me. I'd walked right into one of the *tangueros* I'd been watching all afternoon: a handsome, self-confidant man, a fabulous dancer, the kind I'd sought to impress. And now I had. I'd stepped right on the top of his gray suede dance shoes.

"*¡Oh*, excuse me, *perdón!*" I stuttered. "I'm so sorry," I said automatically in English.

I wanted to disappear, but he was Mr. Cool: "*¡Muñeca!* Doll!" he said folding his arms around me like an eagle with a mouse, "*¿A dónde vas?* Where are you going?"

"*¡Me tengo que ir!*" I said, nervously. "Please forgive me for stepping on your very handsome and talented feet. I am just leaving."

With that he let out a genuine belly laugh. "Your face is rosey, and look at these perfect little pearls of perspiration here on your *frente*." He delicately ran a fingertip across my forehead. "Why don't you sit with us for a moment?" He gestured toward a nearby chair. Any other time, I'd have accepted that invitation in a flash, but I could feel those "pearls" traveling south, and it was definitely time to get out of there.

"No, *gracias*," I said.

"Well, Cinderella, I'm not accustomed to being turned down," he said, without a smile. I looked at him for a moment genuinely afraid that I'd made a terrible faux pas. Then his lips curled into a smile that was so infectious I had to laugh at myself. He was flirting with me.

"Well, I don't want to get into the habit of turning you down,"

I said, "so please, invite me again when I can stay."

With that he nodded his head. "*Okay, hasta la próxima, entonces,* 'til next time."

"I'll look forward to that," I said, and walked out. On my way down the stairs I hoped he'd remember me the next time. Men are fickle in the tango world, and the better they dance, the more fickle they can afford to be. From the visiting Argentines I'd met in California, I'd learned that one day they regale you with *piropos*, artful Argentine compliments, and the next day they look right through you. It's a seductive game, and those compliments can be lethal bait for anyone who takes them to heart.

Back in my apartment, I felt a new relaxation in my body. I had broken the grip of anxiety, and though I might meet it again, I knew I had defeated it. I could come and go as I wished. I made a cup of tea and brought the computer to the sofa hoping for a report from Marta regarding my *madrina's* condition.

After Mama and Papa died, Tía Leti became mother to Marta and me. Sure, we were adults, but there were times, like when our children were born, that we needed her beside us. I hadn't wanted to leave her, but she'd begged me to find Mateo. The only thing she longed for before dying, she said, was the sound of her brother's voice. So despite the excitement of my first Argentine *milonga*, my mind filled now with thoughts of Leti. I opened Marta's email hoping for good news.

Hi Sis,

How is Buenos Aires? I'm dying to hear about your latest adventures.

Tía has had a pretty good day. She rallies when she sees Dr. Shapiro. He was cheery with her, though the latest blood tests weren't encouraging. Nevertheless, she is stable for now and in good spirits. More tomorrow.

XO, Marti

Next I opened one from Carolina telling me that she'd sent messages to her friends hosting *milongas* in Buenos Aires so they'd be watching for me. She encouraged me to go to the club called Gricel tonight because her teacher, who she referred to as *La Maestra*, was having her birthday party there. She'd told *La Maestra* about me, too, so I must introduce myself.

I went upstairs and lay on the bed with my bare soles elevated against the cool wall. In my mind I made little souvenir sketches of the coquettish women provocatively posed at their tables. I traced lines by memory trying to capture the postures of the dancers. I wanted to bring tango into my artist's eye, hoping I could eventually translate the grace of the dance into my paintings.

Then I planned what I'd wear to Gricel, and daydreamed about dancing with Mr. Gray Suede Shoes. The afternoon had given me a sense of vitality I thought I'd never know again after the divorce. I'd made this trip under the pressure of finding Uncle

Mateo, telling myself that tango was just a side interest. But the exhilaration of the *milonga* fueled a sense of anticipation in me that I'd long ago forgotten.

CHAPTER THREE

At 10:30 I took the TU Radio Taxi card from my purse and dialed the handwritten number on the back. "*Hola*, Alfonso," I said, "This is Raquel Carval. You picked me up this afternoon outside *El Ateneo* on *Avenida Santa Fe.*"

"*Sí, sí.* How was the *milonga*?" he asked enthusiastically.

"It was wonderful. Tonight I am going to a place called Gricel."

"On *La Rioja*, no?"

"Yes, 1180 *La Rioja.*"

"Where should I collect you?" he asked.

"The corner of *Chacabuco* and *Umberto Primo.*"

"When?"

"Now would be fine."

"See you in fifteen minutes," he said.

I waited just inside the main door of my building until I saw him pull up.

"*Buenas noches, señora,*" he said, as I stepped into the cab.

"*Buenas noches,*" I said, settling into the back seat. I expected that we'd take off from the curb immediately, and when that didn't happen, I met his gaze in the rearview mirror. "*1180 La Rioja,*" I said, presuming he'd forgotten our destination.

"Yes, I remember," he said, "but I don't know if I should take you there."

"Why not?"

"*Señora,* you must have compassion for the Argentine men."

"What?"

"We *argentinos* are not like the, uh, *norteamericanos.* We live with our heart on the surface. We have a great appreciation for the women. You look so beautiful tonight, you will make the men have a . . . what do you call it? You know, when the heart is fluttering like the wings of a *mariposa*?"

I started laughing. "I think tachycardia is the word you're looking for, but the flutter of butterfly wings is much more poetic."

"Please, *Señora* Raquel, it is not to laugh at," he said, turning toward me.

"Alfonso," I said, "the Argentines are masters of the compliment, and you are a virtuoso. Too bad you couldn't get a job giving compliments."

"Oh, no," he shook his head, "too much competition."

"Let's go, please. I promise to have the compassion of Mother Teresa."

On the drive to Gricel, Alfonso surprised me with a question.

"*Señora*, today you say you are looking for your uncle. Is that right?"

"I'm impressed that you remember, Alfonso, you must transport a hundred people a day. Yes, my mother's brother. Frankly, I'll be lucky to find his grave."

"You know, if he disappeared during *El Proceso*, he will not have a grave."

"What do you mean '*El Proceso*'?"

"That time called "The Dirty War" was officially called by the generals, "*El Proceso de Reorganización Nacional*.""

"Oh, I didn't know that. I have no evidence that he disappeared. He's very old, ninety-one, if he's still alive. He was a priest. In his last letter he was serving a parish here in Buenos Aires."

"Then you can ask at the office of the Diocese, near the National Cathedral, near Plaza de Mayo."

"Yes, that's already on my agenda for tomorrow. Thank you."

When we got to Gricel, Alfonso got out of the cab, came around to my side and opened the door. I'd given him another generous tip, mostly because I liked him so much, but also because he was teaching me a lot. I valued his knowledge. I didn't expect him to open my door.

"Madame," he said, bowing and extending his right hand to assist me from the cab.

"Alfonso, what are you doing?"

"A customer today told me I should get out of the cab for exercise. Also, a beautiful lady should arrive in good style." I took his hand and stepped out of the car.

"Bless you," I said. "It's late, I hope you're going home to your wife and family."

"Very soon, *señora*," he said. "*Buenas noches.*"

Inside Gricel the boisterous crowd was overpowered by a tango recorded by the Juan D'Arienzo orchestra in the 1940's. The DJ and speakers were nowhere in sight, and the music filled the club as if it were a movie scene. I paid at the door, and as there was no host or hostess, I slipped along the edge of the dance floor to the bar. It seemed a good lookout point for spotting my new friends during the *cortina*.

People were in evening attire. Nothing opulent, but plenty of sequins and fringe for ladies, mostly jackets and ties for gentlemen. I'd read that tango is a pure democracy, not only because it requires equality and harmony in the dance partnership, but also because it brings together the wealthy and the poor, the foreign and domestic dancers. I'd seen that democracy in the afternoon *milonga* where there had been a mixture of dancers from all over the world and the demi-monde. In a dance environment social status is based upon dance values, not capitalist, political, or religious values. So even the most common man, like elder pensioners with frayed collars and old suits, can walk onto the dance floor with great dignity due to a respected reputation in the dance.

At the end of the *tanda*, I spotted Fina and Pilar at a table across the dance floor, and settled in with them to study the scene.

"How's the dancing?" I asked.

"Some very good dancers," said Fina. "See that old man in the dark blue blazer, sitting down at the center table?" She pointed casually in his direction.

"Next to the lady in the red dress?"

"Yes, the bald guy. He's a great dancer. He's not with that lady, so try to catch his eye for *cabeceo*."

"Okay. Oh, look," I said, "there's that fellow I danced with this afternoon. Maybe I can dance with him again."

"Watch him," said Pilar, "if he sits with that woman he's dancing with, you can't even greet him, unless he greets you first."

"Why?"

"That could be his wife, and she may not know about his other tango activities."

While I changed my shoes I watched the pair return to their table. They sat together.

"Watch," said Pilar, "he won't dance with anyone else. Maybe a friend at their table, sure, but he won't look around the room."

"Is that part of 'the code'?" I asked.

"Yes, and a healthy domestic policy."

"I know a woman who is a regular at afternoon *milongas*," said Fina, "she wears a wig and everyone knows her as Pamela. But that's not her name."

"Why does she do that?"

"Her family doesn't know she dances tango."

"Does she have affairs?"

"Only an affair with tango."

Just then a well-fed man in a snug-fitting suit approached carrying a vase of roses with a ribbon tied around it. He placed it at the vacant table behind me where a hand-written sign declared it to be, "*Reservado*".

"Could that be *La Maestra's* table?" I wondered out loud. "She's having a birthday party here tonight. You know who she is?"

"Everyone knows *La Maestra*," said Fina, "not personally, of course."

"I think someone at the bar wants to dance with you, Raquel," said Pilar.

"Where? Who is it?" I scanned the bar and found Mr. Gray Suede Shoes looking at me. I flashed him a confident smile to make up for my earlier performance. He nodded toward the dance floor. Yes, I said with my eyes, and stood. As he approached, I slipped out of my jacket and realized that my dress would emphasize my answer. It hugged my hips, and the deep neckline and thin straps revealed the sculptural curves of my shoulders and bosom.

"Whoa, work that dress, Chica," said Fina.

I squeezed between the chairs until I felt the shift from carpet to wood beneath my feet. My tango shoes made me feel sexy and graceful. When he arrived, I looked directly into his eyes. He dropped his gaze to my lips, then took me into his arms. Pressed against his chest, I wrapped my left hand around his neck and placed my forehead lightly against the right side of his face. Instantly we became the model tango couple: one body with four legs.

Secure in his embrace, I closed my eyes. We entered the music, moving in unison, as if by intuition or by some form of prescience. He maintained a path along the edge of the dance floor so that despite the crowded scene, I felt as if we were dancing alone. No one else touched me. All I felt was his body, and the compelling melodies of the tango. In the breaks between songs I learned that his name was Nicolás.

"You can call me Nico," he said softly into my ear.

When he walked me back to the table, he curled his fingers ever so lightly to cup the nape of my neck, and looked into my eyes. He brushed a kiss onto my cheek, gave me a wink, then turned and walked away. As I took my seat, Pilar let out a little whoop. I smiled at her and she raised her eyebrows. I pulled a fan from my purse and put it to good use. Nico and I had not separated between tangos, so my skin was damp. I felt the clinging fabric along my torso, and fanning lifted the fragrance of his cologne from my body. I sat very still for a while, fanning and enjoying the afterglow.

The *tanda* with Nico must have proved my competence, because many good dancers gave me *cabeceo* after that. Two exquisite hours of dancing passed with the swiftness of a dream. I looked for Nico from time to time, and found him always with a different woman. It helped me put my experience into perspective, certain that in spite of the sensations, I meant nothing to him.

"*¿Que pasa allí?*" said Fina, gesturing toward a hubbub at the entrance.

Suddenly a path parted on the dance floor, and everyone stopped dancing as applause broke out across the club. The woman who was undoubtedly *La Maestra* appeared on the arm of the white-haired gentleman I'd first danced with at La Ideal. He was in a tuxedo now, and looked like a diplomat. She was possibly seventy years old, slender and elegant in a midnight blue velvet sheath. She was luminous and beautiful. With her high cheekbones and big expressive eyes, she reminded me of Loretta Young, an actress I'd seen in old movies. Her dark complexion and dramatic eye makeup were offset by a cloud of white hair that framed her face like a halo. For all her glamour, she had a smile like the Dalai Lama suggesting a serene, compassionate, and savvy character. Self-confidence without arrogance. In the couple's wake an entourage of friends carried presents, champagne bottles, and bouquets of flowers.

As they settled in around the table behind me a swelling tide of well-wishers rose up around the lady of the hour. I looked for the right moment to introduce myself, but the arriving waves of admirers seemed endless. Finally, I decided to dive in, hoping to surface within the radius of her embrace.

"*Maestra, feliz cumpleaños*," I said, finally reaching her.

"*Raquel*," said *La Maestra*, as if we'd known each other in another life, "*bienvenida*." She kissed me on one cheek then the other.

"How do you know me, *Maestra?*" I asked.

"Oh, we have more than one friend in common," she said. "You danced with my Paco this afternoon." She placed a delicate fingertip on the cheek of the white-haired gentleman to her right. He smiled at me, and nodded hello. As *La Maestra* took my hands in hers, a deep sense of calm swept through me.

"*Feliz cumpleaños*" I said again, gazing into her eyes.

"*Gracias*," she said. "We shall spend time together soon. Carolina has told me so much about you."

I was speechless. I looked down to witness our hands clasped together, and saw a most unexpected, brutal scar running diagonally across the top of her left hand. I looked back to meet her eyes again, but her attention was taken by the delivery of a large, baroquely decorated cake ablaze with candles. She let go of me.

"Quickly, blow out the candles *Maestra*," someone said.

"Before the fire brigade arrives!" joked another. Everyone laughed.

"I am making a wish now," she said. "Everyone stop thinking so my wish will go straight to heaven." Then, with a deep breath, she extinguished the flames. The uproar from the crowd was deafening. The lady of the evening took a little bow then picked up a large knife and cut a gash through the white frosting and into the cake, its secret interior revealed by chocolate crumbs that surfaced as she lifted out the blade. Champagne corks popped like firecrackers, and plates of cake were passed first around the table, then to anyone nearby with an outstretched hand. When the DJ played a tango waltz for the customary birthday dance, the gentleman I now knew as Paco led *La Maestra* onto the floor. I pushed my way to the front of the encircling crowd to watch them. The diagonal hem of her dress rose to mid-thigh on one side, revealing intricately patterned dark stockings studded with tiny rhinestones. Paco looked so distinguished; he could have stepped out of GQ magazine. They entered their embrace purposefully, then launched into the dance. Like Fred Astaire and Ginger Rogers they made even the most complex footwork seem simple. I studied the precise technique of her *ochos*, the figure eights gliding silently across the surface of the wood. She moved with the grace and quickness of a woman in her thirties. I could have watched them for hours, but a fellow tapped Paco on the shoulder and then one gentleman after another led *La Maestra* successively, until three rounds of the song had played. Short or tall, slender or rotund, the lady adjusted to each partner making every one of them look like a pro (though I knew from experience that some were pretty bad dancers). When the next waltz ended, someone shouted "*¡Evaristo Carriego!*" and everyone applauded, seconding the request. *La Maestra* gestured to a handsome man with salt and pepper hair standing in the crowd. He was at least ten years her junior. Confidently, he stepped in beside her, and the circle widened to give them space.

La Maestra struck a pose and her new partner stepped behind her, wrapping her in his arms. The dramatic opening bars of *Evaristo Carriego* suddenly flooded the ballroom inspiring graceful opening *pasos* that led into complex syncopations. Their deep concentration was evident in quickly executed *sacadas*, a series of quick, almost magical foot displacements that led to a series of windmill-like turns called *molinetes*. *La Maestra's* slender body exhibited considerable strength, making it clear that age sets no limitation in tango. They did no lifts or showy stage acrobatics because this crowd of serious *tangueros* would have been gravely disappointed, maybe even insulted, by the vulgarity of such theatricality. Instead, their performance was pure, intense salon tango, a technically complex choreography, expressing the emotional communion of man, woman, spirit, and music.

When it ended, the crowd went wild with applause and whistles. The couple took modest bows in the four directions of the audience that encircled them. "Señor Luis Viviani," said *La Maestra*, gesturing to her handsome partner. He bowed again, kissed her scarred hand, and they returned to their table. The *milonga* resumed, the floor filled with inspired dancers.

"That was a once in a lifetime experience," said Pilar, when we had returned to our table. "*La Maestra* doesn't perform in public anymore. *Evaristo Carriego* made her famous in 1969 when it was debuted by Pugliese's orchestra. She performed it with her husband Juan Alvarez, it was their signature piece."

"What a fabulous partner she has now," I said, watching Viviani down a glass of champagne.

"Yes, I know," said Fina watching him wistfully.

"He's dreamy," I said.

"I know," she said.

"Raquel," said Pilar, "that was pretty brave of you to go up and introduce yourself to her. You've got guts, girl!"

"Well, *La Maestra* was the teacher of Carolina Guzman, my tango teacher in California," I said.

"Oh, I know Carolina," said Fina, "she came to Chicago to teach. I liked her."

"She's a wonderful person," I said, pulling my attention away from Viviani. "She did more than mold me into a tango dancer. When I met her I was psychologically battered. I'd become a person, not a woman. No, not even a full person, I was a survivor. I'd been through my husband's infidelity and a terrible divorce. I was oblivious to my womanhood. It was Carolina's classes, and her encouragement, that rebuilt my self-esteem and made me aware of my body again."

"Good for you!" said Pilar. "Sounds like tango saved your life."

"In many ways, it did," I said. My eye wandered again to the birthday table. "You know I'd love to dance with that man, what's his name? The one who danced Evaristo with La Meastra?"

"Luis," said Fina, ogling him.

"Luis Viviani," said Pilar.

"Luis. Viviani," I said, settling back into my seat. "I'd love to dance with him."

"He's leaving," said Fina, crestfallen.

"What?"

"Look. He just said good-bye to *La Maestra*."

She was right. I saw him turn toward the exit, then he disappeared into the crowd.

"Damn."

"Oh, chin up," said Pilar pointing behind me, "someone special wants to dance with you."

I looked back to find Paco looking at me.

"*¿Bailás?*" he asked.

"*Sí, con gusto.*" I smiled.

Now it seemed an honor to dance with this gentleman. When we entered the embrace, I felt myself sink easily into a harmonious partnership, glad to have moved beyond being the tense newcomer.

"It seems as if you've known *La Maestra* for a long time?" I said between tangos.

"Many years."

"She's so beautiful and charismatic."

He glanced over at her and smiled affectionately. I wished he were fifteen years younger, but his expression watching *La Maestra* told me he was taken, anyway. Even though I danced a lot after that, only another *tanda* with Nico could have rivaled the joy of dancing with Paco. But whenever I looked for Nico I found him satisfying the tango needs of a series of women. I wasn't about to get another invitation from him.

By four A.M. I'd come to the end of my first day of real Argentine tango. Tomorrow I'd go to the Catholic Diocese office in hopes of getting information about Tío Mateo. I'd need my strength to face the bureaucracy I anticipated there. It was time to go home. I changed my shoes, and bid farewell to my friends. I looked for *La Maestra* hoping to catch her eye, but she was on the dance floor, and Paco sat deep in conversation with a compatriot at the table.

CHAPTER FOUR

Before leaving the Diocese office, I decided to reread the first of Tío's letters from Buenos Aires. It's a miracle they weren't destroyed in the fire that took my house. Looking at it in retrospect, it seems a cruel irony that fire destroyed the dream house we were supposed to grow old in together. As if the universe were striking the set of the future life I'd imagined living. And everything would have been destroyed if the garage had been attached to the house. Fortunately, fifty feet and the skills of the Oakland Fire Department saved the garage and these pieces of family history that have opened a new future. The letters were simultaneously a window on the past and a doorway to the future. I never would have come to Buenos Aires without them.

I was still in a daze when I found them a few weeks after the fire. Up to my ears in insurance business and wearing my sister's clothes, I scanned a few letters just enough to accept the shock of their existence. I couldn't have read through them then, the impact of the moment was even more overwhelming than the duplicity and details of the past.

Now, as I took the letters from the manila envelope I caught a hint of smoke. Was it coming from the paper, or from my memory I wondered. It's a funny thing about smoke, it stays with you long after the fire has gnawed through your life. I washed my hair every day, sprayed my nasal cavities obsessively, I had my car detailed once a month, but the redolent smoke in my mind was nearly impossible to purge. Just opening Tío's letters took me back to the vivid memories of that day.

I had driven my son off to U.C. Santa Cruz. The overnight stay was in itself a welcome change of pace. On the drive home I made a mental list of adjustments I'd make by living alone. David had a new life. I'd be challenged by the silence of his absence in the house, but with less cooking and cleaning I'd have time for myself. I'd already set up my old easel in the garage and felt excited about recommitting myself to painting. Thanks to therapy I'd cut way back on my anxiety medication. I remember feeling calm and optimistic as I pulled into my street, and found it blocked by fire vehicles with great lengths of fire hoses snaked along the pavement. I couldn't see my house at first, and my immediate concern was for whichever neighbor had suffered a fire. I didn't even think of a fire taking my house. I parked a ways away and walked toward my neighbors standing on the sidewalk watching the commotion. The stench of steaming destruction filled my head. Squinting, I tried to wave it away from my face with my hand until suddenly it all came into view. A brigade of firemen surrounded the remains, still pouring water on a pile of ashes that had been the hub of my life. The charred brick chimney stood erect, the lone survivor.

I know I fainted because I remember waking up in the heavily jacketed arms of a firemen. He set me down on my neighbor's front steps. I felt paralyzed, unable to move or even cry in those first minutes. I think it was my neighbor Minnie who said she'd call my sister.

Reflecting on the whole life-changing event from a distance of both time and space, it seemed less dramatic than it had been. The hardest thing was letting go of physical objects that symbolized the memories of a lifetime. I solved the housing dilemma with the purchase of a new loft in Oakland - a temporary solution in my mind. I didn't need another big house in the hills. Too much to clean, anyway. The important thing was that I had a place to sleep, and "a room of one's own" as Virginia Woolf called it. The loft was a space holder for now. When I returned I'd deal with the final insurance issues and make a new home for myself. It was time now to focus on the task that brought me here, uniting Tía Leti with her brother in some way, before she died.

Papa hadn't kept any of the envelopes, so I looked for an address in the letter. I didn't find it, but what I did find began to form a shocking profile of the man I had always thought of as a pious, religious soul.

30 July 1956

Buenos Aires

Felicitaciones Cuñado,

I told you God would bless you with children. You have played your fatherly role as He has declared it. My abuela would be so proud to see a new child named Raquel after her.

Honestly, I am lucky your letter found me. This move to Buenos Aires is, in a way, a promotion. In all the busy details of moving, I forgot to write you. Sorry. But my mail has been sent to me from San Juan, so all is fine in the end.

My new church has a school attached, and an orphanage nearby. I am very busy working in all three places.

I had stopped carrying la pistola for a while. (I named it El Señor.) But since Evita died, things have unraveled here. The Perón regime became very, well . . .not trustworthy. I am sure you have read that the Holy Father excommunicated Peron from the Church. One of the problems is that since the end of WWII this country is crawling with Jews. But we have new leadership now. I think the military is best, it makes the most reliable government. (We learned that in Spain.) Still, things are dangerous now in the capital. So I carry El Señor with me always. I am, after all, a trained soldier of the Lord. I do believe Jesus Christ watches over me at all times, but a little protection on my part makes his job easier.

Write to me at the address on the envelope. I receive my mail at the mailbox of another priest so instead of using my name, address the envelope to Padre Zorrilla. When he sees your return address, he will make sure I get it.

Yours in Christ, Mateo

His other letters bore repeated condemnation of Jews and praise for the military. My uncle, I understood, was an anti-Semitic militarist. A Fascist. Clearly, the Spanish Civil War had continued to have an impact on him. With the war experience added to his tragic childhood, there had to be a complex pathology behind his personality. I never imagined a priest carrying a gun. Well, not in peacetime. If it weren't for my promise to Tía Leti, I'd never go looking for such a man. And I had to wonder if what I found was really going to be a gift at all.

The Diocese office was on Rivadavia near the National Cathedral and the Plaza de Mayo, just as Alfonso had said. I mapped it out, thirteen blocks. I wanted to walk because I feared another anxiety attack, and I wanted to challenge myself to overcome those shameful seizures of insecurity. Choosing to walk was like inviting the dragon out of his cave. If it came at me, I'd just sit down until it went away, I thought, even if I had to sit down right on the sidewalk. Knowing that logical planning was fine in moments of total calm but not easy to act on in the inner chaos of the moment, I also decided to keep some medication in my pocket. Using it would feel like failure, but I needed the last-resort support it gave me.

After three blocks, I'd passed the cobblestoned Dorrego Plaza without incident, and a sense of self-confidence came over me. I declared that I would visit the quaint old Plaza again during the weekend when it fills with musicians, dancers, and antique sellers. I lifted my chin, relaxed my shoulders and took a deep, easy breath. My stride kept time to the tango rhythm of the city, and I felt something new emerge in me. I searched for the word for it. Comfort. Yes, I was comfortable. I fit into this place, and it fit me like a new pair of shoes.

I arrived at the Diocese office, with a victorious smile on my face. It didn't bother me to stand in line for thirty minutes, it gave me time to start reading the book I'd bought with the city map on my first day out of the apartment. It was a book about the history of tango with biographies and photos of those spirits I had seen in the mirrors of La Ideal. Better still, it was in Spanish forcing me to reconnect with the language I had abandoned so long ago.

When it was finally my turn the clerk signaled me with an authoritative wave.

She wasn't what I'd expected for a clerk at the Catholic Diocese. Her hennaed hair clashed with her bright pink silk blouse, and unfortunately, she was a wall of incomprehension. I spoke in Spanish, but she insisted she couldn't follow me, so I resorted to English, and she came to life.

"*Sí, sí,* I speak English," she said. "Also, I need practice."

"I'm looking for my uncle, he's a priest, or he was," I explained. "He lived in Buenos Aires between 1956 and 1977, perhaps longer. I don't know what church he served. He's surely retired, if he's alive. He'd be ninety-one."

"And what you want from the Diocese?" she asked.

"Well, the Diocese is, or was, his employer, so there must be records of him. An address, at least. Or notification of death."

"*Señora,* the Diocese of Buenos Aires covers over 200 kilometers, with 182 parishes. You want information for a priest who was here in 1977?"

"From 1956 to 1977, maybe longer."

"Eseriously?" She rolled her eyes.

"Yes, eseriously," I said. "His name is Mateo Vicente López."

She wrote it down. "Date of birth?"

"February 12, 1912."

"He's born in Buenos Aires?"

"I'm not certain. He could have been born in Spain, and was brought here as a toddler, uh, a baby."

She looked at me quizzically. "Wait one minute," she said, then disappeared behind a wooden door with the word *Privado* written in thick black letters on a pane of frosted glass. Behind me a line of people shuffled their feet and refolded their newspapers impatiently. I considered explaining my plight to them, but decided against it. It took ten minutes for the clerk to return, empty-handed.

"When you heared from him last?"

"1977."

"Ooooh!" She bit her lower lip. "Thousands of peoples disappear in that time," she said in a hushed voice. "I don't find him in the computer."

"If he were receiving retirement benefits, you would have his name, wouldn't you?"

She looked at me with a deep sigh. "I guess so," she said, "but he's not in there. Maybe he is, uh, deceased."

"When he first came to Argentina he served a church in San Juan, in 1954."

"That is not in Buenos Aires Diocese, *señora*."

"I know that. But I cannot go back home empty-handed. Doesn't that detail help you?" I decided to add a little drama to my plea. Looking at her plaintively I said, "My *madrina*, his last surviving sister, is dying. Her dying wish is to have some news of her brother. I have to take something to her. Maybe you can find a baptismal certificate."

"You want that?"

"At least it would give her some sign of him. And maybe once you find that you'll find the rest of his papers. Oh, his church was also connected to an orphanage."

Her expression suggested she was losing her patience. "He was in an orphanage?"

"No, there was an orphanage connected to his church here in the city."

"I will try to find something for you, *señora*," she said, "but if he disappeared there will be no records, and if he died many years ago, he wouldn't be in the current computer information." She indicated the line behind me with her chin. "Many peoples are waiting."

"Let me give you my address and phone number. If you find anything you can leave a message at either of these numbers." I wrote my cell and apartment phone numbers at the bottom of the 3x5 card I'd prepared with Tío's name and information.

"I will send you notice of anything I find," she said. "There may be a fee."

"Fine." I handed her the card and started away from the window, discouraged.

"*Señora!*" she called out.

"Yes?"

"Your name?"

"Oh!" I stepped back to the window. "Raquel Cameron. . . uh, Carval, Raquel Carval." I flinched when Cameron came to mind. No more old identity, I thought. She wrote Carval on the card. "*Muchas gracias*," I said.

"My niece disappeared, too," she whispered, with a sad smile.

I wanted to explain that I had no reason to assume that Uncle Mateo had disappeared, but it was easier to accept her compassion and walk away.

On Thursday morning I was awakened by a knock on the door. I didn't yet know many people in Buenos Aires, and those I knew, didn't know where I lived. Also, the front door to the apartment building should have been locked and anyone who wanted me should have buzzed from the intercom at the street. The knocking was loud even from the bedroom loft, and it was unnerving. I tiptoed downstairs from my bedroom loft, my heart pounding. Barefooted, I approached the peephole to investigate. It was Luis Viviani, that handsome *porteño* who'd performed with *La Maestra* on Monday night. What was he doing at my door? We hadn't even been introduced. How could he know where I live? He knocked again. I took a couple of steps back.

"Who's there?"

"Luis Viviani."

I grinned, but couldn't muster a response.

"Perhaps you remember me," he said, "I danced with *La Maestra* at Gricel."

"Oh, yes, of course I remember." I feigned vague memory. "We didn't meet."

"No, to my disappointment. You see, *La Maestra* is waiting to meet you. I've been sent to collect you." His English was very good.

"I don't have an appointment with *La Maestra*."

"No," he said, "when she decides she wants to see someone, she summons them, and, well, they arrive."

"But I'm not dressed. It's only . ." I checked the clock over the stove, "10:15."

"Yes, sorry. If you need a few minutes I can wait."

A few minutes? I hadn't even brushed my teeth. "Maybe we could meet tomorrow?" I said.

"No. It must be now. You can arrive casual."

I peeked at him again. He was starting to pace. I didn't want to leave him in the hallway, but neither did I want to meet him in my nightie. Clearly, it was an honor to be summoned by *La Maestra*. I had to put vanity aside, and dress as quickly as possible.

"Okay," I said. "Go have a coffee on the corner. Come back in half an hour."

"No. . . that's too long. I'll return in ten minutes."

"Ten minutes! No . . ."

"From what I saw of you at Gricel, even in ten minutes you will look beautiful."

Had he noticed me? Impossible. It was one of those Argentine *piropos* aimed at my ego. "You Argentines and your compliments," I complained, "very charming! Come back in . . . twenty minutes."

"See you in ten!" he said.

I scampered upstairs, ran a comb through my hair and brushed my teeth. "Damn! I wish I were thirty again," I said into the mirror. "It was so much easier to look good."

I tried to get the most benefit from the least amount of effort, and returned to the front door in twelve minutes in a blue dress and white espadrilles. I checked the little mirror by the front door for lipstick on my teeth, then looked out the peep hole. He was leaning against the wall, as if he'd never left. This time I took a moment to look at his creamy caramel complexion, and his thick, wavy salt-and-pepper hair. It looked like he'd run his fingers through it with gel, or it was still wet from the shower. He was wearing khaki slacks and a long-sleeved ecru shirt with the cuffs rolled to just below the elbows. The strap of a weathered leather bag cut across his firm chest, tugging his shirt open at the top, revealing a swatch of soft hair.

"I thought you were going for coffee," I teased without opening the door.

He looked up, startled. "What makes you think I didn't?"

"You haven't had time to go to the café, order coffee, drink it, and walk back."

"But you had time to make yourself beautiful, no?"

Charmed again, I opened the door.

"Aha!" he said, "You see, just as I said, beautiful."

"Alright, that's enough."

"Let's go," he said, with a flirtatious *cabeceo*. I threw my purse over my shoulder and pulled the door shut.

When we passed the building manager sweeping the entrance, I realized how he'd gotten into the building. "That's how you did it," I said.

"What?"

"It was frightening to have someone knock directly on my door instead of buzzing from the street."

"Oh, I'm sorry if I frightened you."

"Once I saw who it was, I was okay." I smiled coyly.

"Then you did remember me."

"Of course. Your performance was breathtaking. Are you *La Maestra's* teaching partner, or her assistant?" I asked, stepping judiciously across the cracked sidewalk.

"Assistant?" His tone suddenly suggested that I'd insulted him. "I am an architect."

"Oh. But you're running this errand for *La Maestra* on a Thursday morning?"

"This is not an errand." He stopped walking. "Maybe I should explain something."

I stood in front of him, compelled to listen seriously.

"It is an honor to assist *La Maestra* with anything. The ego recedes at such times."

"I'm sorry, I didn't mean to . . ."

"To study tango with *La Maestra*," he touched my arm for emphasis, "one must be invited. Perhaps you do not understand this."

"Is that why she's summoning me? Does this mean she's inviting me to study with her?"

"I have no idea, but you should appreciate the honor of being summoned."

He started to walk again. I could see I wasn't making a good first impression. "I am honored. It's just that I'm very new here. I don't know many people, by reputation or otherwise. And I don't know the protocols."

He was stepping briskly and I wanted to calm him down, or redeem myself. "Luis." I said his name to get his attention, but he kept walking. So I stopped. "Luis," I said firmly.

Suddenly he seemed to realize that he'd lost peripheral sight of me and stopped. "What?" He asked, checking his watch.

"Look at me, please."

He turned toward me.

"We've gotten off on the wrong foot," I said. "I flew more than six thousand miles to learn tango from those who cherish it in their souls. I don't want you to think that I'm arrogant or unappreciative about meeting *La Maestra*. Quite the opposite is true. Tango isn't just a dance to me, it's something precious."

He took a deep breath, and the tense line of his pursed lips relaxed into a smile. He nodded. I held out my right hand and took a few steps toward him.

"Truce?"

"Truce," he said clasping my hand in his and giving it a firm shake.

"How did you know where I live?" I asked, as we started to walk again.

"*La Maestra* knew. She called me this morning, and asked me to deliver you to *El Alef.*"

"El Olive? What's El Olive?"

He stopped again, and looked at me incredulously. "*Alef. Alef!* You don't know *El Alef*?"

"I know that an aleph is a Hebrew letter," I said, a little annoyed.

His eyes and mouth widened, seemingly in disbelief. Shaking his head, he resumed his march. "We have to keep moving," he said. We dodged an occasional pedestrian and several dog drop-pings on the narrow sidewalk, placing me behind him at times.

"Well," he said "you must . ." He stopped his thought, maybe to let me catch up, but when I was beside him again, he just strode on purposefully. I quickened my pace to keep up, and when he stopped again, I took a step back, a little startled.

"Does *La Maestra* realize you know nothing of *El Alef*?"

"I have no idea!"

He shook his head in exasperation. "Well," he said, throwing his hands in the air, "she asked me to bring you, and I am bringing you! The rest has nothing to do with me!"

"Okay," I said, marching again an arm's length away.

"It's not very far," he said. "I deliver you, and then I go. That's it. I have appointments."

"I'm sure you have." I gave it half a minute then dared another question. "So what is *El Alef*?"

"A tango school." His words were clipped, but I dared to press on.

"The name is like the Hebrew letter?"

"Yes. See, just up ahead on the left, there is the gate."

I could make out the scrolling ironwork of an arched gate as we got closer. It had an aleph in the center. When we arrived, Luis pressed a button on an adjacent talk box.

"*Sí?*" grumbled a smoky voice.

"*Aquí estamos,*" he said, and a buzzer released the gate lock.

"After you," he said, politely.

I stepped through and found myself in a tranquil courtyard

with potted orange geraniums and hanging ferns. A tiled Andalusian fountain bubbled in the center of the patio, and stone benches offered rest along the whitewashed walls where roses crept toward the heavens.

"I feel as though I've been transported to Spain," I said.

He walked toward the back of the patio as I crossed to visit little canaries in delicate cages hanging in the shade of a canopy.

"These little birds remind me of Córdoba," I said. "They hang their bird cages on the balconies along the narrow streets."

"Raquel."

I heard him say my name, and it sounded like a song.

"Raquel," he said again. I turned to see that he held the door open for me. He'd taken off his sunglasses, and his eyes seemed closed more in restraint than adaptation to the shifting light.

"Sorry. The little birds are so sweet," I said crossing to him. Then we came face to face for the first time. I took off my sunglasses. "Thank you," I said, discovering that he had green eyes rimmed with lush black lashes that made even his impatience captivating. He directed me to enter with a gesture. I stepped into the cool darkness, and was momentarily blinded by the sudden transition from bright sunlight. An arcing crease of light ahead suggested an archway over a curtain. I felt his tender pressure at my right elbow guiding me forward.

"Careful here, your eyes haven't had time to adjust," he said. He led me up four steps, then stopped. Reaching forward, he pulled aside a heavy drape revealing a light-filled salon with comfortable sofas and overstuffed chairs arranged on islands of Persian carpeting. Long brocade curtains were tied away from tall windows with thickly woven silk cords. Several Ficus trees accented the height of the ceiling. He escorted me into the center of the room, then turned abruptly away. "Enjoy your day," he said.

"You're leaving?"

"My buildings need me."

"Thank you."

He nodded, and smiled back. "*Chau!*"

"*Chau!*"

As he pulled the drape closed, I heard a door behind me. Turning quickly I saw *La Maestra* enter wearing a long black skirt. An ornate silver necklace embedded with Lapis Lazuli lay against the bodice of a black blouse, tinkling like a wind chime as she walked. When she stopped in front of me, I felt as if I should curtsy or bow. Instead, I just smiled.

CHAPTER FIVE

Taking my hands delicately into hers, *La Maestra* kissed me on the cheek, and I heard the intimate jingle of earrings hidden within the white curls that framed her face. I was speechless, maybe even breathless for a moment.

"*Bienvenida,*" she said. "Please, sit down." Leading me around the front of a moss green velvet sofa, she nested at one end. A broad ray of sunlight gleamed through the French doors behind her, as if she'd directed the perfect lighting to spotlight her slender silhouette. She slipped off her mules and pulled her naked feet up beneath her with the grace of a cat.

On the coffee table was a thermos pitcher I knew would be filled with hot water for the *yerba mate* gourd beside it. There was also a tall bottle of water, a carafe of red wine, two glasses, a plate of olives, and a circular tortilla española cut into wedges. Several *medialunas,* those small Argentine croissants I had quickly grown to love, were offered on another plate. Forks, and napkins rested on two small ceramic plates with a colorful glazed pattern I'd first seen in Sevilla.

"I realized the hour, and thought that, with the surprise visit from Luis, you might not have had time for food," she said with a gesture toward the still life of delicacies. "Would you like something?"

Fearing that it would seem rude to reject the offer, I stuttered to find an answer. "How kind of you, *Maestra*. Uh, perhaps a little water," I said.

"Help yourself. Nina is an excellent cook. She cures these olives herself, of course. She is the housekeeper and chef here, and my oldest friend."

I poured a glass of water, placed a few olives onto a plate and grabbed a napkin.

"Tell me something about yourself," she said.

"Well, I was born in the U.S. My grandparents came to Argentina from Spain. Both my parents were born here. They moved to California after living eleven years here in Buenos Aires." I bit into an olive. "Oh! Delicious!" I said. The herbaceous tang of the olive danced over my tongue. "Mmmm, really delicious." I repeated. "Even in the States, our family carried on the Spanish and Argentine customs around food. They cured olives, too."

"Ah, I see," she said. "So you come to Buenos Aires to visit family or just to study tango?"

"Well, I should explain a bit. After my divorce two years ago, my sister and brother-in-law took me to Carolina's tango class. I'd refused their invitation at first, but Marta, my sister, pushed me. Honestly, I think without tango classes I would still be hanging onto the past. I told myself that my husband would leave his new wife and baby, and come back to me. Imagine!" I sipped some water. "Tango was my first step toward a new life. I thought it would be just a dance class. It was really the best medicine for depression."

"It cured your depression?"

"Yes, and more. Carolina and tango helped me become my own person again. After twenty-one years married to an *americano*, an Anglo-American I mean, I had lost myself completely. After my grandparents died, and my parents died, I just blended into the mainstream culture. I stopped speaking Spanish. The *yerba mate* gourds just sat on a shelf, decorative souvenirs of the past." I gazed fondly at the gourd on the table.

"Ah! We must have *mate*!" she said, pouring the hot water slowly into the gourd with its silver straw embedded deep into the tea leaves. "You take first," she said, handing it to me.

"*Gracias*." I sipped the warm, acrid tea.

"Your smile tells me you like the memories," she said. "You like the *yerba mate*, too?"

"I'll have to get used to it again," I said. "*Abuela* used to put sugar in it for me." I took another sip. "You know, *Maestra*, even though I was born in California, our customs always made me feel like a person from another place. Once a school friend came to our house and when she saw my parents drinking *yerba mate* she thought they were on drugs! She spread a rumor all over school. I never took anyone home again after that.

"My husband Gordon wasn't much for what he called 'ethnic foods' but he loved *asado*, which he just called barbecue. He never developed a taste for *chimichurri*. So, I cooked American food in our home. When David, my son, took an interest in soccer as a child I knew my father would have been very happy. But Papa had died years ago, and without encouragement David switched to baseball." Suddenly I became very self-conscious. "I'm talking too much! I'm sorry, I do that when I'm nervous."

She leaned toward me. "Not at all. Tell me about your son."

"He's eighteen now. Went away to college this year." I handed her the *mate* gourd. "You have children, *Maestra?*"

"A son," she said.

"Is he a fabulous tango dancer?"

"He disappeared during *El Proceso.*"

"Oh." I felt a dark weight drop into my gut. "I'm so sorry."

"Thank you. It is not an uncommon story here. Please, tell me more of yourself."

"My life seems so trivial by comparison."

"Not at all. Please, I want to know you."

"Well, I'd been a dancer all my life until I met Gordon. He didn't dance, and wasn't interested in learning, so I stopped dancing for twenty years. When I first saw myself in Carolina's studio mirrors, I realized that the woman I saw there was a stranger. I had molded myself into a wife for my husband and a mother for my son, and all the parts of me, whatever they didn't need, had been folded away into a closet somewhere inside me."

"But that woman in the mirror no longer had a husband," she said.

"Exactly! And she had no parents and no grandparents. Everyone who had originally formed my identity was gone. Only my sister and my *madrina,* Tía Leti, knew the pre-Gordon me. I don't think my son even realized that I was a woman." I bit into another olive. "I didn't know who I was anymore. The only constant element in my life was art. Did I mention that I'm a painter? I guess I can still make that claim. I haven't been happy with my work for years. I stopped giving it the time it requires, and then I stopped exhibiting."

"So how did tango change you?"

"Tango put me in touch with my body! Even though my physical presence seemed to be the only solid thing about me, I realized that I wasn't feeling my body at all." This intimate fact suddenly made me feel uncomfortable. "I'm sorry, *Maestra,*" I said, "I don't like talking on and on about myself."

"Raquel, the uncensored flow of your words is a gift of trust. But I do not force you to be uncomfortable. Tell me why you want to pursue more tango studies." She sucked gently on the metal *bombilla* of the *yerba mate* gourd.

"Tango challenges me. I love the difficulty of it. It made me care about something again, aside from my son, I mean."

"Your soul was cut open by the divorce," she said. "Now I

understand why Carolina recommended you to me. Your losses opened you to the spiritual dimension of tango. It is normal for people to feel the sensuous, romantic, and carnal experience of the dance, but some people can also enter a deeper dimension of tango. My husband Juan developed *El Alef* as a place to enter and explore that spiritual dimension. Here we study the dance, of course, but also we explore the spiritual experience."

"I want to know more, *Maestra*. Is there some literature? I'm reading a book about tango history, about composers, and even the history of certain tangos, but nothing about the spirituality of tango. Please tell me more."

"Well," she set the yerba *mate* onto the coffee table, "tell me, where do you go when you dance tango?"

"Well, if I have a good partner, I travel into the music. That's the best answer I can give. When the physical experience of the dance is most sublime, it launches my spirit into the music. It's almost like time travel, except it takes me to a plane of timelessness. Forgive me if this sounds too provocative, *Maestra*," I lowered my voice, "but it's comparable to orgasm, like a spiritual orgasm that connects me with the whole universe. No past, present or future."

"An excellent analogy," she said with a coy smile.

"Very few things fill me as tango does. Occasionally a painting takes my breath away; I think of that as art sex." I covered my mouth. "I've never told that to anyone!" I confessed.

"Your secret is safe here," she said. "I love this excitement on your face, Raquel."

"Well, it's exhilarating!"

"You understand an important foundation of our Tango Dharma," she said. "It's very important, what I've learned about you today."

"Tango Dharma? You mean like the teaching of Buddhism?"

"Yes. Let me explain. My husband Juan was Jewish, but the continual violence in Israel left him spiritually bereft. He felt that if Judaism taught the essential spiritual truth of life, its people would be at peace. Instead, he saw his people suffering, always suffering, and, especially in the Holy Land, so many were violent." Her gaze fell upon the black velveteen of her skirt. She shook her head. "So he decided to devote himself to finding a spiritual teaching that brought people together in peace and compassion. He traveled the world searching for it. In Asia he studied with Buddhists, Sufis and yogis. In the Middle East he found Islamic teachers, imams, and rabbis. He studied the writings of Maimonides and The Golden Age of Spain when Jews, Catholics, and Muslims lived collaboratively in peace. He went to the United States to live among the Franciscan priests, and then among the Native Americans: the Hopi and the Navajo people. In Mexico he experienced the peyote of the shamans. He was away for years. Thank God that was before I knew him. Anyway, he described his initial return to Buenos Aires as a time of deep despair, because no one seemed to have an answer for humanity. He continued to practice Buddhist meditation.

Then one afternoon, as he loved to tell it, he walked on the sidewalk and tango music came, like the aroma of good coffee, out

from a *milonga*. It stopped him, he said, and the music filled his being like a powerful incense. He was stunned into a euphoric ecstasy
right there on the sidewalk. People walking bumped him here and
there," she punched the air with her fists, "but he didn't move until
the magnet of the tango pulled him into the *milonga*. That's how he
described it. All he knew about tango was Carlos Gardel, because
he had been schoolmates with the great tango star, growing up in
the barrio of El Abasto. Imagine, a man seeks for truth all over the
world then he finds his spiritual pot of gold right in his own back
yard." She lowered her voice to whisper, "I think tango was just
waiting for him," she said, "and once he got hooked, she reeled him
in like a fish!"

"And is that where you met him? In that *milonga*?"

She smiled coquettishly. "On another day. We met at . . .oh,
that's not important now, what's important is that inside the *milonga*
he saw people in close embrace, moving counter-clockwise in synchronized harmony, as if aligned with the cosmos. It was the harmony he sought. 'It's one thing for a person to find peace within himself
and with his God,' Juan said, 'but to find harmony with others, that
is the most challenging spiritual task of the human being.'"

The room was silent. "The allurement of tango is such a mystery," I said.

"Yes. Mystery is the right word," she said. "You discovered
that you had no identity, yet tango led you to the map of your full,
authentic self. Right here in your body." She laid her warm hand
on my heart. "The body holds ancestor wisdom in its bones, blood,

sinew, and even tastebuds! When we dance tango we dance with a resonance of the ancestors present within us."

This was very profound to me. "Please teach me more about this, *Maestra*."

"The body carries the resonance of memory. Tango specifically celebrates those who have come before. In that way it is almost a folkloric dance. If you listen to the lyrics, you understand that tango is the oral history of its people. It carries a thousand stories. Our dance, for all its sexy reputation, is really a ritual of remembrance."

Suddenly I remembered the mirrors of La Ideal and the ghostly dancers I saw there. I wanted to tell her about them, but feared I might seem mentally unbalanced. Instead I said, "You know, *Maestra*, from my first tangos here in Buenos Aires, I've had powerfully spiritual experiences. I've never felt that before, and I thought maybe I was, well, a little, uh, eccentric."

"Nonsense! With good partners who connect to the music and to the floor, the spirit of yin and yang comes together. It is a powerful universal coupling. At *El Alef* we talk specifically about tango but it can apply also to other parts of your life. The resonance of memory is in all things."

I took a hungry, lung-expanding breath. "The resonance of memory is in all things?"

"Yes. And in Buenos Aires the walls and chairs and mirrors and floorings have been absorbing tango vibrations for over one hundred years."

"Wow." This was something I wanted to think about and sleep

with. "It's going to take a while for that realization to sink in," I said. "Could I have a glass of wine now?"

"Yes, and tortilla, too. Please join me, suddenly I am starving," she said.

We attacked the food like ravenous peasants. The tortilla disappeared, and half the carafe of wine. Olive pits piled like miniature cairns in the dishes. With the last satisfying swallow of wine I felt fortified.

La Maestra drew a deep breath. "Goodness," she said looking at the meager remains on the table, "I guess we were really hungry." We started to laugh and couldn't stop. Tears rolled off our cheeks, and my stomach ached with pleasure. "This has been a most unexpected experience," said *La Maestra*, gazing quizzically at me. "There is a rising spirit in you, Raquel. I see it the way womanhood can be seen rising in a young girl at puberty."

"You must be seeing the spirit of menopause, *Maestra*," I said, trying to make a joke.

"No, this is not a joke, my dear." Her serious expression was sobering.

"What do you see?"

"Every step of your life created your path to Buenos Aires." She studied my face. "But you will be tested before the true nature of your journey can be fully revealed. You have an enduring spirit, but you must earn the next level of self-confidence. And with it, you will earn respect."

I imagined she had intuited my war with the dragon of anxiety. "What kind of test are you talking about?"

"I don't know, and even if I did, I couldn't tell you about it. It will test your courage. You must be afraid. Fear is the prerequisite of courage. I know you want to dance tango, but I sense that something else has brought you here. What is the burning purpose of your presence in Buenos Aires?"

The battle against anxiety was not the answer to that question. The real purpose was finding Tío Mateo. I told her about the letters, my aunt, and the promise I'd made. I suggested that after the Diocese visit I thought of giving up for lack of information. But La Meastra made me realize that finding Mateo wasn't just important to my *madrina*. Finding him would repair the family tapestry, she said. His life had been torn away, by my grandfather's wrath, and finding him, alive or dead, was the only way to reweave his story back into the matrix of the family, and restore the full picture of who we are.

"You know, I've had a vague fear about this search," I said. "Well, I'm alone in a foreign country, I thought that was it, but now your intuition confirms it. People warn me that Tío may have disappeared, but I have no evidence to suggest that. Did I mention he was a priest? I think the Catholic Church sent him to the Argentine provinces after the Spanish Civil War, later he was moved again to serve a parish with an orphanage here in Buenos Aires. The Diocese office couldn't find him in the computer. That leads me to think that if he's not receiving retirement benefits, he must be dead. That would be great. Excuse me, I don't mean it would be great,

I just mean there wouldn't be any quest or mission, or anything. I could take a photo of his grave and it would all end there."

"But you don't believe that," she said.

"Well, my gut is telling me that it's not going to be that easy."

"So your uncle survived the Spanish Civil War as I did," she said.

"Really?"

"We can talk about that another time. When did your family hear from him last?"

"1977."

"I'm sorry, Raquel, but it's true that this could be an unpleasant search. Many people disappeared."

"I know, *El Proceso*: The Dirty War."

"As if any war could be clean, heh!"

"I think the letters ended in 1977 because of my father's death. If there were subsequent letters they'd have been returned." I thought for a moment. "Did priests disappear, too, *Maestra?*"

"Oh, yes. One of the first people to disappear was the Bishop of *La Rioja*. He was assassinated by a death squad. There was also a massacre of young priests in Belgrano, it was called the Massacre of St. Patrick's. They were liberation theologians. Some clergy were on the side of the people, others were sympathetic to the military machine. Keep that in mind," she said, looking at me squarely. "A search could still be dangerous. Don't forget that 'disappeared' is shorthand for tortured, executed, and disposed of in such a way that there wasn't even a trace of ashes to put in an urn or an envelope."

"I'm sorry if this leads you into painful memories, *Maestra*," I said.

She shook her head. "No, no," the rest of the sentence was a gesture seemingly intended to absolve me of any trespass. "The first day the mothers marched in the Plaza de Mayo, we knew that our voices would never be silenced. That is why they still march, so that no one forgets. Even now, you join thousands of others still looking for relatives. You must know that there are old reptiles hiding under rocks, nesting in filthy secrets. It's dangerous to expose desperate creatures. They are still killers, Raquel. Do not be naïve."

An expression of bitterness had overtaken the grace of her delicate features, and as she pushed a strand of hair from her forehead, I saw the scar that had caught my eye at Gricel.

"It's a real attention-getter, no?" She said, seeing that it had caught my eye.

"Sorry, *Maestra*, it's hard to miss."

"Yes, this scar has been a conversation piece since the night I got it."

"During the *Proceso?*"

"No, no. It has been with me most of my life." A smile graced her face again as she recounted childhood memories of her family's march toward France from the city of Málaga on the southern Mediterranean coast of Spain. "My mother was French, so we hoped to make a new home with her family," she said. "It was 1937, the Fascist military and Church people hunted us like animals." The smile disappeared again like the sun gone behind a cloud. "We stopped in Barcelona before the last march to the border. It was winter, painfully cold. My little brother had a fever and a rattle in his chest. He was five years old, I was eight. I was so happy to sleep inside a building, even on a straw floor. Then, we heard a great *jaleo* outside. Voices shouted, 'Soldiers are coming'. Then gunfire, getting closer. Papa lifted me into his arms; Maman pulled my brother from his cot. We joined a crush of people trying to escape through the narrow street. Papa put me on his shoulders, so I wouldn't get trampled. But that is where a bullet found me. It ripped across my hand like lightening. They wrapped my hand quickly with snow and a strip of cloth." Grinning, she held it out in front of me. "See the pattern of the stitches," she said, 'when we finally stopped outside the city, my mother begged a seamstress to sew my wound."

"God! That must have been so painful," I said.

La Maestra shook her head, and bit her bottom lip. "The snow numbed it. Also, they gave me whiskey. To this day, I cannot stand the smell of whiskey." After a long sip of *mate* she said, "Life is like a big black cat, Raquel, and we are her little mice. She toys with us, tortures us, then tosses us about. This scar reminds me to give thanks for anything good in life. Probably thanks to the whiskey, I slept very deeply that night, despite the pain and the cold. When I woke up to sunshine the next morning, I learned that my little brother had died in the night. The pain of his death completely overpowered the throbbing of my wound."

She offered me the *mate*. I declined. "Sorry to share such a sad tale with you, but now you are saved from wondering when you can ask me about the scar." I grinned sheepishly. "It is natural to be curious about such a thing, do not worry. I am not offended."

La Maestra stood up signaling the end of our meeting. As we walked into the patio, she said, "Remember that the city of Buenos Aires has three million people, Raquel. Documents are not easy to get, and thousands of people still search for loved ones. There is a database now on the missing, even DNA. If it comes to that, maybe Paco can help."

"Paco?"

"Yes, he works for an organization. He can tell you more himself."

"I'm very realistic, *Maestra*. That's why I decided to come with a one-way ticket. I knew it could take time to find Uncle Mateo. I'm driven, frankly, by love for my *madrina*. I don't think my uncle was a great guy, but I want to take her something, you know, for eternity. It may just be a photo of his grave."

She nodded her head. "We have millions of those too," she said.

"You have created a beautiful place here, *Maestra*," I said. "May I ask why you named the school *El Alef*?"

"A very good question. There are three parts to the answer. As I said, Juan was Jewish, and the aleph is the first letter of the Hebrew alphabet. In Judaism the letters are considered to be the basic "building blocks" of all creation. So, the aleph is a cornerstone of creation, and in respect to his heritage it is the cornerstone of our school. It is also the letter that corresponds with The Fool, the first card of the Tarot de Marseilles. The Fool symbolizes the spiritual traveler always searching for meaning. Juan identified with that character throughout his life, and he believed in tango as a constant spiritual quest. The third meaning comes in a story by Jorge Luis Borges called The Aleph. Are you familiar with Borges?"

"I know he was a great Argentine writer, but I confess I've never read his stories."

"Well, he wrote many short stories, and they usually offer life through unusual circumstances or through strange dimensions of reality. In The Aleph, for example, a spot is discovered in the universe where all of time and space meet. That spot is located in the cellar of a building here in Buenos Aires."

"In a foundation?"

"Exactly. So the Aleph from Borges' story signifies the meeting of past, present, and future, and tango is also such a meeting place."

"Wow!" I took a moment to make sure I remembered all three meanings. "I'm going to have to think a lot about that, *Maestra*,"

"Of course. That's why we are a school. Our philosophy deserves a good deal of thought, and study," she said. "And this brings me to my invitation. If you would like to study here, we would be pleased to have you."

"Yes, absolutely! Thank you so much."

"Be advised, Raquel," she said, "many criticize us. Some say what we do is esoteric, others call it heresy. We say we are a mystery school, always seeking the wisdom of tango. Juan believed in tango as a path to world peace so you may think of this as a peace school."

"Thank you for your hospitality, *Maestra*."

"Class begins at 11 a.m. on Saturday," she said. "Use the same entrance; just turn left at the landing. The hall will be lit."

"You're sure I'm a good enough dancer?"

"Well, Paco gave you excellent reviews."

"I'm glad I didn't know I was auditioning! See you Saturday. *Chau!*"

I walked home slowly, *La Maestra's* words and images swirling in my mind. In the cool refuge of my apartment, I recorded her story in my journal wishing I could have recorded her voice just as I still hear it spiraling through my mind like the smoke of an opium dream. Coleridge would have loved it all, I thought. Without the desiccation of a single poppy, I'd gone to a new edge of the world.

CHAPTER SIX

On Saturday morning the gate to El Aleph was open. I nodded hello to a couple chatting beside the Andalusian fountain. A warm breeze ruffled through my hair as I greeted the canaries, remembering our first meeting and my unfortunate interaction with Luis. I'd been thinking a lot about him, planning to redeem myself in his green eyes.

At the landing that had been dark on Thursday, I stepped down to my left into the hallway toward the dance studio. A fascinating exhibition of tango photos along both walls captured my attention. It began with old sepia toned images of dancers and musicians and progressed to more recent photos as I approached the studio. The final photo was a black and white glossy 8x10. Hand written at the bottom I read, "*Juan y Beatríz, 1950*". The luscious young Beatriz was in the arms of a slightly older man whose exotic good looks rivaled Valentino in his heyday. Dark eyes, full lips, a strong chin.

Thick, shiny black hair swept dramatically away from his face, tied
in a ponytail at the collar of a white shirt. He wore gaucho pants
and boots, and around his waist was a broad silver and leather belt.
La Maestra would have been in her twenties, I guessed. She wore a
silky blouse with a scooped neckline that fell off one shoulder. At
the waist it cinched into a floral skirt that clung to her hips before
flaring gently. The gaucho bent over his beloved, holding her close,
her back arched, their lips nearly touching.

"If you like old photos, *La Maestra* has volumes of albums."

"Oh, Luis!" I said, catching my breath, "it's good to see you.
Yes, I love these photos. It's nice to have an image of Juan Alvarez."

"There are many. See." He pointed to the opposite wall. "Those
are later than this one. But you have no time for sight-seeing now,
class is about to begin. Let's warm up before *La Maestra* arrives."

"Thank you." I had ruminated over our original episode, curs-
ing myself for my clumsiness with him. He seemed to have held none
of it against me, thank God. Nevertheless, today I was determined
to concentrate on tango and Luis, maybe not always in that order.

Like the rest of this old building, the dance studio was spacious
and charming. Three sets of French doors opened onto little balconies on the far side of the long room, and a large translucent skylight
brightened the oyster white walls and tall ceiling. The scarred wood
floor welcomed dancers the way a pool invites swimmers of all
abilities. Old bentwood chairs were stacked at the far corner, and
long mirrors made the room appear double in size. Students pulled
down chairs to change shoes and stow belongings. I followed suit.

Couples began dancing to a D'Arienzo melody chosen by the DJ in his nest at the other corner. Some people stretched using the barres along one wall, while others practiced their technique in front of the mirrors. The students were all races, ages, and sizes. I was surprised to see that I was part of the majority, students over forty. The eldest seemed to be at least seventy.

Luis came over, smiling, and I got so lost in his smile that, in spite of his gesture to take my hand, he actually had to say the words: "Would you like to warm up?"

"Oh, yes! Thank you."

Stepping into the close embrace I said, "It may take me a minute to relax."

"I understand," he said. "Do you trust me?"

"Yes."

"Good. Then just close your eyes. In my arms, you are safer than anywhere in the world. Just let your tension drop to the floor."

We stepped into the embrace and I waited for his next move.

"Stop thinking," he whispered.

The gentle firmness of his arm encircled my rib cage. I felt the solid warmth of his chest against mine. Our legs touched softly at the thighs, and beneath my left forearm I felt the muscular curve of his shoulder. We held that tender embrace without taking a single step for the longest time, reminding me of my first tango with Paco at La Ideal. I took a deep breath and it felt as though Luis took that breath with me, simultaneously. Then we exhaled, and my tension just melted away. We adjusted into an even closer embrace, then moved swiftly into a wide step to the right, as if we inhabited a single body.

When that tango ended, we stayed together, stepping into the next one quickly with elegant synchronization. I was calm as the moon. When it ended, he took one step away from me, and smiled.

"Thank you," I said, "that was beautiful."

He nodded, gazing into me, as if he'd seen me for the first time. Just as I thought he might say something complimentary, *La Maestra* entered like a beacon outshining sunlight. All eyes were drawn to her. "*Hola, Maestra,*" "*Buenos días, Maestra,*" said the students. Their greetings layered in the air like a Greek chorus. She stepped into the center of the room, and as she came near, touched my shoulder, and gave me a kiss on the cheek. "*Bienvenida,*" she whispered.

"*Gracias, Maestra.*" I felt nearly breathless in her presence.

"*Vamos a bailar un poco,*" she said, encouraging the students to continue dancing while she observed. Luis was on the far side of the room by that time, so I danced with a round, middle-aged Asian fellow with shaved head wearing a knee length saffron yellow tunic over matching pants. His fingertips rested tentatively on my spine, leaving a space between our torsos. I could feel that his weight was on his heels and he wasn't bending his knees because as we moved he pulled me toward him draping me over his belly and pulling me off balance. He listened well to the music, and stayed perfectly in rhythm, but aside from the forward pull of the embrace, there was no lead. Basically I rode his tummy into each step.

La Maestra came to his side and whispered something into his ear. In the mirror, I saw her place one finger onto the center of his back. As if by magic, he elongated his spine and brought his chest toward me, allowing me to readjust my weight. As we moved through the dance, I felt him struggle to maintain the new posture, forcing me to focus on maintaining my balance. When the tango ended, he took one step away from me, drew his hands together in front of his chest, and bowed. I mirrored the gesture, like a Judo competitor. He turned to bow to *La Maestra* but she was already half way across the room.

Some students sat on the floor, others brought chairs to sit on. I sat on the floor and in a minute the entire class was gathered in a semi-circle around *La Maestra*, seated in a bentwood armchair. She was all in black as she had been on Thursday. Black tights accented the firm calves of her legs, and a leotard was accessorized with a wrap-around skirt that revealed her trim frame.

"Today we welcome a new student," she began. "We could call her a California *porteña* because her parents were born in Buenos Aires. Please welcome Raquel Carval." Heat flashed across my face. I waved and nodded to polite applause.

"Also, we have a visitor, Chen, a student of Buddhism, from Oregon, United States. I believe you will see that in tango yin and yang are more than philosophical concepts. The man and woman must embrace." She was teasing my recent partner a little and he blushed, but laughed good-naturedly.

"The embrace, and the shifting weight of the bodies," he said, "teaches the deep dynamics of yin and yang in a very powerful way, *Maestra*. This is why I come to *El Alef*, to learn the dharma of Buddhism in the cells of the body through tango."

"Yes, the Tango Dharma can only be learned from the mystery of the physical embrace. Tibetan Buddhism, I believe, has a Tantric tradition that also takes the teaching deep into the body, no?"

He lowered his eyes. "Yes, *Maestra*. But I have taken a vow of celibacy, so I come to tango hoping to understand the tantra others may learn in the, uh, carnal union. I must ask patience and forgiveness of the ladies. Dancing with a partner is very difficult. I have much to learn," he said, shaking his head.

"All men bid women to have patience," she said. Everyone laughed.

"Oh, *Maestra*, you wound us," said a fellow on the other side of the room.

"Ay, *pobrecito*," she said, teasing. "I only expose the truth." As the laughter subsided, she continued, "Well, let's get to the Dharma for today. Close your eyes please, calm yourselves, and begin to settle. Take a slow, deep breath." An audible inhalation moved through the group. There must have been twenty-five of us, more or less. I lifted my lids just enough to watch them. As they breathed, they straightened their spines, dropped their shoulders, and visibly flared their nostrils according to her quiet guidance. "Find the center point of your body, and when you are there, open your eyes."

When she had their attention again, she began, "First, my observation of this morning's dancing: I should not hear your shoes swiping the floor. An occasional sound, of course, but swoosh,

swoosh, swoosh! Pleeease! Pay attention to your feet. Caress the floor with the foot, do not sand it." People were nodding and twisting their faces.

"Today we talk about *duende*," she continued. "*Duende* is a dark spirit. It exists in all cultures, but we Spaniards are very good at dark spirits so we got to name it." The group laughed politely. "We find it especially in the dark, rough melodies of the flamenco. In Italy, I find *duende* in opera. For example, in Don Giovanni, which is actually an opera written by Mozart, an Austrian, about a character who suffers what we now call sex addiction. I think we invent this addiction in Spain because this man is famous around the world as Don Juan, but the Austrian wants to put his opera in Italian, so he is Don Giovanni."

The students laughed at *La Maestra's* annoyance and the pride with which she claimed the worst lothario in fiction as a product of her own culture. "Thank you. You get my joke! Bravi! Anyway, in Act Two a spirit comes from the grave, invited to dinner by Don Giovanni. That spirit is, to me, the embodiment of *duende*.

"In Portugal you find *duende* in the lamentation of the fado. In America you also find *duende* in the blues, which grew out of the suffering of African people. Here, in Argentina, *duende* is in tango. Tango was born in the shadows of the city, and grew from the hard life of the poor, struggling immigrants and also those brought here as slaves. All re-invented themselves as *porteños*, the people of the conventillos, the slums along the port of Buenos Aires." She got up from her chair and moved among us slowly, her arms outstretched like threatening wings. "They lived with dark spirits always over the shoulder: hunger, violence, poverty, greed, infidelity, jealousy, and death. From within those slums a character took shape. He came to be known as el compadrito. The compadritos were young men who embodied the shadows. Gamblers, grifters, conmen, and thieves. Respectable people kept their distance from the compadritos, except in the *milonga*. In the *milonga*, these men rivaled each other to be the best dancers. The character of the compadrito sculpted the *emoción*, the dark, erotic emotions of life into tango steps and postures that still reveal the *duende* in our dance.

"This *duende* must be in your dancing. But you do not live as the *porteños* of the past, so how will you find it?" She looked around the room making eye contact with one student then another. "The Spanish playwright and poet, Federico García Lorca," she went on, "said that one must find *duende* 'in the remotest mansions of the blood'. One guitar maestro said that *duende* climbs up inside you, from the soles of the feet. It is important to master technique, but without *duende*, you do not dance tango. Many people just step to music, they may dance tango steps. . . ." In mid-sentence she moved to the black board on the side wall and wrote the word tango. "I use this word, with the small 't' to mean simply the dance, the steps. But Tango," her chalk hit the slate with a sharp squeal as she wrote, "this means all that Tango is. You must know this difference. Our dance is the tango of Tango." She took a breath and looked around the room. "Tango with this capital T, is the history, the music, the composers, the dancers, the stories, the soul that creates the universe of Tango. Do not become arrogant because you think you dance well. There are *tangueros* who do not dance at all, yet they know more about the heart and soul of Tango than you do."

She came back to the chair and looked into the faces of her students. "I can tell you about *duende*," she said, "but I cannot find it for you. I cannot give it to you. You must be like the mystical woman, Persephone, who was kidnapped into the underworld. Dive into yourself, and into every piece of music. You will find the dark, passionate heart, the *duende* of Tango at the intersection of the music and your own shadow."

"How will we know when we've got it?" asked a blond American fellow in a black tee shirt that clung to his muscular physique.

She smiled. "You will cry."

"*Maestra*," he pleaded, "I have a black belt in Karate, I cannot be seen crying on the dance floor or anyplace else. Besides, I don't see anybody crying in the *milonga*. Don't those people have *duende*?"

"Some in the *milonga* have *duende*, others do not. If you see someone dancing and talking, you know that person has no *duende*. He or she does not dance Tango. When you have *duende* the Tango will ache in your soul. When you have *duende* you will feel the ancestors rise to meet you on the dance floor. The cry of *duende* is an ache in the body, not necessarily in the eyes. Watch some of the oldest men in the *milonga*, Steven, those who perhaps once had a physique like yours. Age has taught them the difficult lessons of surrender. To have *duende*, let go of a little bit of yourself. Buddhists also speak of letting go, I believe. Release your ego into Tango. Think about this, and we will talk of *duende* again, another day." She stood up abruptly. "Now, *la técnica*."

The floor was cleared as students formed a circle alternating men and women. The DJ played D'Arienzo again, an excellent accompaniment for *caminada*, walking step. *La Maestra* watched from the center of the circle, correcting postures and technique when necessary. After an hour of review on *caminada*, *ochos*, and *amagues*, we worked on *dibujos*, little circular drawings made with the big toe on the floor.

"Use your core muscles for support," she reminded us.

I thought of dancers I'd seen in California who considered themselves accomplished after six months of classes. Except for visitors like Chen, these *Alef* students were far from beginners, yet *La Maestra* drilled them in the basics, which they obviously knew very well. I realized that serious tango dancers are like ballet dancers whose art demands disciplined repetition and practice of even the most fundamental movements. When the music stopped she said simply, "*parejas*", and everyone paired up.

"Most of you are experienced dancers, so I'm going to push you to surrender to your partner." She smiled at us playfully. "I learned a phrase in English," she said, "relinquish your autonomy'. Do you like that? I worked hard to learn that phrase. Relinquish your autonomy."

We all laughed, and gave her a little applause.

"It's really a good phrase, *Maestra*," said a slender English woman. "It goes directly to the challenge that comes, especially in the *milonga*, when you dance with someone for the first time."

There was a murmur of agreement.

"It is especially difficult for the leader," said *La Maestra*, "he, too, must surrender. First give your ego to tango, then your body."

"But doesn't the woman relinquish autonomy more than the man?" The question came from a *porteño* in jeans and a white shirt.

"It's very typical a man says this," responded *La Maestra*. Everyone laughed, and the *porteño's* complexion turned deep rose. "I know it's the image of tango that the man is in control," she said, "we pretend the woman is his subject. But you know this is not true. Come here, Felipe."

The *porteño* complied quickly. She said something quietly into his ear, then they embraced.

"Now, dance," she said. Instead of following, *La Maestra* lagged behind his steps. As he struggled to lead her, she asked, "What can you do with this partner?"

"I have to slow down, and work to bring you with me," he said. "And I have to mark the lead more firmly."

"Yes!" she said, stepping out of the embrace. "You compromise with the partner, if you are a good dancer. Men, do not use the woman to accomplish your dance!"

"I didn't realize it," he said, "but I do presume I'm taking control of my partner." Felipe's eyes grew wide with discovery. "To me, surrender has always meant a loss of power. But I do surrender when I adapt my lead, *Maestra*. God, I'm not in control at all!"

The group broke into laughter.

"Tango, in fact dance as a whole, is not a competition or a game of control!" she said. "You do not win or lose. Everybody must surrender like a leaf dropped onto the river surrenders to the current. You go, happily. No! What is the word?" She thought for a moment. "Blissfully! Men, at least Argentine men, love to hold women. So men," she turned slowly making eye contact with them individually, "enjoy the embrace. Seduce her and she will go with you willingly. And women, you are not a lifeless ribbon, dance from your heart, let the man feel your body and personality, your substance and spirit."

Everyone nodded and smiled. *La Maestra* gestured to the DJ in the corner, "DeCaro," she said, changing composers. "Now," she said, "let me see the strength of your surrender."

Two and a half hours after we'd begun, the work came to a halt. Whereas other classes I'd taken, from other teachers, had ended abruptly when time was up, the *Alef* class had a closing. *La Maestra* noted the time and asked the students to gather around her. This time she stood in the circle with us. "When you dance tonight or this afternoon, remember to search for the *duende* in the music and in your heart. It may be painful, but this is Tango." Then she blew a kiss with a quick "*¡Chau!*" and left through the door from which she'd arrived.

I was tired, but it was a good tired. I felt happy. While changing my shoes, Luis came over with an attractive blonde woman.

"Raquel, this is Carla, Paco's daughter."

"*Encantada*," I said, shaking her hand.

"It's good to meet you," said Carla, "I lived in L.A. for ten years. I really miss California. You're so lucky to live there."

"Well, I live in the north, San Francisco. You're lucky to live in Buenos Aires."

"How did you like the class?" asked Luis.

I slung my purse and shoe bag over my shoulder. "The class was great, but I'm starving," I said, "would you two like to join me for lunch in Dorrego Plaza?"

"Yes," said Luis immediately.

"We'd love to, I'm sure," said Carla, "but Luis is helping me move a love seat."

"We can do that after lunch," he said.

"No, *corazon*, Mrs. Cortez will only be home until two thirty. We must go now."

"Sorry, Raquel," he said, "another time. Next Saturday, for sure."

"Okay."

As they walked off, Carla took his arm. I stayed behind them, and when they went through the exterior gate, Luis looked back. I smiled. He waved.

CHAPTER SEVEN

It was late afternoon when I got back to my apartment. The place was actually starting to feel like home. The bedroom loft warmed in the afternoon under a big skylight at the center of the ceiling. The kitchen, beneath the loft, was the only dark spot, but there was ample lighting for cooking. At the base of the curved metal spiral stairway, a small dinette set sat beside a frosted window. The living space beyond that had a gray sofa with a chrome and glass oblong coffee table. There was a small desk near the French doors that led to the balcony behind the sofa. The rent included television, stereo and wifi, plus a *mucama*, a cleaning lady, twice a month. Soft light filled the space like a fragrance. The first time I saw the apartment I imagined bringing in a big easel. Canvases could be taken out through the balcony, and lowered to a vehicle in the alley behind the building. I stopped myself there, amazed that the fantasy had so quickly taken shape.

As I lay on the bed with my feet up against the cool wall, I closed my eyes and reflected on the day's events. The first tangos with Luis were still fresh in my mind. We had melted together even before taking a step. That embrace. I could still feel it.

Then there was Carla. "*Corazon*" she'd called him, "sweetheart". And she took his arm. She took it, he didn't offer it. He didn't hold her hand. He turned around and waved at me. The thought of him put a Cheshire Cat-like grin on my face.

My thoughts were shattered by the phone ringing downstairs. The machine picked up before I got there and Pilar's voice met me halfway there. She and Fina were inviting me to a tango show at Café Tortoni. I picked up and got all the details. We'd meet after dinner in front of the café, *Avenida de Mayo*. Hanging up, I felt light-hearted, anxious to see the historic meeting place of international intellectuals and brave journalists. But just as quickly as the invitation had lifted my spirits, the mood turned sharply dropping me into a dark blue shadow. How dare I have a good time when Marta is home nursing Tía, I thought. I phoned to check on them.

My sister was excited to hear of my adventures. Describing the city, I tried not to gush about the grace of the tall purple flowered trees along *Nueve de Julio*, or the multitude of picturesque sidewalk cafes that remind me of Paris. Instead, I sent a few photos I'd taken with my phone through email, and concentrated my report on the frustrations of my encounter at the Diocese. Then I asked a long list of questions about Tía's condition: the results of the last blood tests, her blood pressure, and the state of her mental acuity. Was she having a lot of pain? I worried that Marta's family life might be suffering from the demands of Tía's needs. But my sister is a trooper. With excited curiosity she asked about tango class, and the nightlife. What kind of people was I meeting? How are the men? Had I been shopping? Even though the news about Tía was not optimistic, she immersed herself in my life as if it lifted the weight of responsibility from her shoulders for those few minutes. I hated to hang up, but promised to call again when I had news about Tío. Verbal kisses and hugs, then good-byes.

I don't know how many times Fina and Pilar had been to Café Tortoni, but they walked into the beautiful old place as if it were MacDonald's. I, on the other hand, took a few steps inside and stopped in my tracks. "Don't go so fast, you two!" I said. "This is my first time here. I've read so much about this place. Historically it's one of the oldest and most important literary and intellectual hotspots of South America, even the world! It's like a museum. Let's look at these photos." Victorian glass display cases were filled with framed photos accumulated over decades. "Look, there's Federico García Lorca! Arturo Rubinstein, and Lily Pons. And there are some tango greats, look, DiSarli and Pugliese. And even Hillary Clinton's been here!"

"She's not a tango great," said Fina sarcastically. "Let's go. We want to get good seats for the show."

"See this man," said Pilar, pointing at one of the photos, "that's Atahualpa Yupanqui, a great Argentine folk hero and . . ."

"Jorge Luis Borges!" I said, pointing to another photo.

"Let's go!" scolded Fina.

"Yes, and that's Julio De Caro," said Pilar. "And see, there's Troilo."

"Imagine if they were all sitting here at the same time," I proposed.

"As if time could be manipulated to overlap?" she asked.

"Yes, or they could meet in a spiritual time zone and the Tortoni could be their spiritual meeting place," I said.

"Let's go!" demanded Fina, breaking the surreal imagery of my proposition.

We serpentined around the little tables, where chatting patrons savored food, drinks, aromatic coffee, and conversation. I promised myself a return visit to look more closely at the impressive display of paintings and bronze busts. When we arrived at the back of the café the cabaret doors were not yet open, so Fina ambled over to confirm our reservation while we installed ourselves at a table near the billiards area. Hubbub of the busy café was punctuated by the soft sounds of balls colliding and bouncing off felt.

"Doors open in fifteen minutes," she said on return. "We can sit here while we wait. But if we want good seats we should be at the door when they open it." The conversation went quickly to shopping, and tango shoes with me jotting down recommendations on flimsy napkins until I felt a hand on my shoulder.

"*Hola hermosa*," said Nico, "what are you doing here?"

"*Hola*," I said, "What a surprise to see you. We've come to see the show.' I introduced Fina and Pilar. They each got a kiss on the cheek. "And you, Nico? Do you dance tango in the show."

"No, here I sing."

"Sing?"

"I am in the show. I will make sure you have excellent seats."

"*Muchísimas gracias*," said Fina.

"Raquel, you must have a drink with me later," he said.

"Must I? I don't know about that," I hesitated.

"I have no time to argue, *preciosa*, and as you know, I am not accustomed to being turned down. *Hasta luego, Chau!*" He kissed my hand, a contrived anachronistic act of chivalry I thought, then disappeared behind the cabaret door. I felt my cheeks flush.

"That," said Pilar, still watching Nico's exit, "is 100% Argentine charm."

"Too bad we can't bottle it," I said. "I won't stay after the show."

"Why not?" They chimed in unison.

"He's just a lothario."

"You think he's insincere?" asked Pilar

"Oh, please, he's a lady's man. I'm sure he's sincere about always wanting things to go exactly as he contrives them."

"Well, yes, he's not husband material," contributed Fina.

"I'm not looking for a husband," I said.

"Then why not stay?"

I didn't actually know why, and when we were ushered through the intimate theater to a table right beside the stage, I reconsidered. The waiter removed the reserved sign, and quickly brought us a bottle of champagne. "Compliments of Señor Durman", he said.

"I hope you're planning to stay now," said Fina.

"We'll see." I wanted to convince them that I'd only stay if it was my decision. And maybe I wanted to convince myself, as well.

To the left of the stage were three musicians in black attire: a pianist at an electric keyboard, a guitarist, and a *bandoneonísta*, supporting on his knee the accordion-like instrument that creates the unique sound of tango music. The lights lowered and after the musicians played two lively tangos, Nico arrived in a dark blue suit, vintage 1930's. He entered singing *Por Una Cabeza*, one of the most famous songs of Carlos Gardel, who Americans might describe as the Elvis Presley of tango. With his hair slicked back to a patent leather shine, Nico even resembled Gardel, except that Gardel died at the age of forty-eight, and Nico was probably closer to sixty. He was handsome and charming, and in the first five minutes he had the audience captivated. "The theme of our show," he said, "is the music of Carlos Gardel, the great and tragic king of *tango canción*, tango songs.

"As a singer and composer, Gardel rose to fame like a shooting star, not only in Argentina and Uruguay but in Europe, and then in Hollywood. He was the first true tango star, not like Valentino, an Italian made to look like a gaucho for the silent movies. We Argentines claim Gardel as one of us, a pure *porteño*," he said. "The *Uruguayos* claim he was born in Uruguay, and the French think he was born in France, but we Argentines know he was ours. He grew up here in our city, and we celebrate his life every day. Gardel is our

Carlitos, and tonight I would like to sing for you his music."

Nico wowed the crowd with one beautiful number after another. Between songs he told Gardel's life story, from his childhood in the Abasto neighborhood of Buenos Aires to his European travels. "Gardel was not only a great singer of tangos," he said, "he was also a composer. And in the years before his untimely death, he became also a film star."

As images of Gardel were projected onto the backdrop, Nico was joined on stage by a beautiful young dance partner in a shimmering red dress. I watched his hands cradle her torso as he wrapped her in front of him, facing the audience. His long fingers caressed her hair. I guessed she was twenty-five. The musicians played *piu forte* and the couple entertained with an acrobatic *tango fantasía*. Nico lifted her effortlessly. Her long slender legs cut through the air, then folded into a compact *sentada*, as she perched in a seated position on his knee.

'The world accepts older men and younger women', said a cranky voice within me. 'That's no problem, on stage or off.' My bitter inner divorcee was turning Nico into Gordon, and his dance partner into Bridget, Gordon's paramour. It bothered me that I felt envious of the dancer. Envious of her youth, of her tango skills, and of her proximity to Nico. The emotions of the music, and the sexuality reawakening within me, were meddling with my psychological balance, and I could feel memories and emotions colliding. I took a deep breath and a gulp of champagne, then closed my eyes to clear my mind. When I opened them again, Nico and his partner were finishing their tango with her on one bended knee before him, the other long leg stretched behind her. The audience, small as it was, responded with vibrant applause.

"Gardel was handsome," said Nico, after the applause had died down and his partner had left the stage. "Gardel was talented. Gardel was a nice guy, everybody's friend. His success brought pride to every Argentine the way a child brings honor to his family. But this family was to suffer a painful fate."

Suddenly the backdrop displayed film of a plane on fire on an airport runway. The stage lights dimmed. "June 24, 1935," said Nico, somberly, "the life of Carlos Gardel ended tragically on an airfield in Colombia." There was an audible breath of response from the audience and a minute long silence. I heard sniffling, and people blowing their nose as Gardel's funeral filled the screen. *Avenida 9 de Julio* packed with mourners reminded me of photos I'd seen of Edith Piaf's funeral. Then, *a capella* at first, Nico began to sing *"Mi Buenos Aires Querido"*, Gardel's love song to the city and its people, "My Buenos Aires, My Beloved."

From our close proximity to the stage I could see tears running down Nico's cheeks. The last word in the song was "forgetting," and when Nico finished singing, the audience remained hushed, as if mesmerized. "There will be no forgetting," said Nico, "no forgetting Gardel, no forgetting Buenos Aires, and no forgetting all you lovely people who shared this evening with us. Thank you and good night."

He took a deep bow and the audience broke into passionate applause. Nico bowed again and gestured to the musicians who stood and took their bow. The audience continued, and the dance partner joined her colleagues on stage. More applause, and another bow.

"*Otra! Otra!*" chanted the crowd, begging for another number.

The musicians took their seats again, poised for action. Nico took his partner's hand and nodded to the guitarist who responded with a beautiful opening to the well-known *Milonga Sentimental*. Nico sang several choruses, then he and the young brunette danced to a lively instrumental passage. Finally, holding her in an embrace, he sang the closing line with dramatic pathos. Again the audience responded with heartfelt applause. As the musicians played the final bars, Nico and his partner bowed again, blew kisses to the audience, then disappeared behind the back curtain.

When the house lights came up, animated conversations filled the cabaret. Emphatic phrases rose above the rest. "What a great little show." "Doesn't he have a terrific voice!" "*Carlitos era un genio.*" "*¡Cómo baila esa chica!*" Most of the comments I heard were in English and Spanish, but there seemed to be a smattering of Italian, and even some German.

"Let's let the audience clear out for a minute," said Pilar. "How much did you know about Gardel, Raquel?"

"I knew basic information, and of course I've listened to many recordings," I said. "You know *La Maestra's* husband grew up with Gardel. He was quite an influence on him. I've seen film clips. But Nico really brought him to life."

"Yes! He's very good," she said.

The club cleared quickly, and we got up from the table to leave. For some reason, I didn't believe Nico would really turn up after the show, so I began to put on my jacket.

"You're not going to leave me here alone are you?" he said. I turned to find him standing on the stage, looking down at me. Though his hair kept Gardel's 1930's shine, he'd returned to his personal wardrobe of soft fabrics that accented his lean physique. I looked at my companions, as if wanting moral guidance. I couldn't name the reason for my reticence to spend time with him, he just had a bad boy charisma that smacks of trouble.

"See you in the *milonga*, girlfriend," said Fina. "*¡Chau!*" they said in unison, and walked out.

"Looks like you've been abandoned," he said, descending the stage stairs, "but Nico will not abandon you." He came up close and put his arm around me. "Good, I see you got the champagne."

"Yes, thank you," I said, "but after that champagne I'm really not thirsty."

"Then we can have cognac which is not meant for thirst, but for intimate conversation."

"Alright, since I don't have to drive, I'll have one small cognac."

"Fine. And then I will take you home."

"No, one cognac and I will take a cab home."

"*Bueno.* As you wish."

Upstairs in the café Nico found us a quiet table against the wall.

"You have a marvelous voice," I said, as we settled in.

"Trying to reach Gardel pulls the best from me." He signaled to the waiter with a wave of his hand. "You know what they say about Gardel?"

"No, what do they say?"

"*Cada día canta mejor.* Everyday he sings better." He went into the inside pocket of his jacket and brought out a pack of Marlboro cigarettes. Tapping it to expose one from the pack, he offered it to me.

"No thanks, I don't smoke."

"Oh, I'm sorry, I put us in the smoking section. Do you want to move?"

The tables around us were vacant. "No, this is fine," I said.

"I don't have to smoke." He started to put them away.

"Well, it's an unhealthy habit, but I'm not moralistic about it."

"Sure?"

"Tell you what, if I start coughing, put it out."

"Okay." As he lit up, the waiter arrived. "*Cognac, Humberto, dos,*" he said exhaling the words.

I hated to admit it even to myself, but I liked watching Nico smoke. He had beautiful hands. Soft skin and long, elegant fingers, the nails, delicately manicured. With his hair slicked back he looked like the leading man in an old movie.

"Is this the only place you sing?" I asked.

"Now, yes. But sometimes I sing at *Esquina Homero Manci*, sometimes *Club del Vino*. Many places. The shows change."

"Buenos Aires must have hundreds of tango shows."

"*Bastante, sí.* But I want to know about you, Raquel" He looked at me, and squinted his eyes.

"Honestly, I am surprised you remember my name," I said.

"Why? You are the kind of woman who leaves an impression on a man. That hair, those big dark eyes, those lips."

I loved hearing that, of course, but immediately reset my vanity meter. "I think Argentine men are very susceptible to women," I said.

"Why? Are we different from American men?"

"Definitely." I laughed.

"Why do you laugh?"

"Well, just thinking about comparing the way American men relate to women and how Argentines relate to women. It's comic."

Humberto delivered the cognacs, slid the tab under the ashtray, and vanished.

"Comic? That means funny?"

"Yes, funny. In the U.S. men treat me like a person, not like a woman, generally speaking. There's very little flirtation or sexuality in their demeanor."

"Demeanor?"

"Uh, demeanor means the way they carry themselves."

"*¿Su manera de portarse?*"

"Yes. *¿Quieres hablar en castellano?*"

"No. Please speak English. I need to practice."

"Your English is excellent. You studied in school?"

"Yes, Father made me learn as a boy. Then, I spent a little time in The States when I lived in Mexico. But tell me about you Raquel . . . Raquel *¿qué?* What is your . . . *¿apellido?*"

"Carval."

"Raquel Carval. And what are you doing in Buenos Aires, Raquel Carval?"

"Well, I came for some family business, and also to study tango."

"But you dance very well."

"Oh, I had a good teacher. She's *porteña*. There are a lot of Argentines in San Francisco."

"California? That is where you are from?"

"Yes."

"My father lived near San Francisco when he was young."

"Have you ever been there?"

"No, but I know lots of *americanas*. They come to dance tango and to have affairs."

"And you are happy to oblige, I imagine," I surprised myself by my straightforward response. "You should know I am not here to have an affair." The declaration came out of me without a moment's hesitation.

"Sometimes, I am obliging, yes. What makes you think I put you into that category?" He took a sip from his glass. "You are not married, are you," he asked, shifting his focus to my left hand.

"No. Divorced. You?"

"What, married? Divorced? No, Nico doesn't marry so Nico doesn't divorce. For some years, I thought to be a *priest*."

"Really! I don't think you'd have been a very happy priest. All this charm and good looks gone to waste? No, that would have been a mistake."

"Now you are making fun of me?"

"Not at all. But, you are what we call A Ladies' Man."

"What is that, a gigolo?"

"No, well, not necessarily. It means a man who seduces women, frequently. You've had a lot of women haven't you?"

"Yes," he tossed his head proudly, "I can say I have had many women. This is a bad thing?"

"No, but it doesn't make you a good choice for a husband."

"Ah, and you are looking for a husband?"

"Me? Good gracious, no!"

"Good! Then Nico is a good choice for you."

He came a little closer and gazed at my mouth. With the tip of his index finger he drew a delicate line along the ridge of my lower lip to beneath my chin where, with the slightest pressure he drew me to him. Very gently, he pressed his lips to mine then pulled away. I drew a long deep breath. "I would love to take a picture of your lips," he said, "just to have them with me all day long."

"Tell me," I said quietly, "do Argentine men practice lines like that in the mirror?"

"What? That is not a line, you have beautiful lips."

I laughed and shook my head.

"Fine!" He said, "Let's talk about something serious. How long do you stay?"

"How long am I staying in Buenos Aires?" Repeating the question gave me a moment to clear my head. "Maybe six months. I'm not sure."

"Six months! *¡Belleza!*" He took my face in his hands and kissed me again quickly. "This is wonderful. All this time we will have together."

"Nico, we're just having one drink. And just because you can steal a kiss or two, don't assume anything. I don't know you." I pushed away from the table to get some space but my chair quickly backed into the wall.

"I am Nico Durman," he said, "and you may ask anything you wish. Why don't you trust me?"

"Because, you're a ladies' man. You can't be trusted or taken seriously."

"Now you hurt my feelings." He dropped his gaze to the table. The smile drained from his face.

"Nico, you are constantly on stage. I'm *certain* you practice those expressions in the mirror. Don't tell me I'm hurting your feelings."

"You think I have no feelings?"

"What?" He seemed genuinely hurt, and suddenly I thought I'd gone too far. "No. I mean, yes, I'm sure you have feelings. But I'm a foreign woman in Argentina for the first time, and you are trained to charm hundreds of people from the stage. Up close you're bound to be overwhelming. You're handsome and talented, put yourself in my place, you'd be cautious too."

He nodded, still not looking at me. "So you don't like me. I am a, a . . . *charlatán?*"

"I don't know if you are a charlatan. That's my whole point"

"But so far you like me?" There was a grin and a hint of playfulness.

"I find you attractive, like the rest of the audience."

"Well, it's a start," he said lightheartedly. Lighting another cigarette, he exhaled the next question. "Carval is a Spanish name. You are not *americana*, are you?"

"I was born in the U.S. That makes me *americana*."

He looked at me seriously and without a hint of flirtation said, "I know what you are."

"What do you mean?"

"You are a pilgrim. You came to Argentina looking for home."

I felt a shiver travel the length of my spine. "What do you mean by that?"

He leaned closer. "You came here to find your true home, and now you know that you belong here."

"What makes you say that?"

"If I am wrong, tell me where your home is?"

"I don't like being challenged, Nico."

"I do not challenge, *preciosa*, I simply say to you what I see. I see a woman looking for a home for her heart."

In my mind I saw an image of the crisp black remains of my house in Oakland and the cold, industrial chic estuary condo that housed my sparse belongings. I owned that condo, but it wasn't home. Nico was right, except for one thing.

"David," I said.

"David?"

"Yes. My heart's home is in my son's heart. It is actually the only home I have." I wondered what wise part of me had realized that.

"So, there is another man in your life. When were you going to tell me about him?"

"I didn't plan on telling you about him at all," I said. "But he's everything to me."

"He's a lucky boy. How old is he?"

"Eighteen."

"Tell me about him."

"Well, he's rather tall for someone in my family. He takes after his father in stature. He has dark brown hair and big brown eyes, and a smile that lights up a room."

"Ah! There he takes after his mother."

"He's also very smart, and unusually tender for a boy, I mean even in his rebellious teens he would ask me questions about feelings and emotions."

"What do you mean?"

"Well, most of his friends could tease each other mercilessly without any thought of damaging someone's self-esteem. But David often asked me how to tell when he might cross the threshold of bullying or doing harm to someone. He was a very inclusive kid. He could have just hung around with the beautiful kids, you know, the athletes who get such a big head. He was good in sports and in studies, so he also had some friends who were nerds. They were kind of lumpy kids with acne who spent hours on their computers playing games or whatever they do."

"You are proud of him."

"Of course. And I've worried about him every day of his life.

Gordon and I worked very hard to make him thoughtful and caring, yet his tenderness always surprised me. I don't like being far away from him. But I couldn't be close to him now, even if I were in California. It was time to let him leave the nest, so I just send him my thoughts every day."

"You do like me," he said in his serious persona, "otherwise you would not tell me these touching things about your son."

"I'm going home now," I said, feeling that I'd dropped my guard and let him get too close.

"Why? I frighten you?"

"You don't frighten me, Nico, but your persistence feels, uh, invasive. I want to go home."

"I am sorry. I will not pressure you. Let's finish our drinks with a toast." He raised his glass.

"What are we toasting?"

He seemed to search for the answer. "To . . . Carlos Gardel, and the resonance of memories."

"Where did you get that phrase?" I asked. He just smiled, and downed the rest of his cognac. "Have you studied with *La Maestra?*"

"*La Maestra?* You mean Beatriz Pérez-Alvarez?"

"Yes."

His face suddenly twisted into a sneer. "I wouldn't study with that woman. Why would you ask me that?"

"You used a phrase that I learned from her. It seems strange to hear it from you."

"What phrase is that?"

"The resonance of memories."

"I just said it. I would never quote her."

"Why not?" The hostility in his voice annoyed me.

"Because I don't agree with all that metaphysical mumbo jumbo from that 'school', if you want to call it a school."

I felt uneasy. "I have to go," I said.

"But you haven't finished your drink."

"I don't want it."

"Yes, you must or it is bad luck," he said. "Here, I will help you." He poured a bit of my cognac into his glass, leaving me with just a swallow.

"To Gardel!" he said, putting the snifter into my hand and lifting his own. We took the final drink.

"Thank you," I said, pulling my purse over my shoulder. I wanted to stand up, but my chair was still up against the wall.

Nico lit another cigarette and blew the smoke away from the table. He knew that my chair couldn't move, but he took a long calm moment to assess the tab and put down some pesos. Then he stood up, tucked the cigarette pack into his breast pocket and buttoned his jacket. He took a step back, then moved the table, allowing space for me to stand. Then he extricated my jacket from the back of my chair, and, as I stepped away from the table, placed it delicately across my shoulders.

"I have to make a call," I said, taking my cell phone from my purse.

"Oh, you're not calling the cavalry, are you?

"The cavalry?"

"Like in the movies. John Wayne."

"No, no cavalry."

I slipped away from him and went toward the back of the café now vacant of billiards players. I pulled Alfonso's card from the side pouch of my purse and dialed the number.

"*¿Quién habla?*" said Alfonso.

"*Hola Alfonso*, it's Raquel."

"Oh yes, my lady, where are you?"

"I'm at the Tortoni, how long would it take you to get here? Are you available?"

"*Momento.*" I heard him say good-bye to a fare. "Yes, I am at El Presidente Hotel, just up *Nueve de Julio*. Maybe, ten minutes."

"Great, I'll be in front of the Tortoni on *Avenida de Mayo.*"

"O.K."

Walking back to the table. "Ready to go?" Asked Nico.

"Yes, I've called a cab."

"Why? I could get you a cab."

"I called a *special* cab."

"A special cab? What makes it special?"

"Well, I know the cabdriver."

"Oh, no. Do not tell me you have fallen for one of those guys who gives you his card, and says 'call me anytime'?"

Suddenly, his comment made me question my decision. Was Alfonso a potential villain, and Nico the safer choice?

"He's very reliable," I said.

"And how can you be sure of that?"

"He drives a radio-dispatched taxi."

"Oh, then certainly he must be a true prince."

"Don't make me afraid of him now that I've called him." I stayed ahead of him as we made our way to the front of the café.

"Why not, I still have time to save you from a bad decision. Why don't you trust *me* to take you home? I have my Alfa Romeo just around the corner."

"Nico, I don't know you," I said reaching the sidewalk, "but I do know that you taking me home would not be a safe choice."

"And you know the cab driver?"

"Well, it's his job to drive people home."

"Yes, and now he will know where you live."

"Stop it!"

He broke into laughter, and pulled me into a hug. "I'm sorry, I am just teasing you," he said. "But I hope one day you will trust me as much as this cab driver. You see, I'm already jealous."

"You have no right to be jealous."

Just then Alfonso arrived. Nico walked me slowly to the curb. "I hope to see you again, soon," he said.

"In the *milonga*, I'm sure," I said.

"Why don't you give me your phone number?"

"No, I'll see you in a *milonga*."

He delivered a slow delicate kiss on my cheek, then opened the door to the cab. "*¿Hermano, cómo te llamás?*" he asked Alfonso.

"*Alfonso García.*"

"*Bueno, ya te conozco, si algo le pasa a la señora,*" said Nico, threatening Alfonso with the fact that he now had his name, if anything were to happen to me.

"*Chau, tesoro,*" he said, blowing me a little kiss, and shutting the door solidly.

Alfonso pulled away from the curb, and I gave him my address.

"I'm sorry my friend was so threatening," I said. "He thinks I'm foolish to trust you more than I trust him."

"*Ese señor,* that fellow has the big ego."

I giggled. "Do you know him?"

"Not personally. It's good you called me. I do not trust him, too."

I relaxed into the back seat and closed my eyes, certain I'd made the right decision.

CHAPTER EIGHT

I was still ruminating about Nico the next day as I entered the shopping mall called *Galerías Pacífico*. Descending a grand staircase toward an effervescing fountain below, the splendor of the place took hold of me. The entire domed ceiling was painted with murals like a European cathedral. I must have spent at least ten minutes studying the figures as they turned and moved within each architectural section of the dome. Some daylight falling through translucent glass combined with recessed lighting, giving everything and every one, painted figures and humans alike, a vibrant warm glow. I had to consciously watch my step because the ceiling, marble flooring, and gleaming brass railings seduced me further into the beauty of the place. I nearly forgot I had come here to shop.

Of course, the merchandise did take over eventually, and once I started browsing the enigma of Nico returned. In my gut I didn't trust him. If he was a gigolo, it wouldn't take long for him to realize I didn't have much money, and would quickly lose interest. But then my imagination went into over drive. I imagined that he might want to use me to unknowingly sneak drugs back into the States. Or maybe he wanted to marry me for U. S. citizenship. There are a hundred things a guy like that could want. Did he have another job, something more stable and lucrative than singing tango? He'd been generous, after all: the champagne, and the drinks. And he was always well dressed. Plus he said he drove an Alfa Romeo.

When the boutiques proved to be more seductive than Nico I finally put him out of my mind. I found a few beautiful things for dancing, and fortunately, the frugal side of me had allotted a budget, so once the limit was reached, I went home eager to call my sister.

The soft still glow of the apartment welcomed me as if I were entering a painting. Indirect sunlight poured through the skylight softening edges and muting colors. I stopped at the threshold to appreciate it, and gave it a title, "Interior, Afternoon", I said. I collapsed onto the sofa and inhaled the radiant serenity. When I opened my eyes again I saw the answering machine greeting me with its little red flashing light.

"Raquel, this is Luis Viviani," it said once I'd clicked the MES-SAGES button. "Are you interested in performing a tango with me? We could have a few days to practice. Call me back at 4981-7620. *Chau.*"

My God, I thought, who would ever have imagined such an invitation! He must have gotten my number from the *Alef* sign-up sheet. I was grinning like a kid in a toy store until a part of me worried that the second message was Luis taking back the invitation. I listened expectantly: "Here is Luis, *otra vez*. If you want to, we could practice tonight in *El Alef's* dance studio. Let me know."

I punched the numbers *alegremente*. "Hi Luis, this is Raquel."

"*¡Hola!* You got my message?"

"Yes. I'd love to perform with you. What time do you want to practice?"

"Seven thirty?"

"Fine."

"See you then!"

I went next to email, and found a message from Marta.

"Tía has had a spell today. I'm taking her to Urgent Care. I'll call your cell number later. M."

The message threw a black veil over my freshly revitalized spirit. I imagined Marta spending her day with doctors and nurses, insurance forms, and the demeaning smell of incontinence. What right did I have to be shopping and having fun? I tried to call her, but her phone went to voicemail. I left an anemic message: "Sis, call me A.S.A.P."

The *Alef* gate was unlocked, so I went in and walked down the illuminated corridor toward the studio thinking that Luis might already be there. The room was dark and quiet. I found the light switch by the door, flicked it, then changed my shoes and put my cell phone on the chair. I had placed my left leg onto the barre and bent over it from the waist, when I saw Luis's reflection as he entered.

"Oh!" he exclaimed, "my partner folds into a pretzel?"

"I *have* studied yoga," I said, "but I'm not advanced enough for food poses yet."

I came over and gave him a hug.

"You are early. I am impressed," he said, setting down his shoe bag, thermos and *yerba mate* gourd.

"Just a couple of minutes," I said. "Are we dancing for an occasion?"

"No, the clubs like to spotlight dancers sometimes."

"I'm surprised you aren't dancing with Carla. I mean, I'm just a newcomer."

"You are an excellent dancer, Raquel; people should know you. The choreography is easy to learn for someone at your level. Besides you follow very well, so whatever you forget, we can cover with the lead. We dance to 'Zum', you know it?"

"Pugliese! Of course, I love it."

"Good!" He did a little flexing and stretching as we listened to 'Zum' all the way through. Then he poured hot water into the gourd, and offered it to me.

"Thanks," I said, sipping on the metal straw.

"You like *yerba mate*?"

"It's an acquired taste," I said. "We had it at home when I was growing up. Unfortunately, like so many things, after my parents died, we didn't continue the tradition."

"Well, help yourself," he said.

"Thanks. I should explain that I'm expecting a call from my sister. My aunt is very ill, and she had some type of emergency today."

"Oh, I am sorry to hear that."

"Well, she's very old, and she's been sick a long time," I said. "I feel guilty leaving my sister to care for her, but both of Tía's sons died young, and I'm here on a mission, so Marta is the only one to care for her."

"You are in Buenos Aires on a mission?"

"Yes, it's complicated, I'll tell you another time. Show me the dance."

As we walked through the choreography, I had trouble concentrating. The dance steps weren't the problem, nor were thoughts of Tía Leti. Luis was the difficulty. Each time we touched, I felt a tingle, like an electrical shock. I didn't think chemistry like that was possible past the age of forty. Was he feeling it? Was it just me?

Once we actually started to dance, things improved. I think the *mate* helped my concentration, too. My heart settled down, and my brain focused. I used our reflection in the mirrors to maintain the character of the dance. Luis taught me the choreography in pieces, and we repeated each segment several times without music. The movements sunk into my muscle memory quickly, except for one place toward the end where I had a problem with a *sacada* at the end of a *molinete*.

"My foot isn't in the right place for the *sacada*," I said. "I think the problem is in starting the *molinete* from the back *ocho*."

As we started to work through it, we were interrupted by my phone. I ran to pick up. Even listening to one side of the conversation, I knew he could follow the news. "How is she?" "Did she have a fever?" "The hospital? Was that necessary?" "I know you're doing your very best for her, *hermana*. I wish there was something I could do." "Okay, I'll talk to you tomorrow. *Besos*."

I looked at Luis with a forced smile.

"They put her in the hospital?" he asked.

"Yes. Just overnight, they said, for observation." I put the phone into my purse.

He put his arms around me. "She's very important to you."

"After my parents died, she became mother and father to both of us."

"Were you very young?"

"No. Actually, we were adults, but we lost them suddenly, and both at the same time. It was a blow. Thank you for being so understanding," I said. "Let's continue. Where were we?"

"The dance will take your mind off things," he said. We went through it again and I was impressed that rather than putting the responsibility on me, Luis actually looked to his movements as well. With a few more run-throughs, we seemed to have it and we worked out a dramatic opening that required timing the first several steps just right to place me in his arms in sync with the music.

His hand at my waist

my hand on his shoulder

my right hand in his left.

The warmth of our palms.

"Look into my eyes," he said,

"we are lovers,

separated,

reunited.

Pride, indignation, passion.

This is our tango."

The expressions and movements of our characters took form in the mirror. "You are catching on very quickly," he said. "I like that look of desire in your expression. Keep that." I was quite sure I would. "Let's call *La Maestra* as our first audience," he said. "Besides, she knows we're practicing. If we didn't ask her to observe, she'd get upset."

"Okay, the toughest audience first," I agreed.

La Maestra watched us go through it twice, making perceptive observations and suggestions. When we had trouble with the timing of the *molinete* and *sacada*, she worked us through it over and over until it was right. In close embrace we stepped into the combinations that carried us through the emotional strains of the music. As we looked into each other's eyes, the fictitious love story took shape. The hours of work had brought a deeper dimension to every movement. At the end, we held the pose breathlessly face-to-face, then relaxed and stepped apart.

La Maestra nodded her head, and raised her eyebrows. "You should finish with something more dramatic," she said. "Luis, show Raquel the drop we did for *La Mariposa*."

I didn't want to admit it, but I was starting to feel tired. I countered the fatigue with my determination to learn the movements as quickly as possible. Two turns toward Luis, take his hand and he drops me diagonally in front of him. I support myself with the right leg and my head rests on his knee. He lunges, and we finish face to face.

"Okay, let's do the whole thing," said Luis after we'd walked through it a few times. He touched my cheek. "You're doing great."

Pugliese's music no doubt contributed to the growing emotions of the dance, and we finished with what felt like a very passionate ending. We looked at *La Maestra*. The deep eleven groove of what I'd come to call 'the tango muscles' between her brows were tense with concentration. She nodded, smiling. *"Muy bien,"* she said, finally. *"La venganza de la traspiración."*

I didn't know if it was an old adage, or if she'd made it up, but I swore to remember it: "The vengeance of perspiration."

"Suerte," she said lifting herself like a ballerina from the chair.

"Gracias, Maestra," we said in unison. And she was gone.

I couldn't believe that Luis suggested we run through it again.

"I may have energy for just once more," I said.

"Excellent. Then, I promise to give you a prize," he said.

We got through the whole thing without a hitch, ended with my head down, literally on his left knee. He was in a lunge supporting me, meeting me face to face.

"The End," he said, when the music stopped. But he didn't straighten up.

"Stand up," I said.

"Just give me a minute."

"A minute?"

We started laughing.

"No! Don't laugh," he said. The jostling of our laughter threw us off balance and we started teetering. "Hold on!"

"I can't!"

It was no use. An arm here, a leg there, we cascaded to the floor in a jiggling, giggling heap.

"I have to tell you, I'm starving," I said.

"Good, here comes your prize," he said, "I'm taking you to eat raviolis. There's a little *boliche* not too far from here. They make excellent pasta."

"That sounds great."

It was after ten and the streets were alive with dinnertime pedestrians. I asked about the cop walking the beat, something I hadn't seen in other neighborhoods.

"We are in *El Once*, it is the Jewish neighborhood," Luis explained, "though now, as you see, it is also home to many Koreans. *El Once* has had special police patrols since the bombing of 1994."

"There was a bombing?"

"Yes. In 1988 President Menem, in the wake of what some people called The Dirty War, outlawed racism and anti-Semitism in Argentina. But of course hatred is a hard thing to abolish. Bigots bombed a synagogue and Jewish Community Center near here."

As we entered the boisterous restaurant, a group of men at one end of the place watched a soccer match on a wall-mounted TV. The place was nearly full but we spotted one vacant table against the window. Luis nodded greetings to several people along the way, I guessed they were all regulars. Even before the menus arrived he described the signature homemade spinach ravioli in such luscious detail that when the waiter, who was also the chef, arrived at our table, we ordered immediately.

"*Ravioles, Jorge,*" said Luis.

"*¿Dos?*"

"*Dos. Y una botella de tinto.*"

"*Muy bien.*"

In a moment Jorge returned with an assortment of crackers, "*grisines*" (delicate long bread sticks), and a small complimentary sherry for each of us.

"This little sherry is intended to spark the appetite," said Luis.

"My appetite usually doesn't need much help," I said, "especially not tonight."

We made a quick toast to tango, then sank quickly into a lively conversation to fill the vast void of our brief acquaintance.

"Tell me about your family," he said.

I filled in what he didn't know with a now familiar sketch of my situation: my divorce, my son, my sister and her family, the sad condition of Tía Leti, and the deaths of my parents."

"You lost both parents at the same time?" He asked gently.

"Yes. 1977. Returning home from Christmas midnight mass, they were hit by a drunk driver. It was very difficult. Frankly, I thought I wouldn't survive it. Every time I woke up, it seemed as though they died all over again."

"There is no oblivion for mourning, is there?" he said, wistfully.

"No. But years later, the birth of my son made life beautiful."

"Yes, when my wife died, my two daughters kept me going."

"It's amazing how children can sustain us," I said, "David was born ten years after my parent's death. He changed my whole outlook on life."

Luis recounted his wife's courageous campaign against ovarian cancer, and by the time the ravioli were served we'd gone past the sorrows of our lives and were sharing stories of our childhood. Then I told him about my love of painting, and when we discovered that we shared a passion for the works of the Renaissance master, Caravaggio, our friendship was sealed. We lingered over the last glass of wine until midnight, then he drove me home and said good night with a kiss on the forehead.

CHAPTER NINE

There were six emails from Marta on Monday, and every one of them had an attachment. With Tía Leti in the hospital, she'd had time to scan pictures from one of the old albums. I went through them quickly looking for Tío Mateo, thinking that a photo might help locate him. But these were images of my grandparents dancing tango. I studied them as if I'd never seen them before, though I remembered them, framed and on display in my mother's house. Now I studied their embrace, the placement of their feet, and even the way *Abuelo* held *Abuela's* hand. These images were part of the long chain of memories that vibrate through me every time I dance. I thought I'd lost everything when my house burnt down, but here was my history, a vein of identity, just waiting to be recovered. I encouraged Marta to keep looking for Mateo in the past, to help me locate him now.

Suddenly there was a knock on the door. Checking the peephole, I saw Ernesto, the Building Manager.

"*Buen día, señora,*" he said, with a little bow that revealed the bald spot on the top of his head. "This letter comes for you this morning." He handed me an eight by ten envelope that would not have fit into the mailbox.

"*Muchas gracias.*"

"*No, por favor . . . .*" With a wave of his hand he conveyed both 'don't mention it' and 'good-bye' as he turned and disappeared into the elevator.

The return address told me it was from the Diocese. Something had turned up! I tore the envelope open to find a copy of Mateo's baptismal certificate. There was no note or letter, just the certificate, with a gold seal, very official, suitable for framing. No invoice. I went back to email, and finished off quickly reporting the new arrival, hoping it would encourage Marti to know I'd succeeded in getting something.

That afternoon I returned to the Diocese office with the certificate as proof of Mateo's existence and record of his Argentine life. My hope was to provoke a search for employment records, but all I accomplished was fifteen pages in *El Tango, la otra historia* which I'd begun reading on my first visit. Then, the brief conversation that passed between me and the clerk was so frustrating that it set me storming all the way to the corner of *Suipacha* and *Corrientes*, a distance of maybe five blocks. The brisk pace helped me let off steam and gave me time to consider my alternatives. If I had any solid information that Tío Mateo had disappeared, I could go to Paco with evidence. But I had nothing. By the time I got to La Ideal my heart was pounding and my whole body was damp with perspiration. I was a little early for the *milonga*, and I needed to sit down, so I went into the café.

The scene captured my painter's eye. On the black and white check-tiled flooring, couples and small groups of ladies sat in black bentwood chairs at little tables. They drank from white porcelain demitasse and espresso cups. I inhaled the cool coffee-infused air, and wandered over to the leaded crystal display case where I ogled delicate cakes and pastries decorated with frothy rosettes. A plump little lady in a pink and white uniform paused her handiwork with a decorating tool, and looked up at me. With the lift of one eyebrow she inquired if I needed her assistance. I shook my head and gestured toward the tables to let her know I'd be ordering from the waitress. She smiled, nodded, and returned to her work.

Seated, I ordered water and *una lágrima*, a touching name for a small espresso cup filled with steamed milk and just a drop, literally a tear, of coffee. I didn't need caffeine, just a minute to sit in the refreshing ambiance of the café to recover from the perspiration of my walk. And since I'd be dancing all afternoon I allowed myself the calories of an *alfajor*, Argentina's signature confection: two cookies united by a layer of *dulce de leche* (caramel). Once I'd ordered, I closed my eyes to let go of the frustration and prepare myself for tango.

"Well, we meet again. This is certainly destiny."

I opened my eyes to find Nico standing over me. "It's Monday afternoon, and we're both in La Ideal for the *milonga*," I said. "I wouldn't call that Kismet."

"And what about the fact that I was just behind you the whole length of your march down *Suipacha*?"

"You followed me?"

"I saw you come out of the Diocese building, and I would have accompanied you here if your steps had not become so vigorous. I couldn't catch you without ruining my nice dry shirt. I'm glad you finally sat down."

"Well, I had a lot on my mind."

"Can I ask . . .?"

"No." I cut him off so forcefully that I felt a little embarrassed by my tone. "I'm sorry, Nico. I can't explain the whole thing."

"But maybe Nico can help you. You have trouble with the Church? I have some connections there." He sat down.

"*You* have connections in the Church? Is that from the time when you wanted to be a priest?"

"My father is a priest."

Now he had my attention. "I beg your pardon?"

"I know it sounds funny, but I will explain. I was born just days before a big earthquake. Not here, in San Juan, it's another province. The day after that earthquake a priest found me in the . . .the stones, and the buildings fallen. . ."

"In the rubble, we say."

"Rubble. Yes, in the rubble. He saved my life. As I grew up he came to see me often in the orphanage. He brought me books, and clothing. He made sure I went to school. I was never adopted, and he could not adopt me, but he took care of me all my life. I told you, he made sure I learned English, and studied the voice because I sang in the church choir and he saw I had talent."

"So when you said you thought of becoming a priest, it was like following in your father's footsteps."

He laughed. "Yes. Now you understand."

The waitress brought my *lágrima* and *alfajor.* Nico looked up and formed the word 'espresso' with his movie-star lips. The waitress blushed and gave him a wink.

"Well, that's an amazing story," I said, "but it has nothing to do with my problem."

"Well, tell me what is your problem, maybe Nico can help."

"Those Diocese people are infuriating," I said. "I went there today hoping to speak to the woman I'd seen the last time."

"So you have been there before?"

"Yes, once. But this time I spoke to a man, and had to repeat my story all over again. Then I took out the baptismal certificate I'd just received, and said I needed more information than that. You know what he said?"

"What?"

"He said I shouldn't be asking for more information if they'd already sent me what I requested."

"And you said?"

"I told him that I had asked for more than that, and there had to be more in their files than just a baptismal record. I asked, very nicely, if he wouldn't please try again. But he said it was asking too much."

"And you said?"

"I said that if he didn't promise to dig further I'd be back tomorrow and the day after that and the day after that. I said, 'I can make this into an international incident.'"

"And the clerk said?"

"Well, he went back through that frosted glass door they have, and after five minutes he came back saying that someone would look into it and get back to me."

"But that wasn't enough?"

"No! I said *¿Quién sería? Quiero un nombre.* I wanted a name. I want to know who's going to get back to me, and when." The re-telling had fired up my frustration and I caught my voice as the volume was increasing. Nico's smile made me realize that I'd also been animating with gestures like an orchestra conductor. I started to laugh, and so did he, and suddenly the whole incident shifted from serious to ridiculous. "I guess the whole thing seems pretty funny, doesn't it," I said.

"I'm sure it was very frustrating for you."

"I couldn't just leave defeated, you know, so I decided to wound him just to feel a little satisfaction."

"What did you do?"

"I said, very loudly, in Spanish, that before I met him, I'd been convinced that Argentine men were the most charming men in the world, but our encounter had proven me painfully wrong."

"Oh! You shot him right in his Argentine ego!" he said, laughing.

I shook my head. "Honestly, I just don't know what to do next."

"Maybe I can get information you cannot. I know many priests, maybe they know your uncle."

"Hello," said a familiar voice beside our table.

"Luis! How nice to see you," I said. He had a shoe bag slung over the shoulder of a crisp white shirt, the sleeves rolled up. Gray slacks. I felt my pulse rise in my throat.

"Raquel, I'm surprised you're not upstairs already," he said.

"Oh, I was a little early so I stopped to catch my breath before dancing. Do you know Nico?"

He said nothing but nodded in Nico's direction without making eye contact.

Nico nodded back with a glance that dropped quickly to the table. Was this two bulls meeting in the pasture, I wondered, or was there something more between them?

"Shall I accompany you upstairs?" Luis asked me.

"Uh, yes," I said, with hesitation. Going anywhere with Luis outranked talking about the Diocese of Buenos Aires, but I didn't want to seem rude.

"You go," said Nico, quickly. "I'll be up in a minute. We'll dance."

"Okay," I said, "Thanks for listening. Finish my *alfajor*."

"Thank you," he added, "We can talk later. I'm sure I can help find your uncle."

"I hope so. *Chau.*" As I walked away with Luis, something bothered me. I quickly reran the conversation with Nico in my head. I hadn't mentioned my uncle. I had not said who I was looking for.

Luis and I were barely out of earshot when he leaned closer to me. "*¡Ojo!*" he said. "You have to be careful with that guy, Raquel."

"Why do you say that?"

"He's . . ." he seemed to be searching for the words. "I can't prove it, but I think he deals drugs."

"Drugs? Do you have any evidence?"

As we climbed the stairs he said, "I don't think you want to defend him."

"I'm not defending him, I just want to be fair. Do you have evidence?"

We paid the *milonga* cashier and walked toward the hostess.

"Give me *cabeceo* for the first *tanda*," I said, "I want to hear more."

Anita flashed a warm smile and greeted us each with a kiss on the cheek. Then she looked at us, questioning. "*¿Juntos?*" she asked.

"No," I said. We both knew we'd separate at this point. No one would dance with me if I were seated with Luis. I followed Anita to the ladies' section, and glanced back at him with a smile.

He nodded.

Even though it was early, the place was already crowded. There weren't chairs available in the front, but Anita seemed to look for a place as close to the dance floor as possible. Our path ended at a table a ways back where three women were deep in conversation in a foreign tongue, maybe Swedish. I nodded hello, changed my shoes quickly, then visually scanned for Luis. As soon as our eyes met across the room, he smiled and nodded. I accepted, and we met on the edge of the dance floor. It was a *tanda* of tangos by DiSarli, one of my favorite orchestras. After the first tango, he said, "I hope I didn't come on too strong earlier. I know you are new here. You don't know how Argentine men can be, and you don't know the true character of the people you are meeting."

"Well," I said, "that goes for you too."

"What?"

"I don't know your character either."

"But I am not dangerous."

"How do I know that?" I teased.

"Well, I have references," he whispered before taking me into an embrace. "You can ask *La Maestra*." He smiled and I slipped into a three-minute reverie.

In the interval between tangos we each stepped back just half a step. The dense presence of other dancers held us close, maintaining the shared heat of our bodies. Too vulnerable to look into his eyes, I kept my gaze on the floor or shifted it into the crowd. Whatever conversation we'd had was washed away by the tidal wave that is tango. When the music began again, without a word, our bodies drew together like magnet and metal. The strength of his right arm drew me into his chest. I placed my forehead gently against his temple, and rather than closing my eyes, I focused my gaze on his lips. We entered the music again and blended into the vibration and rhythm that filled the hall. When the voice of Dean Martin marked the end of the *tanda* he walked me slowly back toward my table.

"I didn't finish about Nico," he said, "and I want to talk about our performance tonight at El Beso. Can we warm up at your place?"

Talk of the real world woke me and suddenly the prospect of dancing in front of a whole club full of people flooded me with anxiety. I'd never been to El Beso, but I knew it to be a popular hangout for good dancers.

"We can move the coffee table and the rug. There's plenty of space," I said.

"Great," he said. "And don't worry, you're dancing beautifully."

"Thanks for believing in me," I said. "See you at nine?"

"Okay." We kissed on the cheek and I watched him cross back to the men's enclave across the room. Luis was not a young man, probably around my age, but he could attract women of any age. It said something about his character, I thought, that he was interested in someone age-appropriate. I just didn't know if that was me or Carla. I sat back and took a long drink of water. At home I was a nearly-invisible middle-aged mother, but in Buenos Aires, I'd become a comfortably visible ageless woman. Men were openly flirtatious with me, and I liked it.

Just then I heard my cell phone ring in my purse. "*Hola*, Marti?" I said, anxiously. But I heard no one at the other end. "Hello?" Suddenly my sister's voice broke through the din around me.

"She needs more frequent dialysis," she said, through her tears.

"Oh, Marti, I'm so sorry," I said, "this is so hard on you already." I went out to the foyer to hear more clearly.

"I wouldn't mind, if it were making her well," she said. There was a break in her voice, then silence. My own eyes filled with tears, too.

"I wish I could do something," I said.

"Find Tío Mateo," she said. "She mentions him when she's lucid."

"My trip to the Diocese office was unproductive today, but I may have met someone who can help me. I'll keep you posted."

I looked around for Nico but there was no sign of him. I couldn't help but wonder if Luis's appearance hadn't had some influence on his absence. But my biggest questions about Nico were how he knew I was looking for my uncle, and could he actually help me find him.

CHAPTER TEN

I put on a black dress I'd bought at the Galerias. It had a rhine-stone-studded scooped neckline that dropped to a V at mid-back. The hemline was diagonal, from the right thigh down to the left knee. My legs have always been a winning accessory (even Gordon noticed them), and new tango shoes made me feel extra sexy. Tapered four-inch heels with delicate straps across the ankles, and black lace across the toes. The final touch was a pair of long rhine-stone earrings.

When the doorbell rang, my heart fluttered the way it had when Bobby Gomez picked me up for the Senior Ball. I checked my teeth for lipstick in the front hall mirror.

"*Sí?*" I growled into the intercom, in my sexiest impersonation of *Doña Nina's* voice as we hear it at the *Alef* gate.

There was a moment of silence, then I heard him laughing. "*Doña Nina,*" he said, "*Soy Luis.*"

"*Vení*," I growled back, and buzzed him in. I had never actually seen *Doña Nina*, *La Maestra's* housekeeper and gatekeeper, but the slow raspy quality of her voice had conjured in my mind the image of a magical old woman whose powers far exceeded entry to *El Alef*.

"You're right on time," I growled, opening the door.

"*Doña Nina*, how you have changed!" he said.

"Isn't the real *Doña Nina* a shape shifter?" I asked. "I picture her to have considerable powers."

"Well, she has the power to make a delicious paella," he said, surveying me from head to toe, "but I've never seen her look like that. You are beautiful."

"Oh, glad you like it," I said, "I wanted to look especially nice for my first performance in Buenos Aires, especially with a partner of such stature."

"Please," he said, "I'm not that tall." He walked past me into the center of the living room.

"Very funny! I mean people are accustomed to seeing you dance with *La Maestra!* Would you like a glass of wine?"

"Yes, thanks."

Returning with the glasses I found him studying the design of my apartment. He craned his neck following the upward curve of the windows, and squinted to see the ceiling structure above the suspended lamps.

"I can turn up the lights, if you like," I said.

"No, no. I like the remodel of this building. Those long hanging lights create cozy spaces by night, and the fixtures seem to float in space, their cords disappearing into the darkness overhead."

"Yes, I fell in love with the place the moment I saw it online," I said, handing him a glass of tinto. "In day it's beautifully bright in here, and there's no glare. I could even bring a good size easel in here. I hope you like red wine, it's all I have."

"That's all I drink."

I had the computer on the coffee table. "Look at these," I said, picking up the laptop. "My sister scanned old photos of my grandparents dancing tango."

"Oh, how is your aunt?"

"She's back home, but they have to increase her dialysis."

"Sorry to hear that. But these photos are *maravillosas*. Just as one would suspect, your grandmother was a beauty. Do you know what year this was taken?"

"I don't. The originals might have dates on the back. I'll ask Marta to check."

"This was here in Buenos Aires?"

"I think so. Maybe that's written on them, too."

"Send these to my computer, and I will print them for you."

"Oh, Luis, that would be wonderful. Thank you!"

"It's no problem. We have very good equipment. Not that I can operate it, but someone in the office takes over when I have trouble. Let's send them now. I can have them for you tomorrow. By the way," he said, shifting the subject, "what do you think of "The Olive" now that you have gotten to know people?

"*Alef, Alef!*" I teased.

"*Touché!*" He said, bowing his head.

"I loved the class, but I'd like to ask you about something."

"Yes?"

"Is tango 'a practice' for you?"

"A practice? You mean like a religious or spiritual practice?"

"Well, not religious, but spiritual, yes."

"Tango is fundamental to my life now," he said, "it wasn't always. I told you, my wife did not dance, so even though my mother taught me when I was a boy, I stopped dancing when I got married. Since I met *La Maestra*, tango *has* certainly taken on a spiritual dimension. I have not thought of it as 'a practice', like yoga, but I will give that some thought."

I gestured toward the sofa and we made ourselves comfortable. "What do you tell people when they ask you what tango is?" I asked.

"It depends who I am talking to."

"Well, now you are talking to me."

"Yes, I am." He came a bit closer. "People say that it is a dance about sex," he said. "That is oversimplified. The thing that makes tango sexy is the restraint. When an Argentine man holds a woman, he adores her, not just for the person she is, but also for what women are." He touched my hair, rearranging a strand across my brow. "There is a very strong presence of sexuality," he continued, "but the thing that makes it, what is the English word, "sizzle"?"

"Yes, 'sizzle' means steamy, hot. . ."

"Yes. What makes it sizzle is that we don't act on our feelings.

So the energy is there, vibrating. As in Tantric practice where the sexual energy is circulated throughout the body. It . . .vibrates."

We were so close, I could feel his breath.

"Is that part of the vibration of memory that *La Maestra* talks about?"

"To me, yes. It is the male body's memory of the female body."

"You mean from being *in* the womb, or. . ?"

"Well," he paused as if scanning his body for the answer, "both."

I took a deep breath. "Oh. Okay. And, is that a sacred memory, or is it purely, uh, carnal?"

"It is both. To me, physical love is sacred," he said.

I watched his lips form every word, making each one soft and melodic.

"So, to you, the profane and the spiritual become one?"

"Yes," he paused, "I've never seen the profane and the sacred as separate the way religions would have us believe. As bread is sacred to the hungry, desire is sacred in tango. A kiss can be a sacrament." He looked at my mouth. "And what makes tango sexy," he continued, "is that the dance creates a magnetic field. The kiss seems inevitable, immanent, yet it does not happen." He turned away and took a sip of wine.

I took a deep breath. "I think I understand," I said quietly. "The dance engages the memory of a kiss, and fuels desire. Even in those who just *observe* the dance."

"Yes, of course, all of that is happening deep in our cellular structure and our psychic structure. A tango dancer cannot think while dancing. Do you know that when we are dancing I can feel when you start to think."

"You can?"

"Oh, yes." His lips lifted into a smile, and he came toward me, kissing the tip of my nose. "Shall we practice?"

"Yes!"

He put his CD into the player, and we struck our opening pose. When the *molinete* with *sacada* gave us trouble again, a scarlet heat flooded through me. But Luis was patient, and in two more run-throughs we got it right each time. We ended with him leaned over me, our faces only centimeters apart. The moment was ripe for a kiss. Instead, in a stage whisper, he said, "Tango is our universe! Let us conquer a new galaxy."

"I'll get into my space suit, Captain," I said, as he lifted me from the pose.

"No!" he said. "If you cannot go in that dress, I'd rather stay on earth."

"Oh," I said, unable to conceal my delight, "but will I be able to breathe tango air without a space suit?"

"I promise you, if you have trouble breathing, every man in El Beso will fight to give you CPR."

CHAPTER ELEVEN

The hostess at El Beso was a thirty-something, wearing heavy black eyeliner and false lashes. As she talked on the phone, her glossy red lips reflected a flashing neon sign over the bar reminding me of a kinetic sculpture I'd seen once at the San Francisco Museum of Modern Art. We stepped up to her podium.

"*¡Luis!*" she squealed. Setting down the receiver, she ran out to throw her arms around his neck, air kissing him on both cheeks to maintain the candy apple surface of her lips. She wore a sheer, low cut white blouse over a leopard print camisole tucked into a tight black leather skirt that ended half way to her knees. The bar was crowded, the music was loud, so even though he was just a step in front of me, I couldn't hear a thing they said. She gestured for us to follow her. Luis reached back to clasp my hand, and suddenly his touch revved my pulse so that it throbbed in my throat. We inched our way forward and stopped on the edge of the dance floor, until the voice of Tony Bennett singing Luck be a Lady Tonight marked the *cortina* between *tandas*. The dancers dispersed and the hostess led us across the room. Luis stopped to shake hands, one by one, with a row of men seated together at little tables against the wall to our right. Eventually, we made our way to a table that had been reserved for us adjacent to the dance floor on the far side of the room. While I was changing into my dance shoes several people came by to greet him.

I said, "you must be a regular here."

"I know a lot of people," he said, waving to a woman across the room.

"Who are those men you shook hands with? They look like Olympic Judges."

He laughed, "Oh, they are mostly friends."

"Mostly?"

The new *tanda* began with the captivating music of diSarli's "*Bahía Blanca*." Luis stood up and reached for my hand. I placed my fingers across his palm, and we joined the crowded dance floor. He kept our movements compact and private. I closed my eyes, and the sensations created the imagery of a frothy blue aura rising up around us like champagne bubbles off the ocean floor. The delicate waves surrounding us were set into motion, not by tides but by the electrical current of our bodies.

After the *tanda* we sank into our chairs again, and the energy of my imagination settled around us like flakes in a snow globe. Luis was quiet. I was silent. I imagined that we might not exchange words at all for the rest of the evening. We would just interact intuitively.

"Would you like something to drink?" he asked finally.

"Oh, *yes*." I said.

While he gave the waitress our order, I scanned the crowded room. Across the dance floor I found Fina and Pilar waving to me, and giving me thumbs up. I held up my hands with fingers crossed. When the waitress left, I said, "I was thinking about something you said the other night over dinner."

"What was that?"

"You said that your mother was your first tango teacher."

"Yes. Mother taught everyone in our family to dance, even the dog. Well, sometimes she had to carry the dog. But he was a better dancer than my brother."

His humor and modesty set me completely at ease, and for the next hour we danced and laughed, sharing tidbits and stories from our lives. I became all the more enamored of him when I learned that he actually knew the work of Antoní Tapiès, my favorite contemporary painter. Once we started talking about art we practically had to interrupt our conversation to dance. Around eleven thirty the hostess came over to coordinate the details of our performance, scheduled to take place in fifteen minutes.

I excused myself to the ladies room, not just to freshen up and fix my lipstick, but to take a moment quietly by myself. I thought of the pride my grandparents would've felt to see *me* dance *here* in Buenos Aires. Then I thought of *La Maestra* that night at Gricel. I was so impressed by her self-confident and strong femininity. I looked at myself in the mirror, determined to hold her in my mind and heart as inspiration and role model. I would project *La Maestra's* dynamic presence. She would inspire me to outdo myself.

Making my way back to the table, the crowd was noisey and dense around me. I set my course for Luis and he drew me back to him like gravity.

"You are stunning," he whispered when I sat down. "Just watching you making your way back to me through the crowd, I felt so proud that you are dancing with me tonight. I want you to know that. This crowd will be lucky to see you perform for the first time. Don't forget that, Raquel. You are a beautiful dancer." I know I was blushing, but I lavished in his words. They couldn't have been more perfect if I had written them for him. "They will introduce us from the other side of the room," he said. So we left our table and stood next to a stout gentleman who Luis introduced as Pedro, the club manager. Pedro gave me a kiss on the cheek and thanked me in Spanish for this evening's performance. Then he said he thought it strange he'd never seen me before. Where was I from? Rosario?

"California," I said.

Pedro looked at Luis, then at me, then back to Luis. "*¿Una gringa?*" he said with a mocking grin. "You are performing with *una gringa?*" Luis's expression became stern.

"*Una gringa de nacimiento, no de sangre,*" he said. I thought it was eloquent: A *Gringa* by birth, not by blood. He looked at me and smiled proudly. The lights went up signaling Pedro's introduction. First he introduced us in Spanish, then in English. I wasn't sure if that was customary or added at the spur of the moment for my benefit.

"Ladies and gentlemen," he said, in a heavy accent, "tonight we are pleased to have a performance of the Pugliese tango "Zum", danced by Luis Viviani, who many of you may recognize as the dance partner of *La Maestra*, Beatriz Pérez-Álvarez. Tonight he dances with a new partner," he read it off an envelope, "Raquel Craval." The mispronunciation of my name felt like a pin he'd stuck in me for good measure.

We took to the dance floor with polite applause, and struck our opening pose. I breathed into my vertebrae determined to stretch from 5'1" to 5'6". The music began and I took the three steps into Luis's embrace. We looked into each other's eyes and moved into the music as if it were our natural habitat. We were born to dance tango, and born to dance it together. Our steps coordinated perfectly in length and timing, absolutely with the music. When it came to the place for the *ocho* back into the *molinete con sacada*, he marked it clearly to assure we stayed on tempo. It went perfectly and we finished with the music, Luis pulling me toward him and taking me into a dip that took my body diagonally in front of him. He supported my shoulders on his knee, leaned over me, face to face, his lips only millimeters from mine.

The audience rose to its feet. As we stood together receiving the applause, we saw that even the Olympic Judges were on their feet. I had to cover my mouth with my hand because I couldn't close it. We bowed, and bowed again, and again, and once more facing all four sides of the dance floor. And it was there, in that last bow, that I saw Nico standing at the bar, staring at us with a spiteful gaze. He didn't applaud or smile. He appeared to be a smoldering island of jealousy in a sea of appreciative applause.

Well-wishers surrounded us as we made our way back to the table. Even once we were seated, people came by with compliments. I tried to see through them, to see if Nico was still there, but there was no sign of him. Then, Pedro, the manager, delivered a bottle of champagne from the Olympic Judges, who waved and even made a gesture of tipping the hat.

"Please," said Pedro, "allow me to apologize for my comment earlier. That word, *gringa*, I did not mean . . . *Pero te ves*, I mean, you look very Argentina."

"*Soy española*," I said deliberately in Spanish, "*pero tuve la buena o mala suerte de haber nacido en los Estado Unidos. No me dejaron elegir.*" It was true. Any child taken from what would have been its country of origin, is not given a choice. We are born where we are born, for better or worse.

"Your Spanish is very good," said Pedro.

"One more surprise, no?" I said.

"Yes," he said humbly. "Please forgive me."

"Well, if you promise to pronounce my named correctly next time, it is Carval not Craval, you may consider yourself forgiven."

"*Muchas gracias,*" he said. "I learn something beeg tonight." He walked away, adjusting his jacket and tie, and wiping sweat from his forehead with a big hanky he'd pulled from his breast pocket.

"I'm so sorry," said Luis. "He's really a nice guy."

"Don't worry about it," I said. "This is a glorious moment and I don't intend to let Pedro or anyone ruin it." That included Nico. I pushed him out of my mind.

Driving home, the intimate car interior filled with the vibration of victory. "*La Maestra* is going to be very impressed with you," said Luis. "I'm sure she will hear about your powerful performance even before we see her."

"*Powerful?*"

"Raquel, you were a *force* on that dance floor."

"I was?"

"Why do you think they all stood up?"

"Because we had beautiful technique? Because we were perfectly in sync with each other and with the music?"

Luis stopped the car in the middle of the empty street and looked at me. "Raquel, the people at that club have seen good technique their whole lives," he said. Then, with the softest touch of his index finger under my chin, he lifted my head until I looked straight into his eyes. "You held the attention of the entire club. I knew you could perform that tango with me, but the strength you brought to the dance, the character, was a terrific surprise."

"I just gave it all my anger about Pedro calling me a *gringa*."

"You have to realize that we Argentines have never had a civil rights movement like you had in the U.S. So we are not so politically correct as people in California. *Porteños* use words more loosely. They don't always mean it badly."

"How do you know about California political correctness?"

"Oh, I lived in Los Angeles for a few years, and sometimes I still go there on business."

"You never told me that."

"I am happy to say, there are still many things to be learned about me."

I stared at him, admiringly.

"What are you smiling at?" he asked.

"I think I like you."

"A wise choice," he said, taking his foot off the brake. Back on our way, he asked, "How do you feel about your triumph this evening?"

I shook my head, still reeling from the adulation. "I guess Pedro did me a favor."

"Maybe we should send him a thank you note," he said.

"I'll think about it. You know, it's possible that by putting together the pieces of my uncle's life, I may be gluing my own life back together."

"What? What uncle?" he asked.

"Oh, I've never told you about my uncle?" I hadn't realized that Luis knew nothing of my search. I'd steered away from the subject in the afternoon because I didn't want to mention Nico. "Well, one of the reasons I came to Argentina is to find my mother's eldest brother. It's a pretty long story. I'll tell you another time."

He had eased the car into a snug space across from my apartment building. I reached for the door, but he stopped me with his hand on my forearm.

"Please, allow me," he said, and he jumped quickly out his side. That wasn't exactly what I was hoping for, but it was gallant.

"Now that I know you need to be insulted, I can do that for you myself," he said as we walked toward the building.

"Thank you!"

"Well, we're a dynamic twosome. The stronger you become, the stronger we will be together," he said.

We stepped into the elevator. "On the dance floor, you mean."

"On the dance floor," he hesitated, "and off."

I looked at him and wondered if he realized what he'd suggested, "we", "together." As the doors closed and the lift ascended I decided spontaneously that I couldn't stand it any more. I kissed him. When I heard the doors open I stepped away from him, walked out of the elevator, and proceeded toward my front door thinking he'd followed me. But when I heard the elevator doors close again, I turned to find he was nowhere to be seen. I rushed back and hit the button. When it opened, he was still standing where I'd left him. He looked apoplectic.

"Are you going or coming?" I asked.

"I don't know," he said. "I am in a day. . .a day?"

"A daze?"

"Yes, I am in a daze."

"Come out of the elevator," I said, taking his hand. Three steps put him in the hallway.

"I shocked you. Sorry," I whispered, linking my arm through his. "Just walk me to my door, please."

He was looking at me in such a way that I couldn't read what he was thinking. When we got to the door, I disengaged and slipped the key into the lock, turned it, and pushed the door open.

"*Chau,*" I said, turning to shake his hand. But suddenly his fingers were woven into my hair, and he pulled me toward him.

He kissed me and

kissed me and

kissed me.

He had one hand in my hair, and the other wrapped tightly around my waist. It seemed we'd been waiting years for that kiss.

He guided us inside, still kissing, then shut the door by pushing me up against it. I felt his hands down my hips, as he gently explored my back and buttocks. His lips never left mine, until he created a cascade of kisses careening down my neck to my shoulders. Through the fabric of my dress I felt the heat of his breath on my breasts. In the next moment he lifted me swiftly into his arms and carried me upstairs.

I loosened his tie and unbuttoned his shirt. Pulling it free, I slipped my hands along his soft, warm flesh. It was a mutual peeling, and it made me giggle. His shirt dropped to the floor, then my dress. His slacks. And we never stopped kissing. Every cell of my body hungered for the heat of him. I ran my hands over the long curve of his strong thighs, buttocks, and calves. I explored his taut undulating chest with my breasts. His tongue tasted my nipples and flickered there like a hummingbird at a flower. We turned and trundled, playing and grasping in an unmeasured ballet of desire.

That moment when we came together finally, played out as if choreographed by Aphrodite herself. Luis was everything I ever wanted, and he was there in my arms. We felt as perfect as the modeled figures of a heavenly cloudscape in a Renaissance painting.

Slowly we came to rest in the tumbled territory of sheets and blankets I'd previously known only as a bed. I listened to the heavy rhythm of his breathing as sleep overtook him. Shafts of moonlight shimmered on the contours of his face and torso. I thought of Psyche daring to see her lover in the night, and then a strange thought came to me: I wished my life could end right at that moment, while our world was perfect.

CHAPTER TWELVE

When I woke, Luis slumbered beside me, bathed in morning light. I drew the contour of his arm without touching him, my fingertip tracing an invisible line in the air. He opened his eyes and looked at me without moving a muscle.

"Did I wake you?" I asked softly.

"I felt an angel's wing brush across my shoulder," he said, "was that you?"

"I don't think so, the last time I looked wings did not come with this body."

"Let me check," he said. Turning me onto my stomach, he placed a long strand of kisses from my hip to my neck.

"No," he said between kisses, "no wings here." He turned me over. "Must have been a dream," he said. "Maybe I'm still dreaming. What do you think?"

"Well, if this is a dream, I'm glad we're in it together," I said, kissing his forehead, each eyelid, the tip of his nose, and then his lips. I inhaled the fragrance of our bodies. He nuzzled my earlobe, and I heard myself giggle, echoing centuries of feminine delight.

"Oh my God!" he said, suddenly. "Is that the time?" He double-checked the watch face, still strapped to his wrist. "I'm late! See what you have done to me, you she-devil. Vixen! Temptress!" He lifted me into his arms, the sheets gather up in his grasp. "You are too delicious to resist," he said. "I better reorganize my schedule to leave mornings open. But now I have to run." He gave me one more kiss, then pulled together his strewn garments, dressed and pranced down the stairs.

"I will call you later," he said. I heard the door shut behind him.

I was bursting to share all my good news with my sister, but she would still be asleep. So instead of phoning her I satisfied myself with writing an email. I had told her that the performance would be last night, so I knew she was thinking of me.

>   *Hola* **Marti,**
>
>   **I have such exciting news to tell you. First, the performance was great. Everybody stood up and applauded! Honestly, I will never forget it.**
>
>   **But news about the post-triumph celebration is even better. Luis, the architect, just said goodbye about half an hour ago because he was late for work. I know you are grinning, Sis, I can picture**

you in my mind. Ever since the divorce you've been telling me I needed a new man. Well, it looks like I finally have one.

It was wonderful. Well, he was wonderful. I can't stop smiling. I feel like I'm floating about six inches off the floor.

I'll try to call you this afternoon when I get back from LaBoca, that's the neighborhood with the brightly colored shanties. It's a strange way to have made poverty appealing to tourists. Anyway, it's an artsy neighborhood and there's a gallery I want to check out.

Un fuerte abrazo, Raquel

Anyone who's never been to this city might wonder why it was named for the air. But even the new visitor, in any season, feels the delicate stroke of the slightest breeze. Maybe it was in part my imagination, but as soon as I stepped outside that morning, it seemed that the air surrounded me playfully caressing my skin. I felt positively courageous for not phoning Alfonso and protecting myself like a princess in a carriage, but so much affection had given me courage. That's when I realized that I hadn't had an anxiety attack in days, in fact, in *many* days. I came close before our performance, but anxiety was displaced by anger. Was that what I'd needed all along? Anger? Or was the cure due to Luis, the tango, or just the air? Frankly, it didn't matter. Heroically, I boarded a bus, *el colectivo* as the *porteños* call it, and I found the only vacant seat on it.

It was humid and close, the interior air not so fragrant as the liberated air beyond the windows. In California one would have credited the city with a great diversity of people, but in Argentina the abundance of religious and racial representatives is taken simply as a fact of historical immigrations and conflicts. Surviving indigenous strains continue to surface in the bronze skin and proud profiles of a minority of citizens, while European, Asian, and Middle Eastern immigrants are constantly woven into the cultural tapestry of the city. New riders grabbed the overhead rung for support. Yearning for the cool solitude of Alfonso's cab, I told myself that these humid aromas were the glue that held together our shared humanity. But I confess that I purposely shifted my focus to the *porteños* outside on the sidewalks to keep myself calm. As we approached my stop, I joyfully pulled the cord then pushed through the aisle to land on the sidewalk, heart pumping with a deep sense of accomplishment.

La Boca was a busy tourist scene. The brightly painted buildings provide a picturesque backdrop for tango dancers who draw small crowds of onlookers in the cobblestone plazas. Their recorded music adds a movie-like atmosphere. I walked past the street vendors doing a brisk business selling their crafts. And a living statue painted completely white surprised me when a tourist's donation prompted her to strike a new pose as a graceful gesture of thanks.

Entering the Galeria Marcela I imagined Luis at my side. Just the thought of him fortified my self-confidence. My online research suggested this gallery showed work similar to mine, and though I had no intention of presenting myself as a potential artist for representation, I wanted to appear self-assured. The current exhibit suggested a curator who knew her stuff, and the lighting was well-designed. I imagined my paintings on display there. It's not impossible, I told myself, not at all. The attendant at the front desk nodded good-bye as efficiently as she'd greeted me. I nodded without a smile.

I had just rejoined the street scene when I felt a tap on the shoulder, and instinctively clutched my purse. But when I turned I found Nico nearly on top of me.

"*Raquel!*" he shouted. "*¡Qué suerte!*"

"Oh, yeah, what luck," I said. "What are you doing in this part of town?"

"I am taking pictures with my new camera." He held up a complex looking piece of photographic equipment. "I am a fine photographer," he said, "sometimes I sell my photos to the newspapers and magazines. May I take your picture?"

"You do a little of everything, don't you," I said. "I have to catch a bus, pretty soon. Can you do it quickly?" I lied, of course. I hadn't forgotten his presence at El Beso.

"Of course," he said. "Let's find a good place."

He went into overdrive to find the right spot, then turned me to face one way, then another, testing light and shadows. I posed seated on a huge chain with the deserted old carcasses of rusting ships behind me in the Riachuelo, but Nico wasn't happy with that shot and took at least three more.

"That's fine, Nico," I said. "I really have to go."

"Oh, just one more, please," he said smoothly, "I want to be in one photo, too." He entrusted his camera to a tourist wearing a fanny pack and a pair of yellow shorts asking him to photograph us with the waterway in the background. But after the first snap, Nico wanted another, and then another until the man finally just pushed the camera back into his hands and walked off.

"Raquel, give me your email address, and I will send them to you." He said, handing me a note pad. I jotted down my address.

"This is quite a coincidence to see you here," I said.

"Yes, what luck. Imagine!" He looked at his watch. "I must go now *¡Chau, tesoro! ¡Suerte!*"

With a quick kiss on the cheek, he was gone. I couldn't help but feel that there was something strange about him, and about this encounter. I watched him slither in and out of the crowd. Where was he going? Why didn't he give me the usual seduction moves? A voice inside played Public Defender. Maybe it's just because he was an orphan, she said. He wasn't raised in a family or socialized properly. That's probably the reason he comes off so, the word phony came to mind, but the voice said 'theatrical'. Then I remembered his eerie, almost threatening expression at El Beso. The image of him staring, jealous as Othello, still haunted me.

Just then my cell phone rang. "Luis! Hello!" I felt a warm grin across my face.

"How are you?"

"I'm here in La Boca, missing you."

"What a very special night," he said, "I haven't stopped talking about it all day."

"What?"

"About the dancing, I mean. I haven't stopped talking about your performance on the dance floor."

"Oh, thank God!"

"No, the rest of that evening will stay locked between you and me forever."

I liked hearing him say that. "It was one of those nights that had so many wonderful moments in it," I said, "I wish I could cut it up into little pieces to splice into all the other lonely nights of my life."

Back on the bus, I meditated on our abbreviated conversation. Luis was called away abruptly, and we'd hung up with a quick "*Chau*" leaving me in a kind of melancholy dream state. I watched Buenos Aires through the grimey bus window. As we started and stopped, the song played in my head, "*Mi Buenos Aires Querido*, when will I see you again?" This city, I thought, seduces and teaches her children to seduce. I already loved the old buildings, and the flower vendors, the cab drivers, and those tall trees along *Nueve de Julio* with their passionate purple flowers. In fact, the only person I'd found undeserving of some affection was that jackass of a clerk at the Diocese office. Why did I feel such love for this city after only a matter of days here? I remembered that very perceptive thing Nico had said at the Tortoni, that I was looking for home. He was right.

It's not enough to own a house, it can burn and disappear in a matter of minutes. What's more important, I thought, is to know your point of origin, the home inside you. Beyond that, we live our lives travelling the odyssey of our intentions.

It was early evening when I had another call from Luis saying that he'd made some excellent prints from the images Marta had sent me. We arranged to show them to *La Maestra* together when he returned from La Plata in the morning.

"How about 11a.m.?" he asked.

"I'll suggest noon to *La Maestra*," I said.

"Good, that gives us a little time together first."

"Ah! You read my mind. I'll see you tomorrow. *Un beso. Chau!*"

"*Un beso, hermosura.*" He hung up and I held the phone for a moment, savoring the husky intimacy of his goodbye.

CHAPTER THIRTEEN

At eleven I was dressed and poised to hit the intercom for Luis's arrival. But the phone rang instead. "I'm so sorry," he said, "the inspection took longer than expected, and I have to stop at the office to pick up the photos. Meet me at *El Alef*."

I picked up a little bouquet of flowers on the way and in keeping with my *"gringa"* character, rang the bell at exactly twelve. *Doña Nina*, answered, her voice rough as sandpaper.

"*Sí?*"

"*Soy Raquel*," I said. She buzzed me in without response.

Stepping swiftly through the patio, I pulled briskly on the heavy wooden door. The interior was dark and cool. I pulled back the curtain, and saw *La Maestra*, nested in her favorite corner of the sofa.

"*¡Hola!*" she said. "*¡Entre!*"

"*Buenos días, Maestra.*" I kissed her on the cheek and handed her the flowers.

"*Qué hermosas,*" she said, sniffing the bouquet.

"Luis may be detained a few minutes, *Maestra,*" I explained. "He made prints of photos of my grandparents dancing tango. But he had to go to a construction site in La Plata, and apparently forgot to take them with him. So he has to stop at his office on his way here." She didn't need to know all that, I thought, I just wanted to talk about him.

"Very good," she said, straightening her posture. "Tell me about the performance. I heard it was *espectacular.* How did you feel?"

"At first I was nervous, of course. But you were my inspiration, *Maestra.* Then I got a strange boost of energy at the last moment."

"What do you mean?"

"The club manager learned I was from California, and he called me a *gringa.*"

"Pedro? How rude!"

"Yes. But it got me so mad, that I put all the energy of my anger into the dance."

"*¡Brava!* Perhaps that is why you projected such a powerful persona."

"Well, I don't know if I would use the word powerful."

"That is the word our *Alefos* used."

"*Alefos?*"

"*Alefos* are, how would you call them? Our associates: former students and people who support our school. Many were in the audience."

"*Hola!*" said Luis.

"Hi," I said. He kissed me on the cheek and gave me a quick

strong hug before going to *La Maestra*.

"*Hola, Maestra,*" he said, planting his kiss on her forehead.

"*Buen día,*" she said, looking at him as if he'd shaved his head. Then she looked at me, and back at him. Then me.

"I am so happy!" she said with an impish smile.

"What are you talking about, *Maestra?*" he asked.

"I am so, so, very happy," she said again, clapping her hands.

She couldn't have figured it out, I thought. She couldn't have.

"*Mazel tov!*" she said, getting up from the sofa and throwing her arms around Luis. Then to me, "*Mazel tov, Querida!*" The strength of her embrace conveyed the depth of her delight.

Luis and I looked at each other silently.

"What?" she said, "You think I cannot see that the tango performance had also, shall we say, an encore?"

I felt my face flush with embarrassed laughter.

"Nina!" she shouted. "*¡Traiga una botella de champaña!*"

I wanted to say, "It was only one night," but it didn't seem appropriate. Then Luis came over and kissed me on the lips. I felt my face turn a heated crimson.

"*Ay qué linda,*" said *La Maestra*, teasing me.

"*Por favor, Maestra,*" I said.

"I will not tease you," she said, "but it is very sweet to see that two special people are now also special to each other."

"Thank you," I said. "Did you bring the photos, Luis?" I hoped to shift focus.

"Yes, they are in here." He set his shoulder bag on the chair and pulled out a manila envelope.

A lady who was certainly *Doña Nina* brought out a bottle of champagne and three glasses. She set it on the coffee table looking at Luis then at me, nodding her head with an approving smile. I was pleased to finally meet the sandy voiced keeper of the gate. She was an elderly lady, whose proportions had obviously readjusted with age. Her earlobes were unimaginably long, for example, and her arms, too short for the breadth of her torso. Her face was etched with an accumulation of time and emotion, her hair, gray as a timber wolf. I went around the sofa to meet her and as I got closer the aroma of garlic and fresh onion was almost overpowering.

"*Gracias, Doña Nina,*" I said, "*mucho gusto.*"

"Oh, I'm sorry, I didn't realize that you have not met Nina," said *La Maestra.*

Doña Nina clasped my hand warmly and gave me a kiss on each cheek. I was certain to go away smelling like a *gazpacho*, I thought. Nevertheless, the old woman was immediately endearing. Luis blew her a kiss, then opened the champagne, punctuating our meeting with the joyous pop of the cork.

"*Doña Nina*, won't you join us," he said. "You have only three glasses here."

"*No gracias, hijo,*" she said, and shuffled back to the kitchen.

"*Vamos a brindar por el amor,*" said *La Maestra.* "We toast to love, a blessing whenever and however it comes to us."

Luis and I were certainly in lust, but that other "L" word would not dare come into my vocabulary just yet. He looked at me as we touched our glasses together, then with *La Maestra*, and we sipped the golden bubbles in those still happy moments of our lives.

Luis pulled the photos from the envelope and handed them to me. I turned to *La Maestra* who had already nested back into the cushions. "Are you alright, *Maestra?*" I asked.

"Yes, I'm fine, *querida*. Some days I have some . . . I think it must be arthritis, so I am not so . . . what is the word you taught me, Luis? Esponky?"

"Spunky, *Maestra*," he said.

"I was a little close to it, no? I am not so spunky today. Do not worry. Let me see the photos."

"There are only four," I said. Handing her the first one, I laid down the other three from left to right on the coffee table. "These sepia photos must have been taken right here in Buenos Aires," I said. "I don't know any of the people in this one except my grandparents. It looks like it could be a *milonga*. What do you think, *Maestra?*" She pulled some readers from her sweater pocket, and reviewed the image with a ravenous curiosity. Inch by inch she studied it, as if looking for clues to a murder mystery.

"No date?" she asked, peering at me over the glasses.

"No, that's a copy," I said, "the date might be on the back of the original."

"This looks like Buenos Aires," she said. "The people at the Academia de Tango, above Café Tortoni could place it. It is a wonderful old picture. Which two are your grandparents?"

I pointed them out just to the right of center.

"Very handsome couple. Your grandmother had beautiful hair."

"Yes, and look at my grandfather. With that pointed nose, that mustache and slicked back hair, doesn't he remind you of Snidely Whiplash!" I giggled, and the two of them just looked at me perplexed.

"Who?" They asked in unison.

"Snidely Whiplash. You know, the cartoon villain." They looked at each other quizzically, then back at me. "Well, Snidely Whiplash looked like my grandfather."

There was one more sepia toned photo of my grandparents, posed. *La Maestra* smiled as she studied it. "Did they teach tango?" she asked.

"Why do you ask?"

"Well, it looks like a publicity photo for shows or teaching."

"I hadn't thought of that," I said, "that would explain why no one else is in this picture. I wish I knew the answer to that, *Maestra*."

"Here's a black and white," said Luis, "It looks much later, maybe the 1920's, '30's? Look at the change in the fashions."

"The girl singing is my mother. Those are my *abuelos* dancing. The little girl on the floor must be my Tía Leticia." I handed it to *La Maestra*. "And this lady in the big chair is *Abuela* Eugenia's sister Rosa, and that's Mom's cousin Jorge, I used to call him JoJo. I think everyone in this photo is family."

La Maestra quickly became mesmerized by this photo. She didn't comment or ask anything, she just kept staring at something on the right side of the picture. I looked at Luis and lifted my shoulders as a way of asking him, 'what do you think is going on?' He raised his eyebrows and shook his head.

"Has something caught your attention, *Maestra?*" he asked.

Her brow was knit, and her breathing seemed a little irregular.

"*Maestra?*" pressed Luis.

She looked up at him, breathing hard. She placed her hand to her throat, and gestured toward the kitchen."*Agua.*"

Luis was up and halfway to the kitchen before she finished the word. "*Nina, agua,*" he said, disappearing and returning in a flash. "*Tome, Maestra,*" he said, placing the glass in her hands.

She drank quickly, keeping one hand on her throat as if to help the water down her esophagus. "*No puedo más,*" she said in a whisper, "I am sorry, I cannot do no more today. May I keep the photos?"

"Certainly," said Luis, "I can make more prints."

Nina came in from the kitchen drying her hands on her apron. "*¿Qué te pasa?*" she asked, crossing quickly to the sofa.

"*Chau queridos,*" said *La Maestra.*

"*Maestra,*" said Luis, "can't we do something for you?"

"*Yo te ayudo,*" said Nina.

"I will be fine," said *La Maestra,* "You go now. Nina is with me."

"Are you sure?" asked Luis, but she cut him off quickly.

"Please, go, Luis. *Gracias.*"

We bid her a quick good bye, and slipped out to the patio.

CHAPTER FOURTEEN

La Maestra's turn had left me speechless, but after a minute in the garden I was able to talk again. "What do you think is wrong with her?"

"I don't know," said Luis. "I've never seen her like that."

"That spell came on so suddenly. And the way she stared at that photo. You think the photo disturbed her?"

"It's an old photo of people she doesn't know," he said. "What could disturb?"

"Right. Must have been a coincidence." We stood there for a moment, our bodies apart, even our chemistry at bay.

"Well, let's go to my office," he said. "I'll make new copies."

"There aren't any chemicals in the copy solution that could have caused an allergic reaction are there?"

"I don't know," he said. "I guess that's a possibility. I'll ask my staff."

On the way to his car, he took my hand. "I'm looking forward to seeing your office," I said, "It will tell me things, you can't or won't tell me about yourself."

"Really?" he said. "Then I must kiss you now before my true character is revealed."

Luis's silver Mercedes suggested that the architectural business was enjoying prosperous times.

"Aren't you afraid someone is going to bang into your car?" I asked as he manipulated through the traffic. "No one stays in the lanes here."

He laughed. "Well, I would only get hit if I decided to use the lanes when others did not. I had to get used to that in California."

"How long were you in California?"

"It was a two-year project," he said. "My wife had died two years before, and I felt like I would never scrape the grief off my bones."

"So you found work far away. That was a good idea."

"Actually, it found me. I got an invitation to design a house for someone who had come here to dance tango."

"A woman?"

He hesitated. "A woman, yes. A married woman."

"You can tell me anything," I said, "I won't judge you."

He smiled. "It wasn't a romance, honestly. It was a project. It kept me working and gave me distance from the sorrow of my usual surroundings. My daughters were married. They had their own lives. For me, life had lost its meaning."

He pulled into a parking lot beneath a building in the Recoleta district, and parked in a slot with his name on it. Not only was the garage well lit, the walls were painted with murals. Before pulling the keys from the ignition, he leaned over and kissed me softly. The warm touch of his lips carried me to the vibrant memories of our night together.

"Come along," he said then abruptly, "I will show you my kingdom."

"I can hardly wait."

Up the lift we went to the fifth floor and out into a foyer with marble flooring and walls. The space glowed with light from a large central circular opaque skylight beneath which sat a young, raven-haired receptionist in a business suit behind a tall semi-circular rosewood desk. She sat on a chair raised to the height of a barstool and wore a rockstar-style headset. *Viviani Associates* was announced in raised gold script on the front of the desk.

"*Señor Viviani,*" she said. "*buenas tardes.*"

"*Buenas tardes Lourdes,*" he said as we crossed behind her and through a broad corridor toward the offices, visible beyond. It was a tunnel of cool air with recessed lighting and as we walked I felt my hair flutter like a fashion model in a photo shoot. The scene ahead was a tableau of men and women at work bathed in softened sunlight. Some were at desks with Art Deco dividers of bronze and frosted glass. Once in their midst I saw the drafting department to our left, their tables under another opaque dome of light, and the external windows aglow with translucent shades. Against one wall three-dimensional models were displayed on backlit shelves in glass cases. The entire suite had an ambiance of dynamic harmony, everyone busily at work. Well-dressed young men and women greeted Luis as we passed. "*Buenas tardes, jefe,*" they said.

"*Buenas,*" said Luis.

"*Buenas tardes, Luis,*" said a middle-aged woman in dark slacks and silk blouse. "What are you doing back in the office? I thought you were out for the afternoon."

"We need more copies," he said, not stopping for introductions.

In his office he brought up my photos on the computer and started selecting commands from the drop down menus. His desk was impressively clear of clutter, but the surfaces along the walls were busy with projects and storage. I studied his family photos on the desktop without picking them up. Two frames of young families, I presumed his daughters, their husbands and children. And one, I presumed, of their mother, an attractive woman with dark hair and eyes, and an engaging smile.

"This is a beautiful office," I said, steering my curious eyes away from her.

"Thanks," he said. "Now, if I can remember what we did to get those prints . . ."

"I hope *La Maestra* is okay," I said, thinking out loud. "We should call her."

"I've sent the images to the copier, so I'll leave you here for a few minutes. Make yourself comfortable. Would you like a coffee?"

"No thanks, I'm fine." I was eager to explore the room in his absence. But as soon as he left a sleek young woman came in.

"Hello," she said with a big smile, "I am Jessica."

"I'm Raquel." We shook hands, she gave me a kiss on the cheek.

"Nice to meet you," she said. "You are interested in architecture?"

"Yes. I'm an artist, a painter. I'm fascinated by creativity on such a large scale."

"Would you like a little tour?"

"Absolutely, thank you."

We went from model to model, with Jessica explaining the current projects and their locations as if I knew the city and the country much better than I did. There were homes, and medical buildings, and one large project was taking shape for an a international publishing company.

"Is Luis a good boss?" I asked. "I promise to keep your remarks confidential. I'd like to know another side of him."

"Well, honestly, he has good, and he has not-so-good," she said in a just-between-us-girls tone of voice.

"Oh, what's the not so good?"

"He is a perfectionism," she said.

"Perfectionist?"

"Yes, that's it. Perfectionist. Everything has to be exactly how he wants it, and that is true for everything." As she spoke, I wondered if her perfect application of makeup came under scrutiny, too. "And when we are on a deadline, everyone stays late, until he is satis . .satis. . .*satisfecho*. . .you know?"

"Satisfied."

"That is it, satisfied."

"In The States we'd say he's a 'slave-driver'," I said with a smile.

"A slaves driver?"

"Slave driver."

"I must remember that," she said.

"Have you considered leaving the company?"

"Work for someone else?" Her eyes grew wide. "No! No one would do that."

"Why not?"

"Where do I begin? The reputation of this firm is not like any other. But best of all, as bonus, we can choose money or *fútbol* tickets. You know, soccer?"

"Those are worth a lot of money?"

"You are from United States?" I nodded. "So, you do not know what it means to have soccer tickets. We don't sell them. Vivianis have really *good* seats."

"Oh."

"Yes. In summer we also have *asados* at their house at El Tigre outside of Buenos Aires. Also, we have a profit share plan, and vacation, and . ."

I stopped her there. "I see why you don't mind the slave-driver."

Suddenly Luis's voice broke the gentle lull of the office with an ardent curse. "*¡La puta madre!*" he yelled.

Jessica moved immediately closer to me and raised her voice, as if trying to drown out the epithets coming from the copy room. "But he is a charming slaves driver," she said. "Can I get you a cup of coffee?"

"That damn copy machine," said Luis coming to the door. I peered out at him from behind Jessica who was clearly trying to shield me from another of her boss's faults. "Oh, Raquel," he said, suddenly conscious of his tirade, "I'm sorry. I want to give you copies as good as those I made the first time, and I am having trouble with the borders."

"I'll be happy with leaky borders," I said. "Let me see what you've got."

"No, no, no," he said. "Jessica get Tony."

"Yes, sir," she said, and jumped into action.

"This machine is very expensive," said Luis as I trailed him into the copy room. "It should work on the first try. If it weren't so late in the day, I would call the company right now to come and fix the damn thing."

"Here he is!" said Jessica hurrying back, with the young Tony, I presumed, behind her."

"*¿Qué pasa, jefe?*" he asked. "*¿La máquina otra vez?*" He went directly to work on the villainous machine in the far left corner of the room where countless copies of my relatives lay across a large worktable. I surveyed the multiple images of my mother, Tía Leti, and my cousins, and noticed that behind Rosa in the armchair was a young man I hadn't noticed earlier. He was maybe seventeen or eighteen years old. Half his face and body were cut off.

"*¡Por fin!*" cried Luis. "*¡Antonio, sos un genio! Te debo unos boletos especiales para La Bombonera.*"

Tony beamed with the thought of special *fútbol* tickets.

"*Andate a casa, che,*" said Luis, letting him go home for the day.

As he came past me, the young man nodded respectfully. "*Señora,*" he said.

"*Muchas gracias,*" I said.

"*No, por favor,*" he said, with the typical *porteño* gesture of 'don't mention it'.

Luis was finally satisfied with the prints. "Here we are," he said, "probably almost as good as the originals."

"Thank you for going through so much trouble," I said.

"No trouble at all. As my grandfather taught me, anything worth doing, is worth doing well. Let's take a look at these now," he said. "Why didn't you bring originals?"

"Well, my mother's albums only went back as far as her wedding, and Tía Leti couldn't remember where she'd put her albums, and Marta. . ."

"Never mind," he said, "let's get a closer look." He held a magnifying glass over the image.

"Look at the kid on the far right," I said.

"Looks like he has *un labio leporino*. What is that in English?"

"A harelip. But I don't think that's a harelip. I think it's a scar," I said, taking the magnifier from him. "There's another scar running across his forehead, too. See, under his hair. That's why he seems to be scowling."

"Look at his left arm," said Luis. "I thought he was turned away, but no, he has no arm. The shirt sleeve ends, I see no elbow."

"My God, you're right. This has to be my uncle. The scars and the amputation of his arm are the result of an accident when he was a kid." I pulled out my cell phone. "Let's see if my sister is home," I said, "I can't wait for the email. I also want to hear how Tía is doing today."

Our conversation began as usual, but I had no time to waste. "Marti," I said, "we've made copies of the photos you sent, and I think Tío Mateo is on the right side of the one where Mama is singing. I need you to show it to Tía and confirm that."

"Her eyesight isn't too good now, but when she wakes up I'll ask her. I hate to tell you, Raqui," she said, "but she's starting to lose her orientation. And sometimes, she calls for Mateo like he was in the next room."

"I'm *trying* to find him," I said.

"I know. I'll look for him in other photos, too. How will I know him?"

"You can't miss him. He appears to have a harelip, and there's a scar on his forehead. Also, he's missing the lower part of his left arm."

"A scar, a harelip, and a missing arm? He ought to stand out in a crowd," she quipped. "Sorry, I don't mean to be disrespectful."

"I know. Just send me whatever you find."

"Okay," she said, "Have you seen that hunky architect again?"

"I'll tell you about that another time," I said.

"Is he standing right there?"

"Yes. Gotta go now. I love you. *Chau!*"

"Okay! *Chau!*" She mimicked me playfully and hung up.

"My aunt's getting worse," I said to Luis.

"You are doing the harder job," said Luis.

"Thanks for reminding me. When my mind is flooded with tango - and you - I lose sight of the fact that everything I'm learning here about memory and history and identity is tied into this job to find Mateo. Can I ask you a question?"

"Of course."

"I'm trying to figure out where memory lives. *La Maestra* said, 'It's not the memory of your brain, but the memory of your body.' Do you think memory lives in our skin?"

"I have thought about this, too. I am no scientist, but it's common knowledge that the cellular body renews itself constantly. I figure that memory must live in the weave of our identity, maybe in our DNA. Brain science tells us that different types of memory live in different parts of the brain, but I think our inner *spaces* matter as well." Luis placed his hands on my shoulders. "We are like buildings," he said, "our structure supports our spaces. In architecture, the external lines," he ran his fingertips delicately up to the nape of my neck, "and internal spaces create a dialog. Inside there are chambers, courtyards, tunnels!" He barely touched the skin as his fingers traveled across my face. "Ear canals, and sinus cavities! The body is the ultimate architectural design."

"I get it. We're filled with echo chambers, aren't we!"

"Exactly! The esophagus," his hand descended gently down the center of my chest, "and the lungs, inside those perfectly shaped ribs." His hands wrapped around my torso, thumbs at the base of my breasts. "Our spaces are resonant chambers for the body's memories," he said.

"I see." Our lips nearly touched.

"I didn't think anyone would see this reverberating structure as I do, unless they were another architect," he whispered.

"Well, I often feel emotions vibrating inside me," I said quietly, "so your theory makes perfect sense. I understand you . . ."

"Perfectly," he said, placing the word on my lips.

CHAPTER FIFTEEN

We went to dinner at that little place in El Once, then stopped at an intimate tango club. A couple of people came by to congratulate us on our El Beso performance. Their reviews were glowing, and so were we. I could have danced until three or four a.m., but the restraint of the tango became unbearable.

"Would you like to go home?" he whispered, lips caressing my ear.

"You read my mind." He helped me with my jacket. "I wish *Doña Nina* had let you speak to *La Maestra*," I said.

"She said she was resting."

"I know. I would just feel better if one of us had spoken to her."

In the silence of our journey home I thought about the photo of Mateo. Finding him even in a photo gave me a vague sense of accomplishment. When we arrived on the threshold of my apartment I erased him from my mind. In fact, as soon as I unlocked the door,

Luis and I fell into an embrace that obliterated nearly everything beyond our little pod of enchantment.

"How intuitive is *La Maestra!*" I said.

"Yes, she read the chemistry between us immediately," he said.

"I wonder if she feels her toes curl every time you kiss me."

He laughed. "Well, if she does, she better brace herself for what is yet to come."

"OOOH! I guess I should too!" I said playfully.

"Tonight, for you, a banquet of sensual delights," he said.

"Really? Then why are we here on this sofa? We need a bigger territory."

No need for candles that night, the moon in all her ancient wisdom, rose to a point of perfect alignment with the skylight above my bed. "The ancient Sumerians would have noted this alignment of the moon and celebrated it annually in the temple with a night of lovemaking," I said.

"Really?" He looked at me in disbelief. "And somehow this moment reminds you of your cultural anthropology class?" he asked.

"Well, it's not scholarship," I said, "I'd call it integrated memory. It is rising from those echo chambers you told me about."

"Of course," he said, nuzzling against my cheek. "Then let us reveal our divine Abyssinian costumes," he said, tugging on the zipper of my dress.

"Sumerian," I said. I unbuttoned his shirt.

"Sumerian, yes."

When we lay naked in the moonlight he lifted his head and

looked at me. "Now the goddess is happy," he said, bringing me against the full length of him.

In that moonlight, for the first time in my life, there wasn't a single position that made me hesitate for the sake of vanity or morality. We just followed our instincts, and savored the long night. Just as in tango, we moved together, and seemed to share every breath. Luis wove his fingers into my hair and firmly took hold to guide my movements left and right, back and forth. He pulled me away from him, kissing the length of my neck, adoring my breasts with his lips and tongue.

Even at the beginning of our courtship, Gordon wasn't what I'd call an ardent suitor. Our lovemaking was satisfying, in the clinical definition. I knew he loved me when we married. But Gordon's real passion was discovering something unexpected through a microscope. Well, he'd obviously expanded his interests by the time he met Bridget. I had evolved into a wife by that time, and once we divorced, I felt I had lost whatever sex appeal I'd once had. I never imagined that I would yet become the woman Luis Viviani would choose. Actually, he chose this Argentine Raquel, the woman who dances tango, who flirts with flower vendors and the clerk in the pharmacy. His Raquel has beautiful legs, and a sassy haircut. She doesn't drive her kid to soccer after school, or roll the recycle bins down to the sidewalk and back every Thursday. To be honest, he didn't choose the woman Gordon divorced, he chose her beautiful twin, the one that lives in the land of possibilities.

I woke up Thursday morning fearful I'd turned back into the Gordon-reject Raquel. With the handsome architect next to me, I worried that the sun would dispel the magic his counterpart had conjured the night before.

"*Ummmmm, buen día, Hermosa,*" he said pulling me closer.

"*Buen día,*" I said. "It's eight o'clock. Do you have to run out of here?"

"No, not at all, do you want me to?"

"Of course not, but I'm an unemployed ne'er-do-well. You are a working, creative contributor to society."

"This morning I am not such a hard-working contributor. I am an unshaven Bohemian, a gigolo living to please my American mistress."

Suddenly, I felt his exuberance blossom as he gently pushed his body into mine. The magic had not disappeared, nor had it atrophied in the night.

"Really?" I squealed.

"*Let mee show you what a veery good ghigolo I can be mon amour,*" he said in a throaty French accent. He held me tightly and placed his lips on mine. Once again we followed our passion with all the abandon of moonlight. I was amazed actually, at my own unself-consciousness. He didn't care if I had cellulite, or a scar here or there. And if he didn't care, I wasn't about to stop the machinations of love for the sake of prudence. Besides, I was Raquel's beautiful twin by that time, and she's a pagan.

At nine thirty, he woke from a love nap. I'd been thinking

about the idea of resonant spaces within us because it felt like something metaphysical was happening here. "Unbridled passion" the romance writers might say, but also something beyond the egos of two people. My body wanted him more than she'd wanted anyone. I didn't even know I could feel that depth of desire. It astounded me. Then I thought that to men this symbiosis is probably just what they call a good lay.

I looked at Luis' features slowly coming back to consciousness. Eyes closed, he licked his lips, and twisted his face about. His eyelashes flickered, and finally he opened his eyes.

"*Mon dieu!*" he said, "*Ze Americaine lady, she want more of Pierre?*"

"Relax Pierre," I said, "it's time to get up. Become part of the real world again."

"*Yiu Americaine are so pragmatique! We French are too sensitive for ze world of ze capitalisme.*"

"Just get a shower!" I said, giggling and tickling his torso.

"*Oo-lah lah! Ze madame is steel wanting Pierre, eh Madame?*"

He pulled me into an embrace and rolled me on top of him.

"O.K. Pierre, what if we get a shower together?"

"*Voila! Yiu see how easy is ze compromise!*"

At eleven thirty we stood again at the front door.

"I hate to say it, but I have to go back to La Plata this afternoon," he said, "I will be back late tomorrow. But I'll call just to hear your voice."

Two, no five kisses more, and he left.

CHAPTER SIXTEEN

Saturday morning was fragrant and warm, destined to grow into a humid afternoon. I dressed for the second session of *El Alef,* hungry to go deeper into tango and equally eager to see Luis, who, for some reason, had not phoned since our Thursday farewell. I felt anxious again, and anxious about being anxious. I knew it was inappropriate to feel proprietary, but I did.

Entering the *Alef* courtyard, I greeted the mingling *Alefos.* I wasn't a total newby anymore. I even knew some of them by name. Indoors, I stopped in the corridor to check out photos I hadn't yet seen, honestly hoping that Luis would once again come up behind me. I kept the doorway in my peripheral vision pretending to focus on the photos until impatience got the better of me and I went into the studio alone.

Some couples were warming up to D'Arienzo. I was practicing *ochos* in front of the mirror when I saw the reflection of Luis entering. Carla clung to his arm. She was cooing, and batting her eye-lashes and talking softly into his ear. He was smiling, as if he liked it. Then someone closed the door, suggesting that *La Maestra* would be entering any minute. Luis lifted his head, as if he might have been looking for me, but then Carla said something and they sat down to change their shoes. It occurred to me that if I'd talked with Jessica a bit longer, she might have added fickleness to his faults. Had I made a fool of myself? Maybe it had been just a roll in the hay to him, or however *porteños* put it.

La Maestra entered with Paco, who brought her chair to the center of the studio floor. I had called her on Friday, but again *Doña Nina* said that she was resting and wasn't to be disturbed. Students surrounded her now with the usual greetings. I held back, wishing I were invisible. My emotions about her condition were complicated now by the sight of Luis with Carla. I watched our teacher gently greet each person who addressed her, certain that the malaise we'd seen on Wednesday had not lifted. Paco sat on the edge of the circle across from me. When we made eye contact, he smiled and nodded a quick hello. I reciprocated.

La Maestra led us immediately into deep breathing and a brief meditation awakening the muscles and focusing on our core, where a deep burning ache had nested within me. I saw Luis look back at the studio door a couple of times, then he closed his eyes and seemed to follow the meditation.

"When you are dancing," said *La Maestra*, "the core muscles must be engaged to maintain *la postura*, the posture of pride. Keep this in mind later, when we work on technique."

She seemed unusually brusque, fielding questions with quick, snappy answers. When a woman asked how she could hide her emotions when she danced, *La Maestra* told her not to dance a lie. "Do you dance to deceive?" she asked. The woman looked startled. "Tango is full of deception," said *La Maestra*. "In a strange paradox, I have to say, at least it's good you're honest about it." Everyone laughed. Then she threw out a sharp barb of a question. "Carla, what do you bring to tango today?"

"Uh," Carla seemed startled, "I bring *cariño, Maestra*, affection."

"A coy, but no doubt, honest answer," said La*Maestra*. I read annoyance in her expression, but maybe it was my own. She looked at Luis sitting next to Carla, and I was too far to the side to see her full expression, but she wasn't smiling. Considering how perceptive and happy she'd been with us, I knew she had to be at least a little upset with him sitting beside Carla instead of me. At least, I hoped she was.

"When you are dancing in the *milonga*, each person is carrying a world inside them," she said. "Sometimes we carry problems, anger, or lust. People bring the same emotions to tango that they take to prayer."

Everyone seemed to wake up at that moment.

"*Maestra*," said the Buddhist from Oregon, "would you say that again, please."

"Yes. Many people take what is in their heart to God through prayer. *Tangueros* take what is in their heart to God through tango." She stopped there, looking around the room. "This means that *tangueros* treat the dance as a special, perhaps sacred, place and time. Tango is not rock and roll. It is not swing music. Those are good musics, but tango is not just 'good times Charlie.' This is the *raison d'être* of *El Alef.* I chose each of you to be here because you have a potential to bring more to tango than a new pair of shoes and adequate *ochos.* Know yourself. Do not just walk around in your skin, mindlessly tick-tocking your life away. If you want to dance tango, make it worth something. Knowledge of yourself will bring truth to what you do, especially to your dance. Your body is the instrument of your life, and life is your ultimate tango."

The room went quiet a moment. The students looked at the floor, or studied their hands.

"The better the technique the more truthful, or deceptive, you can make your tango. With good technique your tango can have nuance. Learn to dance *all* the colors of your life."

It was quiet again. I focused with all my might on what she was saying.

"I know the spirit of tango drops its seeds into the heart of each man and woman who loves it," she continued. "Tango feeds the ego. It makes women feel sexy, and men feel powerful. So even those people who dance it poorly want to claim it as their own. But tango is something to achieve. Over and over again. Let it stretch you. Let it make you a better person. A wiser person. Nothing is as offensive as a fool dancing tango. The *milongas* of the world are full of such fools. You will know them quickly: they talk while they dance, they make fancy steps, and when the music pauses, they keep moving!"

She started to pace back and forth in front of the blackboard. "Some people have told me, this school creates ancestors worship," she said, "as if to accuse me of creating a religion. This is absurd!" She teetered and held out her hands to rebalance herself. "*Our* school is a place to learn all dimensions of tango, echoes from the past and the future."

The students were starting to look to each other for solidarity in a growing discomfort. Paco went to her.

"*Sentáte, Maestra,*" he said quietly, then led her gently to the chair. She leaned into him and her head dropped as if she'd suddenly fallen asleep.

"*Horacio, ¡música!*" said Paco. Luis swept in quickly, lifting her. Paco opened the residence door and they disappeared behind it. Marcelo came over to me. "*La Maestra* would want us to practice until she returns," he said. I knew he was right, and we joined the others beginning to dance.

After about twenty minutes Luis, Paco, and *La Maestra* returned. We applauded. She smiled and waved. Marcelo cut the music. "I am sorry to disrupt the class," she said. "I feel not so good today. But we can continue." She gestured to Horacio to play on.

I hoped she would just sit down, but she wandered among the students as they returned to their practice. Quietly she made corrections or suggested embellishments. Luis stayed near her. I tried to make eye contact with her, but she didn't look at me. I knew she knew that I was in the class, nothing escapes her in that classroom. But for some reason she didn't come near me.

"Shush!" she said. "Someone is still sanding the floor with the shoes."

"It's hard to remember everything," said one of the students.

"I know it is, but remember that tango is an earth dance," she said. "It has roots in African dance. Feel the heat of your partner's body next to you, and feel the earth body beneath your feet. Then, step human body into earth body. The foot *caresses* the floor." She was lucid and clear. She seemed to be revived, but for some reason she still didn't look in my direction. She had us change partners repeatedly until eventually I had to deal with Luis.

"There you are," he said, putting his arms around my waist and drawing me into him.

La Maestra spoke up again. "I am giving you some thinking homework this week," she said. "Ask yourself: What does tango have to teach me about living?"

We were all quiet.

"What does tango have to teach me about living?" She repeated it, purposefully. "That is all for today. Now you can have *práctica. Muchas gracias. Chau.*" She waved and left.

Along my eyelids I felt the searing sensation of fury. "What's wrong with *La Maestra?*" I asked Luis, pretending to be following her with my gaze.

"She's not well today."

"She wasn't well on Wednesday either," I said. "Yesterday she wouldn't take my call, and today she didn't even look at me. Maybe she knows something I don't know, and she can't face me."

"What are you talking about?" he asked. "Look at me, Raquel." Instead, I looked at Carla across the room tossing her blonde hair away from her eyes as she began dancing with a new partner.

"Hey!" said Luis, turning my face with his hands.

"We saw how intuitive she was the other day," I said, "and how happy she was to see us together. One doesn't have to be clairvoyant to pick up on you and Carla, Luis. Obviously, *La Maestra* got the message, too."

"First of all, there is nothing with me and Carla," he said. "And secondly, *La Maestra* is not well because she is physically not well. I'm worried about her."

"I'm worried about her too. She purposely did not look at me. There *must* be a reason for that."

"Well, I don't know what it would be," he said. "Let's dance, at least. I've missed you, and tango always brings us closer."

"It can't bring us together if we're not really together," I said. "Isn't that the point she was just making, about dancing the truth. I'm going to change my shoes."

I walked away from him, to the far corner where my shoes waited beneath a bentwood chair. When I looked up, he was still looking at me, then he went back to his seat and started changing into his street shoes, too. I saw Carla finish her dance and move quickly to Luis's side, unbuckling her heels. They were seated right beside the door so I had to walk in front of them. When I got there he took hold of my forearm and stood in front of me barring the doorway. I stared into his chest to avoid his gaze. He wouldn't let go of me.

"Are you going to lunch?" asked Carla. "May I join you?"

"I'm sorry, Carla," he said, "we have some things to talk over. We can't go to lunch now."

"Oh," she said, looking at me, "can I help?"

"No," he said, "thanks anyway."

If I hadn't been so angry, I'd have gloated over the victory of winning Luis's attention. As it was, I was glad to simply leave Carla behind. We walked in silence for a block and a half. San Telmo was throbbing with the noisy weekend crowd. Finally I stopped abruptly in my tracks, and blurted it out, "What the hell is going on?"

"I wish I knew," he said.

"Well, you must know why you didn't call when you said you would, and you must have some idea about why you escorted Carla so affectionately into class," I said. "I seem to have some misconceptions about what has been happening between you and me, Luis. So let's just clear things up."

On the sidewalk people cut around us like stream water straddling a boulder.

"First, I lost my phone," he said. "It has your number in the automatic dialer, so I don't remember it. And second, Carla is an old friend."

"Oh, please, don't insult my intelligence. She was hanging on you and whispering in your ear."

"Yeah, I guess that could seem romantic," he said. "My phone is not at your place?"

"Could? It *could* seem romantic? How else could it be interpreted?" I was trying to keep my voice down, but so much emotion had built up inside me, I was having trouble controlling myself. "If you want things to be casual, okay," I said, "let's put our cards on the table. Tell the truth about what's really going on between you and Carla."

"Carla would like us to have something 'going on'," he said, "but nothing is happening. We are not lovers, if that's what you are thinking. She's been a good friend. She helped me very much when Mari was ill. She was kind to me and to my daughters. Whenever I needed someone in an emergency I could count on her. I don't want to hurt her. But, as you see, she is very possessive, clinging sometimes. This morning she was in the patio as I arrived. She put her arm into mine, and the rest is what you saw: A performance on her part, a fantasy."

I just looked at him, and in my ear I heard my father's old warning regarding my gullibility. 'Don't be a damn fool', he said.

"You're telling me that you just met up with her in the patio?"

"Yes."

I knew I needed to think about this before I decided whether or not to believe him. But now that I had at least a temporary answer, my focus shifted to *La Maestra*.

"What do you think is wrong with *La Maestra*?"

"Wait a minute. Do you believe what I just told you about Carla?"

"I don't know. You didn't call, and then I see you walk in

with her. Let's talk about *La Maestra* for a minute, I'm very worried about her."

"The phone might have fallen under the bed," he said.

"*La Maestra*," I insisted.

"Yes, of course. When I took her into the salon, she was confused," he said. "Nina gave her some medication and some *mate*. She put her feet up for a few minutes, and Paco put a cold towel on her forehead."

"She didn't speak to you?"

"No."

"And Paco?"

"No, not a word from him either."

"Do you know him very well?"

"Yes, of course, he's been with *La Maestra* for years. I met him first as Carla's father, then we became friends at *El Alef*."

"I feel like you know something you're not telling me, Luis."

"No, I don't," he said. "I have seen her have spells in the past."

"What do you mean, spells?"

"Not like seizures or anything, just, you know, fainting spells."

"Well, that could be anything. Lack of food, slow thyroid function, fatigue."

"I know." He looked back toward *El Alef*. "I think I'll go back. I have to know what's going on. She cannot shut me out like that."

"She wouldn't look at me, or come near me, Luis. Are you sure she doesn't know something more about you and Carla?" My voice was starting to crack.

"There is nothing more to know," he said, wrapping me in an embrace. A part of me wanted to fight him off, but tears were burning streaks down my face, a clear sign of resistance meltdown. He stroked my hair and placed his lips at the center of my forehead.

"Maybe she is ill," he said in a frightened whisper. He stepped back and looked at me, his hands placed parenthetically on my shoulders. His expression was lined with dismay. "Maybe *she* misunderstood what she saw with Carla, too. I have to explain."

"I'm going with you," I said. He ran his hand down my arm in a comforting gesture that unleashed an onslaught of new tears. Taking my face in his hands, he said, "We are together, Raquel. *No te preocupes.* Don't worry. *La Maestra* is a complex woman. She has suffered a lot in her life. First the Spanish Civil War, then her husband disappeared, and her son, too. The spells could be psychological. Maybe something has triggered old memories. She has suffered in the past from, in English it is PT, what?"

"PTSD? Post Traumatic Stress Disorder?"

"Yes, maybe that is it," he said. "Let's go see if we can get a few answers."

As we turned to go back to *El Alef* I felt him reach for my hand, but I pulled away. "Let's focus on *La Maestra* for now," I said.

CHAPTER SEVENTEEN

La Maestra was lying on the green sofa, her head propped up on pillows, Paco at her side. The drapes, partially drawn, suppressed the customary warmth of the salon.

"*Maestra*," I said, hesitating at the curtain.

"*Venga, querida,*" she said, opening her arms.

Luis and I went to her. I gave her a gentle hug. "How are you?"

"I am a bit better. Paco does not leave my side, he is such a comfort. He is accustomed to the traumas of war."

"The traumas of war, *Maestra?*"

She looked at Paco, who nodded as if giving her permission to proceed.

"What's going on?" I asked.

Paco spoke up. "Please, have a seat. Luis, you too, please." There was a thermos and *mate* on the coffee table.

"If you want something, please . ." she said gesturing toward the table.

"No, thank you," I said sitting carefully at her feet. "We just want to know how you are, *Maestra*."

"We'd like to know more about the man you are looking for, Raquel," said Paco. "Was he in the photos you left here?"

"My uncle?" I couldn't imagine what he might have to do with *La Maestra's* health. "Yes," I said, "in fact, when Luis reprinted the photos, we were able to see him on the edge of the picture, standing behind Rosa, the old woman in the armchair. I'd only heard him described, I had never seen him before."

"We'd like to know more about him," said Paco.

"Certainly. But what has this to do with *La Maestra's* health?"

"I can explain later, first, tell me about him. His name is?"

"Mateo," I said. "Mateo Vicente López. He's my mother's oldest brother. She had another brother, too, Luciano, he was the eldest. He died very young." I explained the story of Luciano's death, and the accident that caused the loss of Mateo's arm and the disfiguring scars to his face. "Maybe you noticed them in the photo," I said.

"That's a terrible story," said Luis, hearing it for the first time.

"Yes, but the wounds and the trauma of the accident were just the beginning of Mateo's suffering. Luciano was the firstborn son, he was, as his name suggests, the light of my grandfather's heart. The death nearly destroyed him. No matter what Mateo did, *Abuelo* never forgave him for taking that light from his life. Eventually Mateo took refuge in the church where the parish priest made him an altar boy, despite his amputation. That's where Mateo and my father became lifelong friends." I paused at times in case there were questions.

"Even though my grandmother loved him dearly, her loyalty to her husband limited the affection she showed to Mateo. So she was delighted that her son found some acceptance and meaning in the church. But my grandfather was a rabid atheist. He saw Mateo's turn toward the church as a kind of revenge for his alienation. And when Mateo decided to go into the seminary, my grandfather forbade him from returning home.

"He was in Spain during the Civil War?" asked Paco with keen interest.

"Yes. He went to defend the Catholic Church. And, of course, my grandfather supported the Republicans and the socialists."

"There was a violent movement against the Church in Spain even before the war began," said *La Maestra*. "Please, go on, Raquel."

"Well, apparently Mateo sent one letter saying that he'd arrived safely in Spain, and no one heard from him again. It was presumed that he'd died in the war and that was the end of his story. Then, in July of this year, I found letters that Mateo had written to my father. It turns out that they had continued to correspond until 1977. It's possible Tío wrote after that, too, but my parents were killed that year in an automobile accident. So, presumably, his mail would have been returned."

I sat back and took a deep breath trying to read the solemn expressions across the room. "That's it," I said. "That's all I know, except that according to those letters, the Church sent him to Argentina in the 1950's."

"*La Maestra* recognized your uncle from the photograph," said Paco solemnly.

"Recognized?"

She sat up and Paco immediately propped up some pillows to support her. This elegant and energetic woman now seemed as fragile as a piece of Lladro china.

"My memories of the war are still vivid," she began, "most are things I want to forget, but cannot."

"You're saying you remember my uncle from the time of the Spanish Civil War? You knew him?"

"Before I say how I recognized him, I must say something of the war," she said. "It took over our country day by day, until there was blood on every street. Every person looked at every other person suspiciously. Priests and nuns, brothers and sisters, even children were at war. On our street in Málaga the father of my friend Guillermina Paredes was dragged out of his house by another neighbor and killed with a shotgun. Some neighbors, good people, shouted 'That's what he deserved!' They threatened my father for carrying the poor man's body to the mortuary. That is how the war arrived on our street. We could not believe what was happening, but the next morning, before dawn, we walked up into the mountains and disappeared from Málaga. I was seven years old. Nina, and her family came with us. She was fifteen."

As *La Maestra* recounted her story, it was easy to picture her as a small, vulnerable child. Her speech quickened, and the words appeared to grow bitter in her mouth as she described the cruelty of Fascist soldiers waging war against their own people, an untrained country of peasants without uniforms, proper weapons, or even sufficient food to stay alive. She explained quickly that the elected government (the Republicans) had to align with anarchists, Communists, and socialists hoping that united they could defeat the forces of Franco's military and its partners: Loyalists, Carlists, and the Catholic Church. "If the Republicans and anti-Fascists had won," she said, "there would have been a difficult aftermath to unravel the political knots. But the perils of possible success far outweighed the devastation of losing, which they did.

"It is important that you understand the desperation people felt going against a trained army," she continued slowly, "an army that not only had weapons, it had nasty friends with planes and bombs. As Franco's troops flooded into the south, thousands of Spaniards like us fled north on foot toward France. We stayed in the most difficult terrain for safety.

"I will tell you my memory of your uncle, and I hope it is the last time in my life I have to say it." She paused for a long slow breath.

"*Maestra*, please, you don't have to explain," I began to say that I'd believed her without the details, but she protested and cut me off.

"No. You, Raquel, must know this."

She looked straight into my eyes and I took a tense breath, not knowing what to expect.

"We came upon a little town near Jaen, north of Granada. It was called Rio Olvidado. There, we camped behind an abandoned garage on the edge of that town. It was a Sunday morning. I remember the church bells ringing, and Tío Hernán, my father's brother, wanted to go to mass. Our family was going looking for food so we could continue our march again the next day, and my father begged his brother not to go to the church. No one in our party was against the Church, but, as I explained, the Church was now considered an enemy. Well, Tío Hernán was a very good Catholic, and he promised to hide in the back in the shadows where he could not be seen, and he would not receive communion. So, off he went.

"Nina came with us, but her family stayed at the camp repairing shoes and clothing, for the next day of travel." She paused as Paco handed her the *mate* gourd, and took a long sip from the silver straw. "As we returned uphill toward the town," she resumed, "a man who'd also stayed at the camp was running toward us waving his hands. Papa met him ahead of us and signaled us to stop where we were. I could see the man was hysterical. Papa grabbed his shoulders and shook him. When he came back to us, he said that we couldn't go any further, our group had been attacked at the garage. We had to hide, he said. But Nina started to run forward and I ran to catch her, and Papa caught us both. He pushed Nina to the ground but not before she could hear the screams. Crouched down in the tall grass, we all heard them. Screams and gunfire, shouting and yelling. Then, I did a stupid thing, I lifted my head for just a moment, but in that moment I saw Nina's father pushed up against a tree, perhaps he was already dead. He did not fight back at all. He could have easily broken free, the priest appeared to have only one arm."

Suddenly I understood what she was telling me.

"His vestments were covered in blood, and the priest continued stabbing and stabbing with a bayonet in his right hand. Over and over, he shouted, "*¡A la Gloria!¡A la Gloria!*"

"My mother came up behind me then and pushed me down with all her force. I heard someone from above yell, "*¡Adelante!*" and, of course, we were sure they were coming for us. My mother grabbed me roughly and took me to the far side of a big tree down the hill. Immediately she broke pieces of bushes and laid them on top of us."

La Maestra stopped for a moment, and looked into my eyes. "The image of that priest is burned into my mind, Raquel. I saw him very clearly. His mouth, misshapen," she put the fingers of her good hand to her mouth and twisted the top lip, "and he had a deep scar across his forehead. His vestment sleeve flew back and forth with every movement, because there was no arm in it. And that is how he still appears in my dreams."

Her eyes dropped away from my gaze, tears streaking the length of her face. She was trembling. I looked at Paco, then Luis. They seemed to be studying the carpet.

"*Maestra*, you are telling me that my uncle was the priest who killed *Doña Nina's* father? How could that be? I mean, what are the chances . . ."

"Nina saw him, too, Raquel," she said.

I shook my head. "It can't be possible." Luis came over and sat next to me on the arm of the sofa.

"Armed men from the town came out looking for us after that," she continued. "People were hiding up in the trees, inside bushes, you can't imagine. They passed right beside us, beating the tall grass with rifles and machetes. Finally when the sun dropped in the sky, they stopped and wandered back up the hill. Even then, none of us moved or spoke until moonlight lit the terrain. When we began to move as silently as possible, one man sneaked back to our campsite. He returned with the worst news, no one survived. Papa and another man had to pry Nina out of a tree. Her whole family was gone, and she could not even go back to see them. Burial was out of the question. We knew that a single word could kill all of us, so no one spoke for hours. Nina did not speak for more than a year."

I was speechless myself.

"What would be the chances," she said, "of you and me meeting, all these years later, dear Raquel, you looking for the man who hides in the darkest shadows of my mind?"

"It's not possible," I repeated. "It can't be."

"It has happened, Raquel," said Luis.

"So, when you shunned me during class this morning, *Maestra?* Was that your way of saying you don't want to see me anymore, because of that man you think was my uncle?"

"No." She spoke quickly and decisively. "This morning, I did not know how to look at you, because every time I saw you, I saw him."

"Oh God, you think I look like him?"

"No, it was just the memory of the family photo."

I put my face in my hands wishing that when I looked again the scene would be changed, and I'd be waking from a bad dream.

"Raquel, you must speak to Saturnina," said *La Maestra*.

"No!" I said, "I can't imagine that she'd want to talk to me."

"She does. She wants to talk to you. Not today. Perhaps tomorrow."

"No." I said. "No. No. Please, no."

"Raquel," she said. "She needs to see you. You have set her memories to vibrating."

Suddenly she got my attention. "*Maestra*, are you saying that that awful day is now re-animated and evolving through me?" She didn't answer. "Even if that monster was my uncle, I can't undo the loss of Saturnina's family. I have no power to heal her loss, unless you think she can be healed through my shame."

"No, not your shame, Raquel," she said. "You bear no shame. But, you have the power to say you are sorry. And that contrition coming from one of his own people could be powerful."

I never imagined that I could feel a driving need to run away from *El Alef*, but in that moment, that's all I wanted. "I'm sorry," I said, "I have to leave now."

CHAPTER EIGHTEEN

Luis and I walked quietly toward my apartment.

"Could I come up to look for my phone?" he asked.

"I'll look for it," I said. I didn't want to deal with his story about Carla or his story about losing the phone, it didn't even matter to me in that moment. "I need to be alone now."

"I understand. It's just that I really need that phone."

I stared at him blankly for a moment. "Okay, fine. Come up."

My mind was a jumble of images mixed with nameless emotions. I went out to the balcony to think, but even there the sounds of Luis rummaging through the loft was an annoying aggravation. "Luis!" I didn't mean to shout at him, I just couldn't stand the racket.

"Did you find it?" he asked as I came back into the living room.

"No," I said. "Please come down from there. I promise I will look for it, and if I find it, I will call you immediately. I know that phone is like another limb to you."

He came downstairs quickly and though he stood beside me I felt a great abyss between us. "I know *La Maestra's* story must have been devastating to you," he said, "It's very surreal. I wish there was something I could do."

"There is. Leave me alone right now. I have to be alone with my thoughts."

"Of course. I'm sorry I can't be with you to meet with *Doña Nina* tomorrow," he said. "I promised to take my grandchildren to the *Jardín Zoológico*. I cannot disappoint them."

"Don't worry about it. Have a good time." I gave him a peck on the cheek and opened the door.

"You'll call me if you find my phone, right?"

"I promise."

I shut the door and turned the lock. I didn't want to see anyone, not even my own reflection in the mirror. I didn't seem to fit into the human race anymore. I poured a glass of wine and wished I hadn't quit smoking twenty years ago. Why is it, I wonder, that whenever I get bad news or feel uncontainably angry, I want to smoke cigarettes? I knew I could get cigarettes at the quick mart across the street and entertained the idea for about half a minute, then decided against it. My journal was nearby, a pen stuck in the spiral binding. For all its devastating power, I didn't want to record *La Maestra's* story. Maybe I believed that if I didn't write it down, it would prove to have been just a ghostly nightmare. I pulled out the pen, opened to the first clean page, and let my hand draw in abstract movements the anguish and confusion I was feeling. But drawing didn't satisfy me either, so I turned on the laptop and waited impatiently for it to boot up. I had never imagined that my search might uncover something shameful. What was my responsibility to my family now, I wondered. What would I tell them about Tío Mateo? I hoped for email from Marta, or better still, David. But there was only one message. It was from Nico and there were attachments. Probably the photos from La Boca, I thought, and opened it.

Dearest Raquel, Here are the photos I took at La Boca. You are such a lovely subject, I hope I will have many more opportunities to explore your beauty through my lens.

More seriously, meet me tomorrow at the *milonga* at Club Español, 17:00. I have important information about your family member. I must speak to you.

Un Beso, Nico

With the new information from *La Maestra*, instinct told me to stop the search for Tío Mateo. Why go on? He might be dead, but if he wasn't, I didn't want to meet him, anyway. What kind of man could he be? If he's alive, I thought, he's an old man. How has he lived with himself? "Thou shalt not kill." I said it aloud. "Thou shalt not kill, damnit!" He'd broken that commandment over and over, and in a most bloodthirsty way. With that on his conscience he should have left the priesthood. I wanted him to be punished, but his side won the war, so no punishment would have come to him. It had always been an aggravation to me that history books credited the Allies with liberating Europe at the end of World War II, when in fact the Spanish people were left under the Fascist boot of Francisco Franco until the 1970's.

Now I really wanted a cigarette, even though I knew I'd hate the smoke, the taste, and the choking effect it would have on me. Instead, I went to the cupboard and pulled out a box of cookies that had seduced me from the *confiteria* window two days ago. They were chocolate with walnuts, dressed in a dusting of powdered sugar. Before I realized it, I'd devoured four of them. I guessed they had at least eighty calories each. The one redeeming thing about tobacco, probably the only redeeming thing about tobacco, I thought, is that it has no calories. I closed the box and tossed the cookies up onto the highest shelf. Just my luck, I made it on the first try.

After a fitful sleep I woke up early and waited until ten thirty to call *El Alef.*

"*Sí?*" It was the raspy tone of the gatekeeper.

"*Doña Saturnina, habla Raquel Carval.*"

"*Venga a las 11:30.*"

"*Sí señora.*" I answered obediently, and hung up.

On the walk to *El Alef,* I thought about Nico. How did he learn about my search for an uncle? I hadn't kept it a secret, but I hadn't spoken with anyone at the *milongas* about it. Could he have reliable information?

Even though I knew Mateo was anti-Semitic, I presumed that

a priest would have lived a good life, doing good work. Instead, the scenes *La Maestra* described had a brutality equal to those old Sam Peckinpaw movies, and I wouldn't even go see those because of the violence. Clearly, no matter what transpired, I'd have to lie so that Tía Leti could take a fantasy brother to the grave with her.

On the way I stopped to buy *medialunas* and some cookies for Doña Saturnina and *La Maestra*. But as I carried them, I felt stupid for thinking that a polite gesture was appropriate in such a grave situation. In my head I heard *Doña Nina* say, "Your uncle kills my family and you bring me cookies?" All I could do was follow through with my good intention. Sometimes that's all you can do.

I rang the bell at the gate.

"*Entre*," growled the old woman.

The little canaries chirped innocently in their cages, and for a moment I envied the safety of their confinement. I took a moment to breathe in the tranquility of the patio, then went in. The drape was pulled open and the two women, dressed in black, sat in the center of the room. *La Maestra* was in her usual spot, and in the matching love seat to her left, sat Doña Saturnina, her stout little torso held rigidly beneath her shoulders. As I approached I studied her face. She was pale, her eyes puffy, the delicate rims pink with irritation. Her gray hair was braided and wrapped atop her head like a crown. As I approached I saw her fidget with a white hanky, rubbing the intricately embroidered edges between her fingers like rosary beads.

"*Buenos días, Maestra*," I said, leaning in to give her a kiss on the cheek.

"*Buen día*," she said warmly.

"*Señora*," I said nodding politely to *Doña Nina*. On the day she'd brought us the champagne our meeting was very brief, and now I wasn't quite sure of the proper protocol in greeting her. I'd had sincere respect, even before hearing the story of her loss, but I doubted the feeling was mutual. Not knowing what else to do, I gave her a kiss on the cheek. Today she smelled of cinnamon and nutmeg. I held out the offering of sweets. "*Para ustedes*," I said.

"*Gracias*," said Nina, who still had not smiled, even as a polite gesture. She took the box and set it on the coffee table.

"*Siéntate*," she said.

Again, I followed orders and took a seat again on the sofa at *La Maestra's* feet.

"Coffee?" asked Saturnina. Her use of English I knew to be a supreme effort to make me feel comfortable.

"No, thank you."

"Raquel," began *La Maestra*, "we are still in shock by what has been revealed in your photos. Pains of an old past come to the surface. Nina and I are very emotional."

I nodded. "Me too."

Saturnina surprised me by speaking up suddenly. "I want to say, I no hold you *responsable*," she said. "*La Maestra* say you a very nice womans, no worries please that Nina think you *culpable*, guilty of somethings."

"*Gracias, Doña Nina,*" I said, a boulder seemed lodged in my throat choking back all the rest I wanted to say.

"You uncle do terrible thing to me," she said slowly, dabbing at her creased old eyes with the handkerchief. "My mamá, papá, my sister and my little brother, all kill that day," she said, "I have no family after that." She began to sob and I didn't know what to do for her. My own tears were surely useless.

I looked at *La Maestra* who patted her friend's shoulder in a gesture of support. "Raquel, we believe you have come to us as an angel," she said.

"What?" I felt nothing like an angel.

"*¡Sí!*" said *Doña Nina* calming her tears. "Yes, you come to help us get . . .*la justicia.*"

I looked to *La Maestra* for an explanation.

"I have invited Paco to join us today," she said. "He will be here at any moment. Until you came here to find the man of our nightmares, we didn't know he was in Argentina. Through you, we hope to bring him to justice."

"But how? His actions were part of a war that happened in a different country over sixty years ago."

"Paco will explain."

"My uncle may just be dead, *Maestra*. The Diocese sent me his baptismal certificate, and nothing else."

"They did?"

"Yes. But I went there twice looking for more information. I told them that I know he worked in the diocese of Buenos Aires.

They should have some records of him."

"You must tell all this to Paco," said *La Maestra*.

"Each time I've been to the Diocese, the person at the window seemed very uninformed."

"This is their tactics," she said. "Paco!" His presence brought a smile to her face.

"*Hola, mi amor*," he said planting kisses on her cheeks and forehead. Then another on the forehead of *Doña Nina*.

"Raquel," he said, kissing me on the cheek.

"*Hola Paco.*"

He took a seat in the armchair to my right.

"Paco," said *La Maestra*, "Raquel says the Diocese sent her Zorrilla's baptismal record."

He looked at me with surprise. "Really?" he asked sharply.

"No," I said, confused. "Zorrilla? Who is Zorrilla?" I asked.

"Hmf," Paco grunted and lit a cigarette. He took a deep drag and released it slowly, then tapped the cigarette brusquely into an ashtray on the table. "Raquel, I have to tell you that your grandfather is. . ."

"My uncle," I said, correcting him.

"Oh, sorry, your uncle, what is your name for him? I mean, what is his name?"

"López. Mateo Vicente López."

"Hmf," he grunted again. "Well, I have to tell you something." He looked at *La Maestra*, at *Doña Nina*, then back at me. "It's not good news. About your uncle."

Considering what had already been revealed, I couldn't imagine how much worse it could get, and I didn't want Paco playing cat and mouse with me. "What are you talking about?" I asked sharply.

"Your uncle is, I think, a man known in Argentina as Monseñor Sebastián Zorrilla."

"What are you talking about?"

"Do you know that I work for an organization called CELS?"

"I don't know what that is."

"It stands for *Centro de Estudios Legales y Sociales*, The Center for Legal and Social Studies. We recover information regarding those disappeared, *los desaparecidos de la Guerra Sucia*, and information regarding war criminals."

"That sounds like great work, Paco, but why would you think that my uncle would be this Zorrilla?"

"Looking at the photo, and with the memories of Beatriz and Saturnina, the description of your uncle fits that of the priest, Sebastián Zorrilla."

"What did he do?"

Paco was quiet for a moment, looking down at the floor.

"I know it's got to be something bad," I said, "just tell me."

"I wish I could spare you," he said. "He was involved in disappearances, and torture."

His voice seemed to break up as he spoke the words. They came at me, warped, stretched out like taffy. Did he say *torture*? Paco's face seemed frozen into a grimace.

"What are you saying?" I tried to speak, but I wasn't sure if he heard me.

"He aligned with the generals, Raquel."

"He aligned with the generals." I repeated numbly. A dense fogbank had crept into my head like the type I've seen come into San Francisco Bay. It devours everything. When it's thick you can't see through it at all.

I shifted to the front of the sofa. "Paco, you're saying that Sebastián Zorrilla was part of the generals' government."

"Yes. Well, he acted in line with the government."

"I see." But I didn't, quite. He was telling me something else. "And what does that have to do with my uncle?"

"Raquel, your uncle Mateo Vicente López," he spoke very slowly, I thought, "changed his name to Sebastián Zorrilla when he came to Argentina from Spain."

"You think my uncle is that monsignor?"

"Yes. With the information you have given us, it is certain."

"Raquel, the scars make it certain," *La Maestra* said softly. "People have described him and recounted the way Father Zorrilla took part in their torture." It came out of her mouth so gently. She said it as if putting a compress on a wound. "I am so sorry," she said, "you are so . . .so *simpática*."

Hot tears etched into the perimeters of my eyes. "You must think I'm very gullible," I said. "You think you can just tell me these stories, and change an entire life? You think I'm going to believe such things about my own family?"

I got up from the sofa, threw my bag and purse over my shoulder. "Why should I believe you, Paco? And *Maestra*, I'm sure you suffered a great deal during the war, but why should I accept that, against all odds, it was my uncle who caused the death of *Doña Nina's* family? I think you're all looking for neat answers, and here comes a case of a missing priest and now you can fit him to the description of your villain, someone you haven't been able to find for decades. Well, I'm not going to help you condemn my uncle, for all your heinous, unsolved war crimes. That poor misshapen old man suffered first physically and then psychologically all through his life, and now you want to brand him as a war criminal twice over! No! I will not be a part of it!"

I had backed myself all the way to the draperies by that time. It felt as though a collapsing dome of stones was falling in around me. I had to get away. I ran across the patio, and out the gate. On the busy sidewalk I slowed to a walk. I walked and walked the city streets without a single clear thought in my head. All I could do was mechanically put one foot in front of the other. At times the sidewalk became a blur and I watched carefully not to twist an ankle in the broken cement. *La Maestra* wanted me to believe that my uncle, *my* uncle, tortured people. *My uncle!* Someone from *my* family. *A priest.* Not just a priest, now a monsignor! My mother's brother. She wanted me to believe that the troubled young man forced from my grandparents' home had become a monster. He'd been my father's best friend. How could she think I'd believe such a tale? What kind of a person could make such an accusation about someone's relative? He was a victim of fate. He suffered his whole life. Children taunted him. His own father disowned him, and all because of an unfortunate accident in which he was faultless.

I sat on a bench for quite a while, ruminating over the informa-tion I'd been given in the last twenty-four hours. When I surfaced back into the moment I realized it was nearly five o'clock. I had to get to the Club Español to meet Nico. What could he have for me, I wondered. Hopefully it was a death certificate.

CHAPTER NINETEEN

I entered the building of the Club Español at a few minutes past five o'clock. Even with so much on my mind, the beauty of the interior captured my attention. To the left a graceful crimson-carpeted stairway curved behind a black painted Victorian elevator rising with the swift and quiet artistry equal to any modern mechanism. A tango melody wafted like an aroma through the multi-leveled structure. As I climbed the crimson stairs, the music grew stronger.

The *milonga* was crowded. I paid, and changed into my dance shoes in the foyer. Strapped into my four-inch heels I felt the tension in my shoulders begin to melt away. In those heels I felt powerful, desirable, confident. I was in no mood for Nico's games. I waited by the door scanning the busy scene for the host, but before I could find him I felt a hand on my waist.

"¿*Bailamos?*" said Nico, giving me a kiss on the cheek.

"I have my bag," I said. He took it from me and stashed it behind some gentlemen seated nearby. "They will protect it for you," he said, leading me onto the floor.

He encircled my torso with his right arm. I rested my left hand on his shoulder. As he presented his left hand to me, I saw in his palm a folded handkerchief which I read as an antiquated practice intended to absorb perspiration so as not to soil a lady's delicate hand. But as soon as I placed my palm against his, I felt that it was paper, not cotton, and when the first tango ended, he suggested that I read it. "I have the information you are seeking," it said.

I looked up at him. He put his index finger against his lips. "Let's talk outside when this *tanda* ends," he whispered.

I'd always enjoyed dancing with Nico, but on this occasion, he smelled of alcohol, and I felt uneasy in his arms. I was annoyed at him for this stupid game with the note. So at the end of the next tango I turned away from him, grabbed my bag and purse and went out into the foyer. This was a serious breach of etiquette, and it was doubly shocking that a dancer of Nico's status would be left on the floor. I'd only seen women leave partners on the dance floor in the case of very bad dancing, or after verbal abuse. In our case, it appeared that Nico had been a perfect gentleman. I realized he might be furious with me for such an insult in the sight of other men, but I took a seat in the foyer and started unbuckling my shoes. When he sat next to me his response was not what I expected.

He kissed my cheek. "*Tesoro,*" he cooed, "something is bothering you?"

"I am not your treasure, Nico," I said, "and I don't like you using my uncle's life for your annoying flirtations. If you have information, just tell me what it is."

"Ah, yes, the information. Well, it is not good news."

"How do you know that I'm looking for my uncle?"

"Well," he looked at me as if surprised by my attitude, "you told me."

"No I didn't."

"Oh, yes, you must have told me."

"I did not." My teeth clenched and I felt my expression grow stony.

"I cannot talk to you here," he said.

"You asked to meet me here, Nico."

"There is a landing on the next floor down, just behind the elevator."

"You go first," I said, "I'll follow you".

He looked at me, as if to protest, but got up abruptly and left. I finished changing my shoes, then took the antique elevator down one floor. I found him seated on a red velvet Victorian fainting couch.

"Tell me what you know," I demanded, sitting next to him. He put his arm around me and tried to kiss me. "Now!" I said, pushing him away.

"Alright," he said with annoyance. "I work at the Diocese office."

"I thought you were a tango singer?"

"I am, of course, but tango singing does not buy the wardrobe for a tango life." He opened his sport jacket to reveal silk lining and a fancy label. "I also work for the Office of Public Affairs for the Diocese of Buenos Air . . ."

"So, have you known I was looking for my uncle since the beginning?"

"No, just since that day when we talked at the *Confitería La Ideal*. Remember, I told you that I had seen you come out of the Diocese office?"

"Yes, you made it sound like you'd seen me from the street."

"I know. Actually, I saw you inside."

"Why didn't you just tell me?"

"Well, I didn't want to disappoint you if I couldn't find any information."

"So tell me what you found out. No wait, first tell me his name."
"What?"

"Tell me my uncle's name."

"Well, his name is . . .López, Father Mateo López. Uh, no Mateo Vicente López."

At least he had the right guy. Now I hoped he'd tell me that my uncle was dead.

"Okay, so tell me what you know. All of it! Now!"

"Ooh la la!" he said. "I think I like you when you are so tough, so passionate."

"Just tell me, God damn it."

"Okay. I am sad to tell you that your uncle is deceased."

I took a deep breath and dropped my face into my hands. Something told me not to let him see the relief I felt, nor let him hear it in my voice.

"I am sorry," he said.

I put out one hand, asking for a minute to collect myself. He put his arm around my shoulders, as if to comfort me.

"How did you learn this?" I asked finally, looking for a tissue in my purse.

"That is not important. As I said, I know a lot of priests. I went into the records."

"Records? Is this reliable information? Can I trust it?"

"To tell you the truth, I questioned it myself. You see, I found a document that said Mateo Vicente López disappeared in 1977."

"Where'd you find that?"

"What?"

"Where did you find a record of his disappearance?"

"It was in the file."

"A file with his name on it?"

"Of course."

"What else is in that file?"

"What?"

"Do I have to ask you everything twice? I want to know what else was in that file. Were there employment records, for example? Job evaluations? I mean, if you pulled any other priest's file what would be in it?"

He thought for a moment, as if running a search program through his brain. "You know, there wasn't much in there, just a baptismal record, and the statement of his disappearance, and then the death certificate."

"Nothing else?"

"No."

"Doesn't that seem strange to you? He worked in Buenos Aires for decades."

"I didn't think about it. But I can take you to his grave," he said. "I was sure you would want to visit. Take flowers. Make some photographs for the family."

"You know where my uncle is buried?"

"Yes. I can take you tomorrow after work. He's in a cemetery in San Isidro."

"Where's that?"

"It's outside the city. I will drive you."

I was anxious to see the gravesite, but not enthusiastic about going off to God-knows-where with Nico. "I need to think this over," I said.

"*O, tesoro,*" he said, unctuously, "Of course, you are too sad at the moment. Why don't I call you tomorrow? We can go whenever you are ready."

"No. I'll get back to you. I want a copy of the death certificate and the record of disappearance."

"Fine. Yes, I can make copies for you," he said digging into his breast pocket. "Here is my card. My *celular* is on the back." Handing it to me, he took my hand and kissed it. "We will talk tomorrow," he said. When I didn't respond, he tightened his grip. "Raquel, you seem not to trust me. I want to help you. I want to *know* you, and I want you to know me. You are a beautiful woman. Please, give me a chance."

"You haven't been honest with me, Nico," I said straightfor-wardly. "That doesn't make me want to know more about you. I don't feel that I can trust you."

"I will prove myself to you. You will see. I did not want you to be disappointed, that's why I didn't explain it all before. Now I know what I can give you, and I am sorry it is the saddest possible outcome." He took my hands in his. "I have serious feelings for you, Raquel. Genuine feelings. I hope I can make you see that I am re-ally a good man. I am not always the actor on the stage. I am just me. I had no mother, no father to teach me how to love someone, so I just do the best I can. I had no parents . ."

"Okay, Nico." He was telling me what I'd told myself about him. "I'll try to keep an open mind."

"That is all I ask. I know you are upset now. I will leave you. *Chau*." He planted a tender little kiss in the center of my forehead, and went back upstairs.

I stayed there for a while watching the elaborate elevator deliv-er its passengers. In my rumination, its vertical rise and fall became symbolic of my brief life in Buenos Aires. I felt like a modern Alice in Wonderland chasing the shadow of my uncle like the white rab-bit. As Alice would have said, the chase was becoming curiouser and curiouser. What was true and what was illusion? How could I separate fact from fiction? That name, Zorrilla, was echoing in my head, as if I'd heard it before Paco had pronounced it. I needed to talk to my sister, but when I called, I got her recorded message.

Then another name came to mind, someone whose number was already in my speed dial.

"*Hola*, Alfonso."

"*Señora* Raquel, how are you?"

"Alfonso, I'm at the Club Español. Could you come pick me up here?"

"Sure. I just dropped a fare at El Abasto. At this day it could take maybe twenty minutes."

"Fine. I'll be on the sidewalk."

"You can't believe it, Alfonso," I said getting into the cab. "This search for my uncle has become a frightening mess."

"I am sorry to hear this, *señora*," he said. "Where do you want to go?"

"Go? I have no idea. What do you suggest?"

"What do you want to do?"

"I want to think."

"Uh, Recoleta, is quite safe for thinking. It has a beautiful park, and it is an expensive neighborhood. You fit very well there. Very classy."

"Thanks for the compliment."

"There is also a nice café where you can sit and think."

"Do they sell alcohol at that café?"

"At La Biela? Yes, of course."

"Perfect," I said, "that's exactly what I need. I knew you were the man to call."

The backseat of Alfonso's cab had a strangely soothing effect on me.

"Today I have CD's," he said. "What tango you want to hear?"

"Surprise me," I said.

"Okay. De Angelis. The violins are very soothing."

After a few bars of the tango named appropriately, "*Mi Dolor*" (My Pain) a sense of calm crept into me. "I've just learned that my uncle is dead, Alfonso."

"I am so sorry."

"Don't be sorry. It looks like he wasn't a very nice guy. I was hoping he was dead."

"Oh!" Alfonso seemed as shocked as if he'd known the old guy.

"I've been told he was a religious fanatic and even a killer. And if you can imagine the coincidence, he is said to have killed the family of someone I know. Years ago, in Spain."

He responded with an audible gasp. "No!" he said. "*¡Qué golpe!*"

"Yes, that's how I feel, like I've been kicked in the gut. At first I just refused to believe it, but it's sinking in. I think it must be true, and the news has thrown me off balance."

"When I meet you, you say maybe he disappear. That is how he died?"

"I don't think so. But there is a document that says he disappeared. I haven't seen it yet. And supposedly, there's also a death certificate, and a grave."

We were at a stoplight, so Alfonso turned to look straight at me. "You think the grave is empty?"

That possibility hadn't even crossed my mind. "My God, that would make it the perfect ruse, wouldn't it."

"Alfonso does not know what is a *ruse*," he said.

"A ruse means something false created to steer people in the wrong direction." "Good vocabulary word!" He grabbed his notebook from the passenger seat. "How you spell it?"

"R-U-S-E," I said, watching him jot it down quickly and shift into motion as the light changed. His suggestion plunged me deeper into thought. I wasn't sure I could even imagine all the possibilities of this situation. Obviously, a death certificate and even a grave, did not insure that my uncle really was dead.

"Here we are *señora*," said Alfonso.

I hadn't even noticed the change in scenery as we'd gone from the city center to the posh neighborhood I'd recently visited with Luis. Even that day I hadn't noticed the little boutiques and expensive cars parked everywhere.

"That is La Biela," said Alfonso, pointing to the spacious outdoor café on the corner. "This is Evita Peron's neighborhood. Maybe you can have a chat with her."

He flashed a roguish smile.

"What are you talking about?"

"Evita is buried just around the corner in the Recoleta Cemetery."

"I'm *so* glad I called you, Alfonso. You're a real professional: a great DJ, a good listener, *and* a fabulous tour guide! Thank you."

Although it was almost six o'clock, the days were long now, and the sun was still high in the sky. A cemetery walk seemed quite appropriate for my ruminations. Argentine cemeteries often rival the cities of the dead found in Italy, where the tombs of wealthy families compete for size and drama. Recoleta Cemetery is a fascinating little city of tall sculptures and impressive mausoleums. It didn't make me think about death, so much as immortality. The dead here have a powerful presence, and it didn't surprise me to know that Evita was among them. I wandered for a while, juggling the pieces of my uncle's supposed life in my head. Then I asked a caretaker for Evita's tomb, and, following his instructions, found myself in a narrow pathway where the structures were more conservative than those on the main avenues. I was surprised that, unlike Evita's attention-getting life, her family mausoleum is settled quietly away from the public eye. Its polished dark stone exterior maintains a dignified architecture offset by a flat bronze cross and ornate bronze grillwork on the door. I read the medallions attached to the tomb, each expressing the undying affection and appreciation of civic associations and trade unions. A few fresh flowers had been recently threaded through the grillwork and others were laid at the base of the door.

Like Nico, Evita was a chameleon. On one hand she had tenacity, intelligence, and charisma, on the other, she was self-serving and power hungry. There are probably more myths and stories about her than any woman of the twentieth century. I envied her in a way. She never lost sight of herself as I had. Her ruthless determination won the wealth and power she hungered for since childhood. Did that ruthlessness make her evil? She appeared to have believed that whatever was good for her would ultimately be good for her people. Uncle Mateo too, must have accepted that brutality was necessary, a part of his commitment to the Lord, I guess. He praised Franco because he fought to protect the Catholic Church, so he certainly considered himself an agent of the restoration and maintenance of the holy order. He probably saw himself the way a policeman sees that his violence is justified by his commitment to being a "peace" officer.

In reality, each of them was blinded by the work of reversing the equation of their own life. Mateo grew up beneath the godless judgments and vengeful force of his father. Eva grew up at the bottom of the heap, looked down on by the glamorous celebrities she adored. It was, I suppose, only natural for each of them to form an alliance with those who had the ultimate power to accomplish their personal vendettas.

Leaving the cemetery I contemplated Mateo's alleged death. Why would Alfonso think that the grave could be empty? Because Alfonso had been schooled in the ways of the Dirty War. The false story of Tío's death could easily be fed to me by Nico, complete with documents and gravesite.

I wanted to believe he was dead so that the story and the search could end there. I wanted to send a photo of his grave to Tía Leti, and let everyone believe he died in Argentina after a life of good work. Everyone, that is, except me.

CHAPTER TWENTY

In any other circumstance, this would feel like the perfect evening for getting lost in one's thoughts, in the eyes of a sweetheart, or in the stars overhead. As I sat in the outdoor café, the soft twilight air caressed the world with a delicate touch, yet the *porteños* around me seemed oblivious to the air, the twilight, and in some cases even to those at their table. This was an upscale crowd: Well-dressed men and women with expensive haircuts. It surprised me that those talking with companions were nearly outnumbered by others on cell phones. At one table there were three businessmen, each one on his phone.

I had situated myself at a table along the outside edge of the café near the shrubs and trees that border the park. It felt a little uncomfortable to be seated alone, especially on such a lovely evening, but I had *El Tango, la otra historia* in my bag, and if I got too self-conscious I could read or at least pretend to read under the dimming light. I ordered an *empanada de acelga* and *a tinto*, then leaned back to watch the scene. Soon I was sketching little portraits of the people around me on the paper napkins from the dispenser with my fine point felt pen. Drawing helped me think. While I sketched I came to accept the reality of my situation and the shocking nature of my uncle's character.

The thin white patches of napkin I had been drawing on proved less than optimal, and before long a breeze came up sending them adrift like autumn leaves. I gathered them up quickly and just as I captured the last drawing under the table, my attention was drawn to the feet of a couple arriving nearby. The woman wore such elegant shoes, I glanced up to see the rest of her outfit. But it wasn't her clothes that captured my attention in that second glance. From my position under the table I watched, frozen in place as Luis drew his left arm tightly around Carla's waist. She was giggling and whispering in his ear. They sat down with their backs to me, so I lifted myself slowly using the metal support of the chair. Carla ordered wine. Luis asked for two coffees and a ham sandwich. She leaned into him and kissed him on the cheek. They talked confidentially, *tête a tête*. When the sandwich arrived, he held it to her lips and she took little baby bites.

Hot tears streamed down my face, and instinctually I dabbed at them with the napkins I'd just retrieved. When I noticed the ink on my hands I realized what I was doing and reached into my purse for a clean tissue. I dabbed some more, sopping up the unrelenting tears and hopefully cleaning off any residual ink that might have been smeared onto my face. Then I pulled out *El Tango, la otra historia*. It made a fine visual partition, but no barrier to emotions. Luis had told me there was nothing between them. I had asked him point blank. She was just an old friend, he said. He was taking his grandchildren to the zoo today, he said. The sense of betrayal was paralyzing. I lifted my book and pretended to read. When the type cleared enough to form words, I looked up from the page to see her stroking his face, and the scene became a blur again. Raising the book once more, I turned the page as if deeply engrossed in its content. In my peripheral vision they remained a single form.

The lovers stayed at the café for the longest half hour of my life. When they finally got up to leave, I watched them walk out to the sidewalk. Carla clung to his chest, as Luis encircled her waist.

In the refuge of my apartment I crumbled under throbbing waves of disappointment. How could I have been so gullible? In spite of my age and the depth of my experience, I had let it happen. It was my fault. I had put myself into a vulnerable position, and I had to extricate myself from it. I had to erase Luis from my heart and my mind. There was too much turmoil in my life. I couldn't spin my wheels over a fickle-hearted jerk. I needed the support of someone trustworthy. I visualized his name written in the sand in big letters, and with each pass of imagined Pacific waves L U I S faded slowly away; the salt of the sea collaborated with the wash of my own tears.

And the stories about my uncle were so confusing. I had no

way to decipher fact from fiction. Was he a criminal of two wars, or a victim of *el proceso*, disappeared like so many others? Did he change his name to Sebastián Zorrilla, or live and die as Mateo Vicente López? The man had gone from being a total stranger to someone whose life cast a long, dark shadow across my own identity. As much as I wanted to return him to his mysterious oblivion, I had dug him up, so I'd have to stay with the search until the whole body of truth was revealed.

Tomorrow, I decided, without Luis in my life, I would begin a commitment to truth in *all* things, no matter the pain it might cause.

By Monday morning the weekend activities in San Telmo had subsided. No outdoor antique stalls, no dancers performing on cobblestones, no tourists abuzz with excitement. Wandering through the shops I was able to clarify things in my head. I decided to accept the news of my uncle's death, and the decision calmed me. Maybe I chose to believe it because it simplified my responsibilities and I could end my search with a sense of closure. The circumstances of his death might have been complex, but I didn't need to go into them. His disappearance during the junta didn't fit with what Paco had told me, and it seemed unlikely that the Diocese could have retrieved his body if he'd been abducted, whether by Montoneros or by death squad. From what I'd read, most of the disappeared were not found, and not many were returned for burial. So what if he'd collaborated with the junta, wasn't it all old news, water under the bridge? It seemed certain that Uncle Mateo's coffin, if indeed he had one, was sealed with lies, but once I'd seen his grave, I could take a photo back to my family, and leave the old man buried deep within his secrets.

Unfortunately, that notion of the resonance of memory kept running through my head. I worried that if there was any chance my uncle was innocent of the brutality he was accused of in Argentina, I was the only person who would ever care enough to clear his name. That is the American way, after all, innocent until proven guilty. If I didn't insure justice one way or the other, our whole family would live in the shadow of his sins, not because of his name, whatever it was in the end, but because he was one of us. He was of our blood. If it turned out that he was guilty, then even one anemic apology would be a heartfelt attempt at making amends. I'd know that I hadn't backed down when the truth proved distasteful. I represented my whole family in this; I had to be the one to do it. That's when I knew that getting to the truth about Tío Mateo's life would also solidify the new foundation and purpose of my own. I had to speak to *Doña Nina*.

I stood on the sidewalk in San Telmo. I might have been standing there for a minute or an hour. I'd lost all sense of time. My whole life before that moment could have been a dream, and I was finally waking up. The scene around me had a clarity I'd never experienced. Across the street an antiques merchant was arranging a display in his shop window. I watched him assemble and reassemble the objects until their placement pleased him. A Victorian picture frame, two porcelain statuettes, a small beaded purse, a kerosene lantern, and finally he placed a lady's fan, open and half resting on the purse at the front of the window. Suddenly I understood that memories are both currency and vehicles for the time travel of the soul. That's why people buy and love antiques. The secret memories in each of those *objets d'art*, whether inherited or purchased, vibrate with the life of those who came before, the long line of humans whose chain of kinship leads to the locus of identity that transcends our own personal physical world. Identity is a longing to revisit the womb of our origin, not necessarily our maternal womb, but that place in time and space where we began. Suddenly I understood the aleph that Borges placed, or discovered, in the subterranean foundation of Buenos Aires. And I understood why Juan Alvarez named his school *El Alef.* He realized that there is a vibration in tango that takes us to our origin, in the depths of our bones. It is a vibration he could not find in the religions of the world.

I went directly to *El Alef* without phoning. I rang the bell at the gate, unsure of *Doña Nina's* current opinion of me. When I said my name she just hit the buzzer without saying a word. The interior door was unlocked so I entered.

"*Maestra?*" I called out from behind the drape, then pushed it back to see if anyone was in the salon.

"Come in, Raquel," she said from the armchair facing away from me, "you are always welcome here." As I came around she closed her book and set it beside her.

"Thank you, *Maestra,*" I said, facing her. She held out her arms, and I gave her a hug.

"How are you feeling today?" I asked.

"Better," she said, in a guarded tone.

"I hate to say it, but you don't look a great deal better."

"No, really, I am better. Sit down."

"I'm sorry for running out of here yesterday. May I speak to *Doña Nina*?"

"Nina!" she called out weakly.

"*¿Sí?*" growled Nina at the kitchen door.

"*Venga.*"

Nina came to the back of the sofa drying her hands on her apron.

"*Siéntate, mujer!*" *La Maestra* commanded with enough force to bring Nina around to sit in the love seat. The aroma of fresh cilantro and garlic came with her.

"*Buen día*" she said to me with half a smile.

"Good morning, *Doña Nina*," I said. "I've come to apologize for escaping as I did."

"Hmf," she grunted, and nodded her head.

"I understand so much more now. Yesterday, I learned that my uncle is dead."

They looked at each other, then at me. "How do you know this?" asked *La Maestra*.

"Nico told me. I learned that he works at the Diocese. He can take me to my uncle's grave. It's in San Isidro."

They were both silent.

"I thought you'd like to know," I said.

"Be cautious about anything you learn from the Diocese, or from that Nico character," said *La Maestra*. "Your uncle was not the only clergy involved in the junta. There were many."

"But you said many clergy also disappeared or were killed," I said.

"Yes, there were clergy on both sides. And those involved have certainly woven intricate fabrications to protect themselves."

"Nico says there's a document that records Tío's disappearance in 1977."

"Do you have it?"

"No. I told him I wanted to see it. He's supposed to give me a copy and a copy of the death certificate."

"Nico told you that your uncle disappeared and that they have a death certificate? And he has a tidy little grave somewhere?" The two women looked at each other skeptically.

"It seems unlikely?" I asked.

La Maestra folded her arms, and looked into my eyes. "Very unlikely."

"Oh, I hope you are wrong, *Maestra*. I've been thinking about the resonance of memory, and I realize that I must either clear my uncle's name, or learn the reality of his cruelty. And, if possible, extend an apology to his victims. I accept what you told me about him in Spain, but maybe he turned his life around here in Argentina. Maybe he did some good things. I have to learn the truth."

"Raquel, you are an artist," said *La Maestra*, "you know that a self-portrait has to be created by the artist himself. You can only uncover the portrait he has left you to find." I nodded to let her know I had followed her so far. "You had a devil in your family. I am sorry for that. But you are not responsible for what you find. You can say he was one of us, but he is not us. The most important thing is to know yourself. Take him as a teacher."

"A teacher?"

"Yes. If it is in your power to bring kindness or justice where he cast hatred and brutality, then you have learned to turn knowledge into compassionate action. But if you do not follow through now to know the truth, then you may forever fear that some way you colluded with him. In that way you failed to prove that he was more the product of the tragic events of his life than an expression of your genetics."

"I want to untangle him and cut him out of me."

"You can do that. But keep the memory of him alive to fuel your humanity."

I looked at Nina, her eyes downcast beneath a heavy, contracted brow. I knelt at her feet, laying my hands over hers. "Nina," I said, "I am so sorry for the brutal deaths of your loved ones. I don't know if my remorse, all these years later, can have any impact on you at all, but what's in my heart is all I have to give you."

"*Gracias, Raquel. Muchas gracias.*" She looked into my eyes. "I do not hold you *responsable.* How could I?" She put her arms around me, and placed her fleshy cheek against my forehead.

"What will you tell your aunt, Raquel?" asked *La Maestra.* "And your sister, and your son?"

I returned to the sofa, shaking my head. "I don't know. I've been thinking of what I can say."

"If you stop your search now you can simply say he died, and that may be true. But a dark shadow stretches across that assumption, and beneath it you will live with the possibility that you may help him go undetected, so you will have allowed him to do more harm in the world."

"But he's so old," I protested.

"You think evil has an age?" *La Maestra's* voice was calm and soft, but her words were brutal. "Can you live inside a set of lies constructed to protect him?"

"I'm still not convinced of his actions here in Argentina, *Maestra.*"

"We can show you evidence of that," she said.

A vast emptiness opened up within me. I felt like a human canyon, stripped of substance, thoughts and words. I walked over to the French doors and watched the *porteños* meeting the demands of their day. I wanted to be one of them drenched in the quotidian dilemmas of life: What dress should I wear to impress my future mother-in-law? How will I get that wine stain off the armchair? Suddenly a question came up. "What's the name of the organization Paco works for?"

"*Centro de Estudios Legales y Sociales.* The Center for Legal and Social Studies. They gather information and search for the truth about the disappeared and their captors."

"Zorrilla can never be an innocent man," said Nina, oblivious to the conversation happening around her. "We seen *you* family pictures, but where is Nina's family? No photos. No family." Then she got up suddenly and came to stand in front of me. "What you say before . . . I know you sorry," she took a firm grasp of my hands, "but you can do *more*."

"Help bring a criminal to justice," said *La Maestra*.

It was a challenge, and also the solution to my dilemma. Even though he can never be punished for what he did to Nina, I thought, old Father Mateo could be held accountable for criminal brutality in this country. Bringing him to justice would prove the allegations, and if they were true, I couldn't risk the possibility that he could still do more harm. Whatever power I might have to bring him out of the woodwork, I had to step up to the challenge.

CHAPTER TWENTY-ONE

Arriving home, my head was throbbing. The labyrinthine trail to find Tío Mateo was disorienting. It made me wish I could call my father. He was the best navigator in the family. *Please Papa,* I prayed, *help me find your old friend.* But then, I wondered, how could the two men have been such good friends? Papa was a peaceful man. He would not have approved of Mateo's Fascist leanings, or his anti-Semitism. I wished I could read the letters Papa wrote in response to Mateo's. Surely, he'd have tried to reason with him. Suddenly I remembered that there was another box of unexplored things at Marta's house. I called her immediately.

"There's a big box of Papa's stuff in your garage, Marti. We stowed it there just after the accident." Of course she wanted details about everything, but I steered the conversation to what I needed. "Send me one or two of the latest photos possible," I said, "I need them *now.*"

"Sounds like you're doing *real* detective work," she said. "I wish I could be there with you. How's it going?"

"It's not as much fun as it sounds, believe me," I said. "Go through that box and send me photos tonight. Oh, one more thing, have you talked to David?"

"No. I don't think he wants to bother calling his aunty."

"I haven't had email from him in days," I said, "Guess I better get used to my son thinking of me less and less. After all, he's begun his own life now. Thanks for your help, *hermana*. I love you." I clicked off just as I heard her begin a question about Luis. More than anything I would have loved one of our sit-downs, pouring out our hearts to each other. But revisiting my heartbreak was a luxury I couldn't afford. And that is why I also didn't relish listening to the messages flashing red hot on the machine. Finally, I relented.

Call number one made me wince: "*Hola*, it's Luis. How are you? Call me." Same with call number two: "Where are you? Call me." And finally, "I'm getting worried, why haven't you called me back?" I erased them, and took out the Diocesan business card that read: Nicolás Durman, *Departamento de Eventos, Calendario*. I dialed the number.

"*Oficina de Sr. Durman*," said a pleasant female voice.

"*Señor Durman*, please," I said, "this is *Señora Carval* from the American Embassy." It was time to find out if Nico was being used to pass false information, or complicit in this trail of misleading lies.

She put him on immediately. "*Señora Carval*," he said softly, "what a pleasure. How are things at the embassy?"

"I said that so she'd put me right through."

"I will give her orders to always put you through quickly, and save you the lie."

"Thank you." I had to sound just alluring enough to manipulate him. "I'm calling to set up a time to go to the gravesite."

"Oh, *tesoro*," he cooed, "I am so sorry, I have a meeting this afternoon. But I do have something for you." He lowered his voice to a whisper. "I got a copy of the death certificate, and of the statement regarding his disappearance."

"Good." I caught myself, "I don't mean to sound happy about the death certificate, Nico, It's just . . ."

"I understand, it's just better to know the truth, isn't it."

"Yes, exactly. Thank you for understanding."

"You know, I do not have a show tonight," he said, "why don't you have dinner with me. I can give you the documents then."

Yesterday I wouldn't have accepted a Tootsie Roll from Nico, but the painful image of Luis and Carla flashed through my mind like a neon sign, and today the world was new. Besides, I had to learn more about this guy; may as well let him buy me dinner.

"That would be lovely," I said.

"Yes?" He seemed shocked.

"Yes."

"Wonderful! May I pick you up at nine?"

"Fine." I gave him my address and hung up. A pang of fear rumbled through my stomach, but in my mind a voice said, *Hey, maybe I've been just as wrong about Nico in one direction as I have been about Luis in the other. Give it some time.*

"*¡O-la-la!*" said, Nico when I opened the door. He took me into a tango embrace and twirled me across the threshold. When we stopped, he kissed my hand, and a breath of relaxation rippled through me. Despite his questionable character it was difficult to maintain the iceberg defense against Nico. Tonight, I thought, I could afford to thaw out a bit. I'd decided to wear my red dress with the halter top that ties in a soft bow at the neck, with cascading tails down my back. The diaphanous layered chiffon skirt falls just above the knee, so when I walk it floats on the air current. Even my women friends have told me I'm the bomb in that dress. Nico seemed to agree.

"Tell me, *señora*," he said, looking me up and down, "do you have a license to wear this dress?"

"I didn't know I needed one."

"Oh yes, and insurance for the cars that could crash when you walk down the street."

I was thawing quickly. He looked like Adonis in a three-piece suit. My husband Gordon was not a bad-looking man. In fact, in a suit and tie, he could actually qualify as handsome. But Nico was over-the-top Hollywood grade gorgeous. I suspected the color of his hair was closely regulated. He managed to keep it soft black with graying at the temples. He had big dark eyes, dimples when he smiled, and a cleft in his chin, like Cary Grant. I decided to be careful with my wine consumption, or I could get easy very fast, especially if the image of Luis and Carla crept into my mind. So instead of offering him an aperitif, I just grabbed my bag, jacket, and keys.

"That is a large bag," he said, "can I hope you have tango shoes inside it?"

"Here in Buenos Aries, I hardly ever go out without them."

"Great!" he said, "Fernández Fierro is giving a concert tonight at La Ideal, we can catch them after dinner."

He took me to a place called Casa Arabia, an upscale Middle Eastern restaurant in the tony neighborhood known as Barrio Norte. Certainly Nico knew more than he was telling me, but I'd have to manipulate information out of him. Unfortunately, I wasn't even sure what to ask.

"I keep this place in mind for special occasions," he said.

"And the delivery of a death certificate qualifies?"

"In this case, it does," he said, nuzzling close to me.

I let Nico order from the menu of exotic offerings, and each time the waiter poured the wine I was quick to instruct him. "Just enough to cover the bottom of the glass, please." As my companion turned up the charm, I wondered how an orphan boy could have such a perfect smile. Dental care would have been expensive. And his manners were so studied, so smooth, where did he learn them? He lit a cigarette and reminded me of Paul Henried in that old Betty Davis movie, *Now Voyager*.

"Do you mind?" he asked, gesturing to the cigarette.

"No. As I said, it's not a habit I recommend, but it's your life."

"Yes, yes. The latest American invention: tobacco phobia."

"It's not a phobia, Nico. It's a fact: tobacco is a toxic substance."

"Even love can be a toxic substance, no?" He blew the aromatic cloud away from me. "Does that mean you stay away from love, too?"

"I haven't thought much about love since my divorce, frankly," I said honestly. "Life has had too many challenges and demands."

"But now you are away from all that, and ready to enjoy life again. How lucky to meet you at just the right time."

His gaze dropped from my lips to my bosom, and he brought his face close to mine. He smiled and took a deep breath. "You smell like a flower in sunshine," he said. "Did you know that when the flower heats up, her aroma rises and fills the air around her." He stroked my hair softly with the back of his index finger. I had to admit, he was heating my petals, and it was getting hard to disguise the effect.

Mercifully, the waiter arrived and I was able to shift the conversation. "Nico, I hope you don't mind me saying this, but for an orphan you've made quite a life for yourself. Somehow you cultivated very good taste."

"I have to credit the Father," he said, "he made sure I got an education."

"What was your childhood like?"

"Oh," he stuck a hefty piece of bread into his mouth, giving him a moment, I presumed, to choreograph his answer. "I don't like to talk about it," he said, after a swallow. "It can seem that I am begging for sympathy."

"Okay, I promise not to sympathize," I said. "I really want to know you."

"Well, it was cold. Big, drafty, dormitories. No mothering. The nuns were weak on cuddling, strong on obedience. They believed that beating a boy strengthened his character. And the food! Thank God that Father made sure I had decent food, not just orphanage food. Sometimes I would eat at the residence with the priests. Also, one housekeeper was very good to me. She had two sons, so I got any clothes they didn't wear out. Usually suits were outgrown before they were worn out so they got passed around a lot. The worse thing was being sick. You know flu, measles, those childhood diseases. The sisters probably did their best, but no one ever held my hand or tucked me into bed."

"That's very sad," I said. "Oh, sorry, I promised not to sympathize."

"Well, kids adapt, you know. I knew nothing else." He gazed off into the chandelier for a moment. "But when I was an altar boy, children came to the communion rail in their Sunday clothes, with their mother or father. Those mothers smelled so sweet." His words drifted off on a current of memories. "So I made up a mother. You know, the way kids have invisible friends. She smelled divine, just like the ladies at the communion rail. And I imagined her holding me at night until I went to sleep in her arms."

"I am sorry that you, or anyone, has that kind of childhood," I said.

"Oh, plenty of kids had it worse than me." He shrugged. "Some kids with parents have worse childhoods than I did. I was born right after an earthquake. Many kids lived in packs through the streets of San Juan. Father watched out for me. When he was transferred here to Buenos Aires, oh, that day I thought the whole planet had been pulled out from under me." The words caught in his throat. He took a drink of wine. "But he promised to get me transferred to live in an orphanage here, and he did it. In my teens he arranged for me to live in the *residencia* with him and other priests. That housekeeper, Rosario, was a wonderful woman, the closest thing I ever had to a mother."

"How'd you get so worldly?" I asked.

"I went to university in Mexico City."

"Why Mexico?"

"I got a scholarship, and Father arranged a place to live in a nearby seminary."

"Were you still thinking of becoming a priest?"

"No! In fact, once I almost got married."

"That makes more sense. But you said you've never been married?"

He stared into his plate. "No. Once I thought I had found a woman superior to the rest. But she was unfaithful to me."

"And that's when you thought of becoming a priest?"

"No!" He laughed. "The priest thing was earlier in my life.

High school. First, I became a Peronista, then I thought to become a priest. I wanted to join the *Movimiento Sacerdotes Para El Tercer Mundo*, a Liberation Theology movement, kind of left wing. It really upset Father. That's when we had our first really big argument. I had always been very agreeable. I adored him, but a kid needs a rebellious period."

"But your Father was a priest. Didn't he want you to become a priest?"

"Not that kind. For him, I may as well have been a Communist."

"Oh. He was or is conservative? Is he still living?"

"He is both living and conservative, very conservative. That's when he found me the scholarship to University of Mexico."

"So, he pulled some strings, you think?"

"I don't know. There was another fellow from the same orphanage, Esteban, he also got a scholarship. I never thought I would go to college," he shook his head pensively. "Father said if I still wanted to be a priest after college, I could do that. That's what Esteban did."

"What did you study?"

"Performing Arts and Literature."

"Oh! Of course," I laughed, "perfect preparation for the priesthood."

He actually blushed, laughing at himself. "Maybe I wasn't too serious about that," he admitted. "I sang in the choir in church. And I have always been 'a big ham', that's what you say, right?

"Yes."

"Besides, I was always interested in women. I almost married a second time, too. That one was *Americana*, from Texas, but I came to my senses."

As the meal progressed, Nico introduced me to the delicacies of Middle Eastern cuisine. I had to admit, I was having a lovely time with him, but my agenda was set to extract as much information as possible, and I didn't falter.

"So when you came back to Argentina after university, what kind of work did you look for?"

"Oh, Father found a job for me with the Diocese."

"Was that the kind of work you wanted?"

"Look, Father saved my life. If he wanted me to work for the Diocese, I did it. I could sing in shows in the evenings, I was content. Besides, the Diocese job supports my passion for clothing. See, my friends at university were, you say, 'well off'? They gave me garments they'd worn once or twice, like the hand-me-downs I got from the boys in the orphanage. But those second hand clothes were of excellent quality. So I fit in with the university in crowd. And I learned to look for quality in everything," he said, putting his arm around me, "especially in women."

"I didn't think the Church paid that well," I said.

"Enough of this," he said, and turned the conversation to my life. I gave him the standard version bio: Masters Degree, museum job, birth of son, dedication to painting and fine arts. He didn't ask much about Gordon except for his profession.

"Brain research." I said. "I thought I was marrying a

healer but as soon as he finished his residency, Gordon applied for a research fellowship."

"Why did you divorce?"

"He set aside brain science, to study the anatomy of his lab assistant."

"Oh, I see! So now, son is grown, husband gone, and you come to Argentina."

"I want to go back home at some point, of course. I miss my sister and my niece, my aunt, and certainly, David. I wish I could bring them all here."

"When will you go back? How long will you stay in Argentina?"

"Whoa! So many questions! I planned to stay just long enough to find my uncle."

"And now, sadly, you have found him," he said, softly.

"Yes, thanks to you. I must return soon, I think, to see my aunt before she dies, and show her the photo of Mateo's grave."

He took my right hand into his and, lifting it gently to his lips, kissed away little deposits of powdered sugar that had accumulated like snow on my fingers after the *bastilla*. The flicker of his tongue on my fingertips was very seductive. I watched his mouth caressing my skin.

"I would like you to stay," he said, kissing my palm.

"*Eh, couscous, señor,*" said the waiter, returning our attention to the food.

The five-course meal gave me ample opportunity to learn

more about Nico, but by the time I stood up to leave, the red dress was closing in around my waist. The evening *milonga* would be the perfect antidote to such a feast.

On the dance floor Nico was creative and challenging, never repetitive with his patterns. There were breathless pauses of suspended balance, and playful quick steps in animation with the music. Between tangos, Nico kissed my hands, and deposited little kisses at my temples. But my spy work remained foremost in my mind no matter how difficult it was to focus. Even though my questions moved from one life situation to another, I could not detect discrepancies. Only one discrepancy bothered me: I didn't believe that a church job could fund such expensive clothes and fine dining.

By the time he took me home, there was little of the iceberg in me. I'd had a wonderful evening. I didn't fault him for being seductive. Latin men are much more blatant in their flirtation than most North Americans. I presumed Nico's advances were customary by Argentine standards. In fact, it's possible that an Argentine woman could feel insulted if a man *didn't* press his affections as far as he could.

I inserted the key and opened my apartment door. "Thank you, Nico," I said. "I had a wonderful evening."

He put his arms around me and pulled me into a long passionate kiss. I felt the heat and musculature of his torso beneath the luxurious weave of his suit. But as the embrace tightened, I began to feel frightened. Suddenly I remembered being pinned into my chair at Café Tortoni. I pushed away enough to catch my breath, but he pulled me closer and kissed me again. This time the kiss was so soft

I thought I'd cry from the tenderness of it, but then his fingers were clutching me.

I pulled away. "Goodnight, Nico."

"Do not send me away, Raquel," he said, his hand cradling my head at the nape of my neck. My pulse pumped forcefully in my ears.

"I'm really not ready to get involved more deeply," I said.

His embrace tightened again, pressing me to his chest with his left arm while his right hand traveled to explore the contour of my waist and hips. His cologne, once pleasant had grown acrid and I couldn't catch my breath. Through the soft fabric layers of my dress I felt the pressure of his hand rubbing my thigh and I tried to push away from him. When his hand reached beneath the fabric to stroke my skin, I struggled earnestly to break free.

"Please," I said, raising my voice.

"Oh, you want more?" he whispered. I felt him pull on the halter tie that released the bow from my neck. As he started to lift the fabric away from my breast, a sense of panic ran through me.

"NO. Stop! Please stop." I didn't care about the neighbors. In fact, I hoped one of them would open their door. I gripped his hand on the halter, trying to pry his fingers away.

"Just let me inside," he said, softly. "You've been promising this all night, Raquel. Don't be a tease. It could be so good."

"No I haven't. Honestly, I can't. Not yet. Please, let go."

There was a moment of paralyzed silence, then his embrace relented. His right hand smoothed out the surface of my dress.

He took a deep breath and a step back.

"Please understand," I said catching my breath, "maybe an Argentine woman would act differently, but I'm very vulnerable. I am alone in a foreign country."

He was silent, staring into my cleavage. His jaw clenched.

"Nico," I said, trying to capture his gaze, "Please don't be angry. It's been such a lovely evening." I placed my fingers under his chin hoping to meet him eye to eye.

He pulled away. "I will call you tomorrow about the time to leave for San Isidro."

"Yes, fine."

Another step backward, and he turned to go.

"Nico!" I said intentionally stopping him with my voice.

"What?" He shouted lifting his hands in the air.

"The documents."

"Oh!" He came back toward me, reached into his breast pocket and pulled out an envelope and held it to his chest. "For a moment I hoped you'd changed your mind," he said looking into my eyes.

"*Buenas noches,*" I said, plucking the envelope out of his long fingers.

"*Chau.*"

CHAPTER TWENTY-TWO

The next morning I showered, dressed, and made coffee before laying the documents and letters out on the table with the deliberation of a Tarot card reader. First: the death certificate. It gave Mateo's date of death as Sept. 20, 1977. But his last letter was dated October, 1977. Suddenly, something else occurred to me. "Zorrilla!" I flipped back through the noisy onionskins.

"Yes!" I held up the letter I'd read before my first trip to the Diocese. There it was: *I receive my mail at the mailbox of another priest, so instead of using my name, just address the envelope to* Padre *Zorrilla. When he sees your return address, he will make sure I get it.*

Paco believed my uncle was Zorrilla, but maybe Zorrilla drew Mateo into working with the junta and somehow he was mistaken for Zorrilla. It seemed to me a credible possibility.

The document of disappearance was nothing more than a statement on Diocesan stationery.

To Whom It May Concern,

This is to certify that Father Mateo Vicente López disappeared from the city of Buenos Aires, Argentina, the night of August 26, 1977. Police searches failed to find Father López, and the Church has never received a single request for ransom, nor any correspondence regarding his abduction. Montoneros have been suspected of his abduction, though no proof was ever found.

The letter didn't even have a date, or a signature. Why would the Diocese lie about Tío Mateo's death? And why would Nico give me both these documents? What was he expecting me to believe? It would have made sense to give me one or the other, but the two together made the whole thing seem like a farce. I decided to reread Tío's last letter, hoping it would give me a clue about the real events.

The dates on the documents, and the appearance of Zorrilla in my uncle's letters, added more disturbing elements into the weave of my evening with Nico. I'd tried to give him the benefit of every doubt, but any affectionate feelings had been overshadowed by the goodnight skirmish at the door. It was time to confront the probability that Nico was a fancy decoy designed to distract my attention from the truth.

Because of their connection to my father, I cherished my uncle's letters no matter their content. The old writing paper, thin by manufacture, seemed thinner still by years of handling. How many times had my father's eyes glided over the scrawled letters of his boyhood friend, I wondered. The occasional smudge suggested he'd wept. He must have worried about Mateo. About his health and his sanity. Why did they keep this correspondence a secret, and how did Papa feel about keeping that secret? The questions were moot; the answers taken with my father on a cold December night, traditionally intended for celebration.

I lay the letters on the coffee table, then curled up on the sofa to read the last one.

> *22 octubre 1977*
> *Querido Fredo,*
> **Things are difficult at the moment. A lot of violence in the city and in the whole country. El Señor is always with me.**

I was startled then, by a knock at the door. Checking through the peephole I saw Paco, with Luis at his side. My feelings for him were far too complex to decipher, and I didn't have time to sort them out, so I took a deep breath and opened the door.

"Paco," I said, "I'm glad to see you."

"I hope you don't mind my coming by without phoning, Raquel," he said. "*La Maestra* told me that you are determined to prove your uncle's innocence, and I have information you should know. It is important you listen to what I have to tell you."

"I'm simply determined to learn the truth," I said. In my peripheral vision I saw Luis leaning toward me as if expecting me to talk to him. "And Paco," I said, "what is Luis doing here with you?"

"You're asking him?" said Luis. "Why don't you ask me?"

I looked at him quickly then dropped my gaze. The sight of him made my stomach burn and blood throb in my head.

"Raquel?" He stepped forward and I stepped back. How could he not know, or at least guess that I might have seen him or heard about him and Carla from people in the tango class?

"Well, Paco," I said, "I can't leave you out there in the corridor. Please, come in. And I guess you may as well bring your friend with you." Escorting them to the sofa, I offered a beverage.

"Nothing for me, thanks," said Paco.

"I'll have tea," said Luis. I shot him a withering glance, then went into the kitchen to put on the kettle. He followed me.

"What is going on with you?" he asked. "Why haven't you returned my phone calls or emails?"

I pulled tea bags from the drawer, and dumped old tea from the pot into the sink.

"Come on. At least an explanation!" he said in a stage whisper. When I turned from the cupboard with the sugar bowl he stood in front of me. I looked down to avoid him, but he lifted my face gently with his fingertips. I closed my eyes. Unfortunately, that released the tears I'd so far managed to retain.

"Tell me!" he said, taking hold of the sugar bowl.

"Alright!" I said, looking at him through a wet blur. "I saw you with Carla at La Biela."

"With Carla? At La Biela? When?"

"Sunday evening. You told me you were taking your grandchildren to the *Jardín Zoológico* that day."

"Yes, I did." He seemed to be replaying the day in his head. "Oh, right. Carla tried to invite herself along. When I told her that I wanted to be alone with the children she said, 'Then you must have dinner with me.' I felt like I'd rejected her for the afternoon so I met her at La Biela. We were supposed to go on to dinner from there, but she'd been out with friends, and she'd had absolutely too much to drink." He lowered his voice even further, I imagined because Carla's father was in the next room. "She gets, uh, romantic when she's drunk, and a little aggressive. So instead of having dinner at her apartment, which she suggested, I kept her at La Biela and ordered her a, uh, . . ."

"A ham sandwich," I said refreshing his memory.

"Yes. And I had to feed it to her. Oh, I see. That could have looked, uh, intimate."

"You think?"

"You have to believe me, it was not what it seemed, honestly. I also ordered coffee to sober her up. If you saw us, you know I ordered coffee."

"You've got an answer for everything," I said.

"We have to talk more about this, Raquel, but right now you must listen to Paco. Can you at least be civil to me?"

The kettle let out a high-pitched whistle behind him and he flinched.

"I'm not unwilling to listen, but I am skeptical," I said. "Now move aside and at least let me take that kettle out of its misery."

Luis carried the tea tray into the living room where I saw Paco standing over the letters.

"Those are private letters," I said, defensively.

"I know. I'm sorry. I didn't read much. Have you learned anything from them?"

"I was just beginning to reread them. Sit down, please. I'm sorry if I seem possessive of the letters, it's just that so much is happening and I feel so out of control."

"I understand," said Paco.

"I have to tell you what's transpired since the last time I saw you," I said. Before those minutes in the kitchen I would have embellished Nico's gallantry and left out his lascivious nature, but some of my vengeance had evaporated. Even though I recounted the events of last night's date with a more circumspect attitude, Luis seemed pretty agitated about it. He paced while I talked.

"How could you go out with that guy?" he said.

I threw him a sideways glance. "The defining moment came," I said to Paco, "when I opened the death certificate this morning." I went to the table and handed it to him. "It declares my uncle dead a month before he wrote the last letter."

The two men looked at me incredulously. I nodded.

"What do you make of that, Raquel?" asked Paco.

"Well, obviously, someone wants me to stop looking for him. I don't know if Nico engineered this, or if it's just given to him by a higher ranking official."

"Look," said Paco, "we came here to convince you to meet a woman who had a painful experience with your uncle, eh, with Zorrilla. Her name is Carmina Perraza. You can bring your photo, and see if she recognizes him."

"I'm trying to get a later photo," I said. "Also, I want to read through all the letters carefully. I can't imagine what reason the Diocese would have for falsifying this document."

"It's very difficult to get a meeting with Carmina," said Paco. "She's not exactly in her right mind since her abduction. She is paranoid about new people coming to her home, so I'll have to arrange a place and time that she will agree to. I'll call you when I know. You should go to the gravesite, also."

"Find out where it is and I'll take you," said Luis.

"I'm going with Nico," I said abruptly.

"No! You can't do that. It could be dangerous," he said, red faced. "You can't trust that guy."

"But" said Paco, "it would assure him that she buys the whole story he's selling. It's possible, Raquel, you could find a criminal we've been hunting for over twenty years."

"The letters indicate that the Spanish Civil War turned my uncle into a Fascist," I said, "but I worry that he could be innocent of crimes you attribute to him. He should be *proven* guilty."

"Meet Carmina. If she doesn't give you enough evidence, nothing will. I'll try to set it up as soon as possible. It will be after dark. She never goes out in daytime."

"Okay. I'm waiting for a call from Nico to set the time to visit the grave."

Luis took a noisy gulp of tea and pushed the cup against the sugar bowl on the tray. Paco stood up and headed for the door, Luis and I behind him.

"Thank you for coming to see me in person, Paco," I said.

"I cannot pretend to know how you feel, Raquel, but you are in a rare position to help us. That phony death certificate is further evidence that Zorrilla is alive."

"I'm still not convinced that he and my uncle are the same person. His first letter from Buenos Aires confirms that he knew Zorrilla because he mentions him." I went for the letter and showed it to Paco who just nodded and handed it back to me.

"Bring your photos to Carmina," he said. "She will tell you."

"Oh, I forgot to show you this," I said retrieving the declaration of disappearance from the table. "Obviously it was placed in the file to throw someone off. I have a feeling it wasn't meant to go out with the death certificate. I mean, it seems strange that Nico gave me both documents."

"This is very strange," said Paco. "I don't know of any family receiving such a document. I wonder if it was intended to be given to you. Perhaps Nico's feelings for you are making him sloppy in following orders," said Paco, "which can work in our favor. I'll see if I can set up the meeting with Carmina tonight." He started to leave then turned back. "I should warn you: her story is a brutal one. And, she has scars. It may be uncomfortable for you."

"Well, I need to be 100% sure that Zorrilla is my uncle. Once I'm sure, I'll have to find him. It's the only moral choice. I don't expect any of this to be easy."

He gave me a hug and a kiss on the cheek. "Luis, are you coming?"

"May I stay?" He looked at me with a forlorn expression.

"Why?"

"I need to explain what you *think* you saw."

"I know what I saw. Maybe you can explain why it happened."

"Yes. I can."

"Raquel," said Paco, "could I speak to you alone for a moment." Luis looked at him curiously.

"Sorry, *amigo*," said Paco, "it's important."

"Sure," said Luis, "I'll drink more tea." He walked back toward the coffee table.

In the hall, Paco pulled the door ajar and stepped close to me. "I have to ask you, forgive me if this is too personal, but we are swimming in dangerous waters. How intimately involved are you with Nico Durman?"

"Oh, that." Suddenly I understood the delicacy of the issue, and I was glad he'd asked to speak to me alone. "We're not lovers, if that's what you're asking. He does have feelings for me. Well, only lust is for certain. I had to fight him off last night."

"Good. You can use that. If he thinks something is growing between you, he will probably protect you from harm. You should cultivate his feelings."

"You're making me feel like Mata Hari." I made a joke of it, but not because it was humorous.

"Sorry, I'm sure you never expected to be in such a position."

"I certainly did not."

"Well, the other thing I wanted to say, is that you should not be seen with Luis."

"What?"

"If you want Nico to think you could be serious about him, you don't want to be seen with another man. Has he ever seen you with Luis?"

The sneer on Nico's face on the night of our performance at El Beso flashed in my mind. "He saw us together at El Beso," I said.

"Then you better be careful."

"I thought jealousy made a man want a woman more."

"In this case, we can't afford to test the theory. Now you have to explain this to Luis," he said, "I mean, I could do it, but I think it will be better coming from you."

He didn't realize that I was still questioning Luis's character, and the role his daughter played in our relationship. Was this going to send Luis back into Carla's arms?

"Do you want me to talk to him?" asked Paco.

"No, I'll do it."

"*Bueno. Chau, Hermosa.*" He walked slowly to the end of the hall and disappeared down the stairs.

Luis sat forward on the sofa staring into his mug.

"Would you read the letters with me?" I asked, stacking the pages and straightening them into a neat pile.

"Are you sure you trust me?"

"I can trust you with letters, it's my heart that's in question."

"That was a long powwow you had with Paco out in the hall."

I tried to collect my thoughts but they were too unruly, so I just started talking. "I have to explain something."

"Okay," he said.

Part of me wanted to hurt him with what I had to say, and part of me hated to hurt him. "Paco thinks we shouldn't be seen in public until this whole thing is over."

"Why?"

"Because Nico has feelings for me, and Paco says we should take advantage of those feelings. He thinks Nico will protect me from harm if he's, uh, if I'm ..."

"His woman?" He stretched his neck and his head like a periscope.

I looked him in the eyes. "No. Well, yes. Well, what does "his woman" mean? I just can't be seen with someone else."

He jumped off the sofa and confronted me face to face. "Are you sleeping with him?"

"NO."

"Well, you must be pretty close if he's thinking you are his woman."

"I am not sleeping with him. Should I ask you that question about Carla?"

"Go ahead and ask it! I'm not."

"Well, maybe it's just as well that you've been seen amorously with her in public."

He turned away, paced into the kitchen and back.

"I want you to know," I said, "this was Paco's idea, not mine. But, hey, maybe Paco wants you for a son-in-law, and he's working on Carla's behalf."

"I don't love Carla. We're old friends."

"Old friends? Or old lovers?"

He was silent.

"Okay. Guess I got my answer."

"It was a very long time ago. She made herself indispensable after Mari died. The girls felt comfortable with her. She became part of our lives. Then it seemed . . . Well, we tried it. It didn't work. I don't love her."

"But she loves you."

"I am not responsible for how she feels or what she wants."

"And I'm not responsible for what Nico wants."

We stood about ten feet apart and looked at each other. I wanted to trust him with all my might, wanted to harbor myself in his arms. But every rational inch of me said, No.

CHAPTER TWENTY-THREE

"I've been afraid to show these letters to anyone because it's easy to jump to conclusions," I said.

"You mean *you* jumped to conclusions when you read them?" said Luis.

"I suppose I do mean that. Just promise to keep an open mind."

"I will do my best."

We perched side by side stiffly on the sofa at first. Relaxing slowly, we finally settled back for comfort until Luis grimaced and jerked forward as if someone had pushed a gun to his back.

"What's wrong?"

"What did I just sit on?" He reached between the sofa cushions, and pulled his cell phone out into view. "You see! I *told* you I'd lost it. God, I've looked everywhere for it. Now do you believe me?"

"Yes, okay, I see that you were telling the truth about the phone."

"And I was telling the truth about the rest of it, too. Carla met me in the patio of *El Alef* just before that class, and she was drunk when I met her at La Biela. You have to believe me now."

I reflected quickly on the events in question, and since I didn't have time to study the potential nuances of the deception, I relented. "I suppose those things are all possible," I said.

"They are more than possible," he said adamantly, "I plead not guilty, your honor, and the evidence proves my innocence." He held up the cell phone as an undeniable truth.

I rolled my eyes. "Yes, though it's not conclusive, the evidence *does* point to your innocence," I conceded. "So, can we drop this and get on with the real case at hand?"

"Absolutely," he said, taking his seat again on the sofa.

"The first letter is from Spain in 1936." I began.

> *15 agosto 1936*
> *Zafra, España,*
> *Querido Alfredo,*
> *Words cannot describe what it's like here. I never imagined anything so grotesque, so horrible. God knows I have suffered a lot with my wounds, physical and emotional, but I have already learned that any life lived in peace is a sacred gift.*
> *I need to build up a tolerance for violence, but I don't know how to do that. I cannot even stomach the smell of it. I've seen many convents and churches destroyed or burnt to the foundations. I knew*

that because of the anti-clerical movement, there was a lot of violence and destruction to the Church, but I had no idea of the human toll.

Everywhere there is a stench of burnt and decaying flesh, urine, feces, and ashes. The devil is among us, hermano, and the world smells like Hell. His agents have killed sisters and priests. We have had to lift their mutilated bodies, and sometimes body parts, out of pools of blood. There is no way to give them individual burials.

Fortunately, I was sent to this place where the army came early and was victorious. Now soldiers hold the peace, but hatred for clergy is so high that I live in fear every minute of the day and night. They will move me soon, I know I am needed elsewhere.

I don't know if I can survive this, hermano. If I die, it will be a blessing. I am ordered to carry a pistol at all times. The soldiers trained me to shoot it. You know me, I couldn't even kill pigeons when we were kids. Remember how disgusted my father was with me? Now, I may have to kill human beings, and all in the name of God, all for our Church. I wonder if Papá would finally be proud of his Mateo if he knew how the war is 'making a man' out of me.

Pray for me, brother. I've enclosed another

short note to Mama to let her know I've arrived
safely. Explain that I sent it to you because I knew
Papá would throw it away if he saw it in the mail
before she could read it.

    Yours in Christ,
    Mateo

"How old was he when he went to Spain?" Luis asked.

"He was born in 1912. So he was twenty-four in 1936. Just out of the seminary, I suppose."

"That war must have been quite a turning point in his life," he said. "He seems to have been a gentle kid. I mean, most boys enjoy learning to hunt. It's the kind of thing that bonds a boy to his father."

"What horror he encountered," I said, "He was a tender soul. That's why I hold out hope for him still. I can't imagine how my father felt reading this. Papa never hunted, either. I guess they shared other interests. Do you have brothers, Luis?"

"Yes, one. I'll tell you about him some time. Let's go to the next letter."

    Río Olvidado,
    12 abril, 1937
    Hermano,
    One of the parishioners promised to take this
letter for mailing. I pray he lives long enough to

get to the mail. I am in a tiny town near Jaen. Rio Olvidado is an appropriate name because the river that once ran through here has been dry so long, there's not a living soul who remembers it.

There are diabolical forces at work here, Fredo. Every day I am tested to meet the demands of the Lord. You should see me. I am no longer the weak invalid you knew me to be: That boy who needed help carrying the communion wine. Remember him? Old Father Teodoro in San Leandro would not recognize me. I have fulfilled the oath of my confirmation, and the vows of my priesthood: I am a real soldier of Christ now.

I am never without a gun, and sometimes I even wield a knife or a bayonet. We use whatever is at hand when we have to. Eight months of war, and I am skilled in finding the enemy and killing him. Yes, God forgive me, I have taken human lives. The enemy doesn't wear a uniform, you know. Here the devil is disguised as normal people. Just recently they came right into the Mass! Nothing is sacred to them. As soon as I recognized the devils, I screamed at the parishioners and together we drove them from the church. We pushed them out, and then we found a whole camp of them behind an old garage at the end of town. We killed every one of them for the glory of God.

I was sent to this defenseless little town to serve and protect the Church and its relics. I have had to do violent things, brother, but la gloria del Señor is in me. Each time I am called into action, I become filled with the Holy Spirit. He makes me ferocious. Yes, me! I become ferocious in the service of the Lord.

Someday I hope to return to being a man of peace, but as long as I can see the devil at work, Jesus Christ will have a dedicated soldier in me.

I pray you are well, Alfredo. Blessings and health for the family, but do not tell them you have heard from me. Papá will make it hard on Mamita.

Yours in Christ, Mateo

We were silent for a minute. "That phrase "*la Gloria*", I said, "*La Maestra* used it."

"Yes, and he mentions the old garage. . ."

"Are you thinking what I'm thinking, Luis?"

"That this letter is about the day Saturnina's family was massacred?"

"Yes. *La Maestra* said it was near Jaen. Her uncle went to mass. I think this could be Mateo's version of the same story."

We sat there staring at the page.

"Why did I ever do this?" I said. "Why didn't I just come to

Buenos Aires to study tango? I could have presumed, as everyone else did, that he was dead."

Luis put his arm around my shoulders, and to my consternation, the feel and the fragrance of him eased my mind.

"Don't forget your aunt," he said. You had to do this for her, if no one else."

"Yes, and I never could have imagined this situation."

"Your uncle paints a powerful self-portrait," he said, looking back at the letter. "The boy, rejected by his father, then pushed into violence for a sacred cause. I can see how Mateo became Sebastián, one of the great martyred saints."

I hadn't thought anything of the name, but he was right. "It fits, except in this incarnation Sebastián is one of the most blood thirsty martyrs around."

"I'm so glad you let me in," he said. "Reading these letters is a painful project."

He picked up the next letter, and began to read.

> *Teruel,*
> *29 febrero 1938*
> *Querido Fredo,*
> *My brother, I thought I would never write you*
> *again. I have been in the city of Teruel since Decem-*
> *ber, and it has been a bloody two months. I dont wear*
> *the collar anymore, it is too dangerous. So I appear*
> *to be an invalid, a simpleton. Whoever would have*

thought that my scars and my lost arm would be a blessing! Now, they make an excellent disgise.

At the beginning of january the Republicans overtook the city. They torched the church and shot out its beautiful windows. Parishioners hid me in their basement where I said Mass each morning. But there were anarchists barging into houses nearby, so I had to leave. For two weeks I moved from one place to another, finding food as best I could. I was just the cripple guy to most people. A miracle I managed to keep the chalice from the church with me, untouched.

I cannot tell you the joy we felt when Franco's army rescued the city. I hope you have learned the good news: the Vatican has recognized Franco's government. With the city under Nationalist control now I hope to begin to put the Church back together, unless I am given orders to move again.

I still carry the pistol always. I try to be optimistic, but even with the soldiers ocupying the city, this is a savage world.

Pray for España, Alfredo. Pray for El Caudillo and his good Catholic soul.

Un abrazo, Mateo

"We cannot imagine what it is like, to hide in fear of your life every day," he said. "Imagine, being both a priest and a soldier at the same time, carrying a chalice and a gun."

"These days he must feel like a fugitive again, don't you think?" I said.

"Well, he may be in hiding, but he can't be moving from place to place at his age."

"Right. At least he's not a moving target," I said.

Luis held the letter up to the light as if searching for a secret message. "It's hard to believe he thought Franco was the savior of the Spanish people," he said. "I mean, the man was responsible for the German Luftwaffe bombing and strafing innocent Spaniards."

"I know," I said, "but a lot of people agreed with him, many still do." I started to pace the room.

"It's history now, *querida*," he said. "What's bothering you?"

"Luis, even if by some miracle, my uncle is not Sebastián Zorrilla," I said, "he was a Fascist, and probably still is. He fought against his own people."

"It was civil war. He fought alongside other Spaniards. These letters really open my eyes to that war. I mean, no matter what side a person was on, they fought with their *compañeros* against their countrymen." He shook his head and picked up the next letter. "This next one is dated seven years later." He started reading.

20 enero, 1945
San Juan, Argentina
Brother Alfredo, Maybe you think I died in Spain. I don't remember the last time I wrote you.

I had serious problems. I could not take the chance to be found. Finally, it was safer to leave the country, and as you see, I am now back in Argentina. San Juan has had much destruction by earthquake. Buildings are in ruins, many are dead, many homeless, children orphaned. Can you imagine, hermano, I found a tiny new baby, just a few days old. I heard his cries and dug him out of the rubble. It was a miracle to find a little life surrounded by so much death and destruction. Yet, despite the chaos it seems peaceful after the war. These people cannot understand how I remain calm. They do not know that I am grateful no one is shooting at me!

If my mother still lives, she has certainly buried me and mourned my passing. Do not dig me up. Let the world presume I died in Spain, fighting for Our Lord.

I am hungry for news of family: You, my sisters, and Mamita.

Write me at the address on the outside. Don't use my name. Address it to Padre de la Iglesia de San Juan.

Yours in Christ, Mateo

"Seven years," observed Luis, "no wonder everyone thought

he'd died."

"I'm wondering why he left Spain," I said. "His side won, after all. What kind of problem could he have had? Why come back to Argentina? He could have gone to the U.S."

"Was he born in Spain?"

"No, he was born here. I think. The Diocese sent me a copy of his baptismal certificate. I didn't ask for a birth certificate. Of course, *anything* they send could be a fraud."

"Now you sound like a real *porteña*."

'What do you mean?"

"We Argentines don't trust documents, or the people who make them."

"You mean because I'm tired and cynical, I'm becoming ac-culturated?"

"Exactly," he said, "*and* you want the truth."

"Yes. I do."

"That's how we all felt during those unending years of *El Proceso*."

"I'm getting a very small taste of what it was like, and I don't like it."

"You know," he said, looking at the letter again, "your uncle seems to have returned to being the man of peace he said he wanted to be. At least in this letter, he is doing good work."

His observation brought me a sudden feeling of exhilaration "You're right! He's helping during an earthquake," I said. "I knew there was some good inside him."

"What do you think this is all about: *Write me at the address on the outside. Don't use my name. Address it to* Padre de la Iglesia de San Juan."

"My God!" I said, "San Juan!"

"Is that significant?"

"Oh, my God."

"What's going on?"

I felt like a pin ball game was chiming and lighting up in my head as memories of Nico's life story lit up.

"Raquel, talk to me. What's on your mind?"

I looked at him wondering if he could listen objectively. "I have to tell you something, it's about Nico. Please just listen, okay?"

"Yes, okay. What is it?"

"I think my uncle is the man that Nico calls Father."

"What do you mean?"

"Nico told me that he was found after an earthquake in the rubble of San Juan, by a priest. And that priest looked after him his whole life. Even though he lived in orphanages, his 'Father', as he calls him, made sure he got an education, even university."

"Why do you think your uncle was that priest? Must have been lots of babies . ."

"It's just too great a coincidence," I said.

"What's his Father's name?"

"I don't know. He's never mentioned him by any name other than Father. Also, Nico works at the Diocese office, and he's the one who gave me the death certificate and the notice of disappearance. And he's going to take me to the gravesite. The clerks at that office couldn't even find a file under my uncle's name, but Nico came up with documents and important information."

Luis was silent, his brow furrowed. The possible connection between my uncle and Nico rendered us both speechless.

"Read the next letter," I said.

> *febrero 1947*
> *San Juan, Argentina*
> *My dear brother,*
> *Your news hit me like a meteor. I am so happy to know that Mamita continues in good health. I wish I could send her a hug, but it is best to leave me dead and buried in the dust of war. I am no longer the son she knew anyway.*
>
> *I never imagined that you would actually become my brother-in-law. You were always my brother, anyway, but, well, welcome to the family, such as it is. Someday I hope we can raise a glass to celebrate.*

"This was obviously news of my parents' marriage," I said, feeling a bit agitated.

> *Though it has been eight years since the end of the Spanish war, I dream of it every night. I still carry the pistol at all times, and I jump at the slightest noise. I wish I could have stayed to put my country*

back together. But it was too dangerous for me. I was lucky to get posted outside the country.

Here, we are encouraged by the presidency of Peron, though I question the character of that woman he married. Still, The Poor love their Evita and she keeps them optimistic. She is perhaps the winning paradox: a beautiful Fascist with a talent for altruism.

I go now to say evening mass. God bless you Fredo, you are more a brother now than ever. But it is best not to confide in your new wife. Our correspondencia must remain a secret.

Yours in Christ, M.V.L.

"I don't want to read any more today," I said, "I'm tired."

"There are six more," said Luis, shuffling through them. "What's bothering you?"

"I don't understand why they kept their correspondence a secret."

"Maybe your uncle became paranoid about being found. That would make sense."

As the light shifted in the apartment, soft shadows accented the masculine contours of Luis's face. Captured in his green gaze, I couldn't even remember being angry at him.

"I have an idea," he said, "have you been to El Tigre, yet?"

"No. What is it?"

"It's a river resort area. Very pretty. Lots of boats, people swimming, fishing, sunning. Lots of *asados*."

"And your idea?"

"I have a place there, well, it's a family house," he said. "It's very relaxing. And at night, on the deck, there are lanterns, and under those lanterns there is a little table with candles and flowers."

"It sounds like a movie set," I said.

"It could be the set for our movie," he said, inching closer to me. I could smell the fragrant tea spices on his breath. "When all this is over we can have our own dinner for two on that deck, and our own *milonga*, dancing to our favorite tangos."

"It sounds wonderful," I said. "I wish we could go tomorrow."

The phone rang, abruptly invading the fantasy of our future. I went quickly to pick up presuming it was Paco with details for meeting Carmina Perraza. "*Hola!*" I said.

"*Hermosura*," cooed Nico.

"Oh, Nico!" Suddenly I felt frightened, as if he could see that Luis was beside me. As if he could read immediately the plan we were hatching. I got up and paced while we spoke. "What can I do for you?" I said, trying to sound sweet but remote. Luis shot me a look and I bounced it right back at him.

"Are you well today?" asked Nico.

"Yes, thank you."

"I am calling to ask if you can go Thursday afternoon to the grave in San Isidro."

"Thursday, uh, the day after tomorrow. That will be fine. Thank you."

"I can pick you up at your apartment around sixteen . .uh, four o'clock."

"No! I mean, I won't be here. I have errands and appointments on Thursday so I'll be out. Pick me up," I had to think of an easy place, "in front of Club Español."

"Club Español? Are you sure that is convenient?"

"I'll be in that neighborhood, and I know where it is, so I won't get lost."

"Fine. Four o'clock at Club Español. Bring an umbrella, it's supposed to rain."

"Oh, thanks, I'll pick one up when I'm out."

"*Hasta jueves, belleza.*"

"Yes, until Thursday. *Chau!*"

A dense silence filled the room. I walked the handset back to its cradle just to give me time to think. Returning to the couch I watched Luis staring at one of the letters. "Did you discover a new clue?" I asked, nonchalantly.

He looked at me sternly. "I guess I have no right to ask you about your date."

"That's right."

"I have to trust you," he said, "and I have no choice but to put away my fears or learn to live with them."

"Honestly Luis, though a part of me would like you to feel jealous, I am telling you that you have nothing to fear. I have to focus on finding Zorrilla now. And I realize that it may be a bit dangerous. I need you to help me keep up my courage."

"I am absolutely here for you," he said, "I will do whatever you need."

CHAPTER TWENTY-FOUR

It was arranged that we'd meet Carmina Perraza that night at a secret location. Even though I protested, Paco pressured me into arriving there *escondida* under a blanket on the floor of Luis's backseat.

"Raquel, you are threatening to uncover brutal and desperate people," he said. "When you meet Carmina you will see just how ruthless they are."

Nevertheless, I tried to make light of it, until the moment came to crouch under cover in the chilly no-man's-land of the darkened Mercedes. There reality set in, and suddenly, I felt fear. I started to sweat and tremble, and begged Luis to keep talking to me. He put on his cellphone earpiece so he'd appear to be talking on the phone.

"What shall we talk about?" he asked.

"You were here in Buenos Aires in the years of the generals," I said, "tell me what it was like." There was a long moment of silence and I wondered if I'd wandered into painful territory.

"For two of those years I was in Italy," he began. "My father sent me to our office in Milan. Probably he wanted to protect me, but when he had a heart attack, I had to come back." He was quiet again, as if choosing how much he would reveal. "It was a shock to find my neighborhood under surveillance when I returned. Not just my neighborhood, every neighborhood. It was common to see men, with guns drawn, leaning out the windows of big black cars or green Ford Falcons. They drove slowly through the streets, just watching you. They wanted you to know that they knew your house, and even where you shopped. They knew what school your children attended. We never got used to it. Just the sight of one of those cars turned otherwise happy, active people, into timid animals, like deer who hear the hunters' footsteps in their forest.

"You could receive a notice in the mail to show up at the police station. It happened to me. My appointment was at ten in the morning. They made me sit there all day. I didn't even know why I was there. They could have put me in a prison cell, or just reminded me to renew my auto insurance."

"What did they want? Did they put you in jail?"

"At three in the afternoon, they called my name. I was hungry and tired, and, yes, frightened." He took a few deep breaths. "They put me in a room with no windows, like an interrogation room. I sat there waiting another hour. Then two men entered and showed me photos of my car doing 50 in a school zone."

"Were they giving you a citation?"

"Oh, nothing so simple. They asked me if that was my car. If that was me driving. Where was I going on that day? They asked if I drive that route very often. I answered the questions, and I don't mind telling you that my shirt was soaked with sweat."

"I can only imagine!"

"They talked to me about the vulnerability of the children, and the destructive power of an automobile. 'Do not speed there again,' they said. 'We will be watching you.' Then, at six in the evening, they let me go."

"You must have been so relieved."

"Relieved. Yes. I left, mopping the sweat off my face. But later that night, I became furious. What right did they have to threaten me like that? What right did they have to take my entire day, and punish me like a child at the principal's office? I pay taxes. I contribute to society. What right did they have to reach their menacing fist into my life? Raquel, you have no idea the magnitude of threat we lived with. I know people who went in as I did, because they'd received the same notice; they were interrogated, beaten, and even tortured. Some were never seen again. Loved ones and colleagues disappeared from our midst every day."

The muffled sounds of the city filled the car interior, and we rode like that for a while. I wanted to know if he'd lost anyone close to him, but I was afraid to ask.

"Hey," he said finally, "it's awfully quiet back there. You're not too afraid to talk are you?"

"Yes."

"We'll be there soon," he said in an upbeat tone. "Just remember, you are in the Buenos Aires of 2004, not 1982. There are still plenty of war criminals at large thanks to ex-president Menem, but as far as we know, they are not in charge of anything anymore."

"I don't quite know what to expect from this meeting," I said. "I think Paco wants to make an impression on me. As if all this hasn't already done so. Do you know this Carmina?"

"No. Never met her. We're just arriving now. Stay down until I tell you."

I heard the tires rolling across loose gravel as we came to a stop. Luis got out, locking the doors as he left. I stayed as still as possible, shivering and listening with ravenous ears. Soon I heard gravel-crunching footsteps. More than one man approached. They stopped just outside the car. The locks clicked and the door to the back seat opened.

"Raquel," Luis said quietly, "you can come out now."

I lifted the blanket and breathed the fresh night air. There was Paco next to Luis, the stress of his years emphasized by the garish interior auto lights. I lifted myself and stepped out, taking Luis's hand for support. The surrounding area was nearly pitch black. I gave Paco a kiss on the cheek. He embraced me.

"You are a brave woman," he said.

"Don't give me too much credit," I said. "I don't think I have a choice anymore."

The three of us followed Paco's flashlight beam into the side entrance of what seemed to be a warehouse or a garage. Once inside we moved gingerly through the dark interior toward a lit office on the far side of a densely arranged collection of cars in various states of disrepair. Entering the glass-encased office, I was glad to feel the warmth from a noisy space heater. Several desk lamps turned upward cast eerie shadows across surfaces and faces alike. A man I guessed to be in his forties, dressed in clean work overalls greeted us.

"Raquel," said Paco, "this is Ernesto García, Carmina's brother."

"*Mucho gusto,*" I said, extending my hand. I guessed that this might be his shop, or that he, at least, worked here.

"My sister should be here soon," he said shaking my hand. "Would you like water?"

He had several bottles of water on the desk with paper cups.

"Thank you," I said. He poured some water and placed the bottle near me on the front desk. Paco and Luis declined.

"Please, sit down," said Paco. We each found a desk chair or a stool from an assortment Ernesto had brought into the cramped quarters of the office. He sat on a desk at the back. We sat there silently for ten or fifteen uncomfortable minutes until we heard the side door open. I could just make out two figures moving through the maze of cars with a flashlight as we had done. Paco stood up and opened the door, and a small woman stepped into his embrace. She was only about five feet tall, a round figure in a black coat and scarf, her face was hidden from view as she nestled her head in Paco's chest. A burly fellow came in behind her. Paco shook his hand then stepped aside to allow him into the office.

"Carmina," said Paco, "this is Raquel Carval, the woman I told you about."

I stood up, and took her outstretched hand in mine. "*Encantada,*" I said, biting down on the word as she dropped the scarf, subjecting her face to the garish light. Her jet black hair was pulled into a ponytail at the neck. Our cold hands clasped together and she gave me a light kiss on the cheek.

"*Mi hermano Felipe,*" she said, introducing me to her stocky companion. He wrapped my hand momentarily in the calloused musculature of his own, then stepped back.

As Carmina unbuttoned her dark raincoat I heard the soft clatter of beads that I presumed came from a bracelet. Felipe pulled the coat over the back of the chair beside me and she lowered her soft frame carefully into it. We sat in a tight, irregular circle in the deep shadows and skewed colors of the dim light bulbs. Carmina cradled a large leather bag on her lap with her left arm, revealing rosary beads wrapped around her hand, the shiny crucifix gripped between the thumb and forefinger. With her right hand she reached into the bag and pulled out a pack of Marlboro cigarettes and a lighter. She freed one from the pack with a gentle toss, and took it between her lips. As she flicked the lighter aflame, I assessed the facial scarring that met her each morning in the mirror. Despite a mask of heavy foundation, circular craters in the skin were visible along her cheek. There were more beneath the irregular fringe of bangs that fell over her forehead. I wondered how she could smoke cigarettes with their obvious implementation so ominously gouged into her skin. Perhaps in an attempt to take attention away from the scarring, she had applied heavy black liner around her eyes and dark metallic eye shadow across the lids. An iridescent blush across her cheeks caught the light.

Paco placed an empty glass ashtray on the desk in front of her. "We are grateful for this meeting, Carmina," he said. "As I told you, Raquel came very innocently from the United States to find a lost relative, and she has walked into a spider's web with Monsignor Zorrilla at its center. We believe he is her uncle."

Her gaze suddenly shifted to me, her eyes narrowed into slits. "*¡Tu tío es el hijo del diablo!*" Her words came at me hot and rasping. If he'd been the one who'd tortured her, I couldn't blame her for thinking of Mateo as the devil's son. I marveled that she could trust me at all.

"Of course, Raquel wants to be certain that Zorrilla is guilty before we go further to apprehend him," Paco continued, "and I know you can prove his guilt to her, if you would agree to recount your experience of him."

She took a deep drag, and released the smoke thoughtfully. The intricate lines and creases around her eyes and mouth twitched. She swallowed hard, and the corner of her mouth drew downward. After a long look at me she asked in a husky voice, "If you think that devil is your uncle you should run out of Argentina where no one can find you. Why do you want to know him?"

"More, I would like to know that my uncle is *not* Zorrilla. Then I can welcome him back to our family and let him speak to his last surviving sister. She is old and ill, I came here to connect them before she dies." She squinted at me incredulously through the tobacco haze. "Regrettably, there is evidence that my uncle, whose name was Mateo Vicente López, may have changed his name to Sebastián Zorrilla when he came here from Spain after the war, the Spanish Civil War."

"He has a big scar here in the head?" She gestured bluntly across her forehead.

"Yes."

"*Y le falta un brazo?*" She made a chopping motion on her left arm.

I hated to admit that she was describing my uncle, but I knew I couldn't deny it any more. "Yes, he lost his left arm in an accident when he was a boy," I said.

"He is a monster," she said, looking into my eyes. "I will tell you. In English so I know you understand. You say when you know enough, so I can stop." She put out her first cigarette in the ashtray and lit another.

"Twenty-four of March, 1978: I am putting my little girl to bed when mens break into my house. Four of them," she began. "I am alone. My daughter has four years old. First, they open drawers, throwing things onto the floor. They throw books, smash things. Then one picks up a photo and says, 'This your brother?' I say, yes, my older brother Fernando. They grab me by the arm and push me to the wall. 'Where he is?' they shout. I don't know, I say. Then one kicks me in the legs, and he pushes a gun to my, uh, ribs.

He screams again, but I say I have no seen Fernando for months. I don't know where is he, or what he does.

"Then one picks up Tanya. Four years old, and she is crying and screaming." Carmina looked at me directly. "I say leave her alone, she is a baby. And one of them hits me very hard in the side of my head. Next I know, I wake up on the floor of a moving car, my head in a sack, my hands behind me . . *esposadas* . ." She gestured her hands handcuffed behind her back.

"I understand," I said. "And your daughter, was she on the floor with you?"

"I hear Tanya cry. She is on the seat. I feel her little feet on my back. A man sits there, too, his big feet on my legs, heavy shoes scraping into my skin."

"It sounds terrifying," I said. "Carmina, I don't want to put you through this, but I need to know more about the man, the priest. He does sound like my uncle."

She tossed off a long ash, and I have to admit that an old part of me looked longingly for a second at that cigarette, even though my eyes already burned and itched from the smoke. When I started to cough, Ernesto turned on a fan.

"Sorry," I said to Carmina, "I'm not used to the smoke."

"Yes, my daughter tells me to stop," she said. I hoped that meant that Tanya, too, had survived.

"They kept me alone in a cell first. The torture beginned slowly. A dirty cell, almost no food, water with a few beans or peas. They called it soup. Maybe a piece of bread. A bucket for the bathroom. The mattress was just a hotel for bugs, on the floor. But there is no sleep at night, anyway; the screaming keeps me awake." She took another drag, as if the tobacco fueled her voice.

"First, they stop bringing the 'soup' and bread. They do not answer when I ask for Tanya. They take me in a room. They say my brother is a Montonero and I must give them information. Then they beat me. But I say I don't know him doing such a thing, so I have nothing to tell. But they didn't believe me. They cut off my clothings with a knife; in places it cut my skin. But still I have no answers. That day, they took me to the cell with no clothes. I wear only shame.

"They left me in that cell for days. Others were out and in, also naked. Sometimes they were bleeding, crying, shaking, moaning. I was crazy with fear for my Tanya. No one answered my questions about her. And always the screams, at night. Screams of women and mens, and even children." She stared off into space. Though her voice remained calm, tears streaked longitudinal lines down the thick makeup. I began to understand that once she'd started talking, she was incapable of choosing isolated parts of her story. We were listening to the story that ran like a loop in her head.

"Then two soldiers come for me," she continued, "they grab me by my. . . elbows." She paused and looked into my eyes, her arms akimbo. "I could not cover myself," she said, "I could not cover myself." She rubbed the beads and crucifix in her left hand. "They take me to a room with a table, like a doctor's table, you know, to lay down. And there was medical things there: Blades and needles, other instruments. And a machine was on the side, I did not know what it was. The guards pushed me onto that cold metal table, then leaved the room. I hear them outside talking. Laughing! I could smell their cigarettes' smoke." She lit a fresh Marlboro from the glowing butt of the last.

"When the door opens again, a priest walks in and hands me a cover to wear. I feel so shame. I smell bad, look bad, and a priest! So he looks away and I wrap myself quickly. I say 'Father I am so grateful to see a priest' (though he was a very ugly priest). I been only praying for those days and nights so alone. He introduce himself, '*Padre* Sebastián'. That's when I notice he has only one arm. The scar on his face was like someone hit him with hot metal across the *frente*, uh, forehead, over the eye." She pointed to her left eye. "And his mouth, he has a mustache, but still, is not right. The mustache grows funny. Poor man, I think, maybe someone torture him, too. We make the sign of the cross and pray the Our Father and Hail Mary. When we finish he say, 'You know, my dear, these people must have the information. They will not stop until they get it.' I say '*Padre*, I told the truth. I don't know where is my brother, but I am sure he is not Montonero'. He put his head down like this, looking to the floor, and shake it slow, like he does not believe me. 'Perhaps,' he says, 'you want to make a confession. Everything you say is confidential. Your brother will never know.' 'I have nothing to confess,' I say. I went to confession and communion the Sunday before they took me."

As she took another drag, a long ash fell onto her purse. I was spellbound. I thought of that bizarre term from Joseph Conrad, 'the fascination of the abomination.' The images she painted were too awful to think about, yet everyone in the room seemed mesmerized by her nightmare.

"Then he say, 'You have a daughter, no?' I say, 'Her name is Tanya,' and I beg him to find her. He say he could try to find her if I cooperate. I say I am cooperating, I know nothing. He shooked his head again, then he knocks on the door and the guards come back with a *comandante*. I screamed, '*Padre!* Do not leave me'. He says, 'These good men are here to help rid you of the devil. They will lead you to tell the truth.' Then a man dressed like a doctor, with a white coat, enters. The guards hold me down, and another attaches wires to my feet. The doctor put this on my arm, I don't know what you call it, *para la presión* . . ."

"The blood pressure cuff?"

"Yes, then the *padre* watch them send electric shocks in me. He watched my legs . . . twitch. He hears me scream. He makes the sign of the cross," she gestures the cross, cigarette smoke trailing the motion, "and he goes!"

In my peripheral vision I saw the burly Felipe wipe his face with the back of his hand. I took a deep breath and dabbed away my own tears with the cuff of my sweater.

"Next day he comes to my cell. He says he seen Tanya in the other side of the camp. She didn't look good, he says. She is thin, very sad, and she coughs. If I want to help her, I must cooperate. He signals to the guards to take me from the cell." Without letting go of her rosary, Carmina unbuttoned the cuff of her right sleeve displaying an arm covered in scars, some like the burns on her face, some worse.

She looked into my eyes again, "In the room he gives me a cigarette. I think he is being kind. He says God wants me to be on his side. I should tell him everything. I say again, I know nothing. He says he knows I am a good woman, but the devil keeps me from saying truth, so he is going to take the devil out of me." I braced myself for what was to come. "The guards hold my arms, and the priest takes the cigarette from me and puts it in my face." For the first time in her monolog, Carmina's voice faltered. Fresh tears meandered slowly down the cratered surface of her cheek. "He tells me to say with him the Lord's Prayer."

"*Basta, Carmina,*" said Paco. "Enough. You are confirming that *Padre* Sebastián witnessed the electric prods used on you, and that he, himself, administered cigarette burns. I think Raquel cannot doubt the truth." He looked at me squarely. I nodded.

Carmina clutched my forearm with three fingers, a dense stream of smoke curled upward into my face. "I had no information to give, so I could not say what he wanted. You understand? No matter how many burns. No matter what he did to my daughter, I had nothing to tell."

"I understand," I said. That Tanya had also been tortured had not occurred to me.

"The last thing he say to me," she seemed not to have heard me, "before he leaves me there in that room: 'Do not worry, Carmina,' he says, 'God knows that man is not perfect, but he is perfectable.'"

The tiny room fell silent except for the soft rattle of rosary beads in Carmina's trembling hand. I noticed then that the crucifix beneath her thumb had been rubbed nearly smooth. She didn't wipe her tears. I wondered if she could even feel them.

"Raquel, show her the photo of your uncle as a young man," said Paco.

"But I can describe him," said Carmina. "I have already done so. How many mens has a mustache that cannot grow across the lip because of a big scar here?" She held her index finger diagonally below her nostrils.

I pulled the photo from the envelope, and handed it to her. "He's on the . ."

"I know the Devil when I see him." she said. "He lives in my head! He creeps into my sleep, and into the nightmares of my Tanya. He is there!" She pointed at him in the photo as if to burn his image away with her wrath. "*¡Hijo de puta!*" she whispered and spit on the photo.

I broke into tears. "I am so sorry," I said. "I've never met my . . .uh, Zorrilla, but I see he is a monster who was once my uncle. In his letters from his early years of the Spanish Civil War he describes himself as a boy who wouldn't even hunt for birds. It was the accident, you see. His brother was killed and his father blamed him for that. Then the scars. He was teased and tormented . . ."

"You want me to be sorry for him?" She cut off my meaningless attempt to explain the twisted bent of his being.

"No! Oh God, no!" I said. Words caught in my throat. "I just want you to understand," I said, but my voice fell into a void. What did I want? I wanted her to *forgive me.* Forgive me for sharing the blood and DNA of the man who had tortured her. How could I say that? "It's been difficult," I began, "to accept the truth about him, Carmina, but we are a good family. Good people, you understand? I don't know what I will tell them about him." I swallowed hard. "Every member of my family would beg your forgiveness if they could, as I beg your forgiveness now. All I can do is try to bring him to justice. And I promise you, I will do everything in my power to accomplish that."

"Forget that he is your uncle," she said. "He is not a man, he is a poison snake."

CHAPTER TWENTY-FIVE

Ernesto allowed us to stay in the office after Carmina and Felipe left. With the door ajar, fresh air replaced the lingering smoke, though the dark spirit of Carmina's demons were not so easy to exorcise. We hadn't yet spoken a word when Ernesto came back with a bottle of brandy and more paper cups.

"*Dios te bendiga, pibe*" said Paco. Though I'm sure he'd heard it before, it seemed that Carmina's stunning monolog had shaken him as it had me. Paco poured the first draft and handed a cup to each of us.

Ernesto tossed it back with a hard swallow. "*Gracias,*" he said to Paco, "*buenas noches.*" He shook my hand, and looked me squarely in the eyes. "*Señora,*" was all he spoke, but the look on his face said, "Kill the bastard."

We sat in the office, each of us lost in our own thoughts. The clanking echo of tools on metal suggested that, despite the late hour,

Ernesto was rerouting his anger into constructive energy.

"Carmina did not tell you what they did to her little girl," said Paco, handing me the next cup.

"Enough!" said Luis. "She's heard enough. Let's get on with it!"

"I just wanted. . ."

"*Basta!*" The close space reverberated with Luis's command. I'd never seen him like this; his body was trembling. "*Cristo!* It's cold in here," he said, pacing toward the little heater at the back wall.

"Raquel, I just want to be sure you understand," said Paco quietly, "if you go forward you could be in real danger. You must cooperate with us completely. Trust us to protect you, and let us guide you each step of the way."

I assured him that I was now sufficiently frightened that I'd follow every instruction. He wanted to see the letters. I promised to make copies for him the next morning. Then we outlined our plan: Paco would follow Nico and me into the cemetery and pretend to be another mourner visiting a grave. I'd leave flowers tied with a yellow ribbon on top of the gravestone so it could be seen from a distance. Paco took my hand, "If you should be taken to him, Raquel . . ."

"Taken?" Luis sprung at Paco like an attack dog. "What do you mean taken? You just said you'd be there to protect her."

"*Ché*, you know that all possibilities need to be discussed."

Luis growled under his breath.

"Raquel, I want you to know something about the *Guardia Sagrada*," said Paco.

"What's that?"

"Followers of Zorrilla, mostly young priests, became a kind of personal army. He's probably protected by a strong circle of them, though there can't be many left now. Of course, just because the Guardia went underground, we can't presume that younger members haven't been recruited. Maybe Nico is a scout for them."

"Oh," I said, realizing that I really knew nothing about the situation I had gotten myself into. "I can't imagine I'd get close to them, Paco," I said. "I mean, Nico expects that the grave will be my final assurance that my uncle is dead. I imagine that he plans on taking me home, as if my search is finished."

"That's the reason you may have to provoke him to go to the old man once he drops you off in Buenos Aires."

"Provoke him?"

"Yes, we want him to report back pretty quickly and in person, so we can follow him. Of course, if Nico has orders to take you directly to Zorrilla instead of the grave, then, whether the old man is happy to see you or not, he will have to do something with you. Once you've seen him, he will consider you a liability. That's why it is important that Nico is fond of you. We'll be behind you anyway, so we just need him to protect you until we move in. I'm guessing he'd probably drug you before hurting you."

"Drug me?" I hadn't thought about potential scenarios.

"Maybe you should carry a gun," said Luis.

"A gun?" I gasped. "I wouldn't know what to do with a gun. And if they were to drug me, that *Guardia*-whatever-you-call-it could use the gun on me." The gravity of the situation was soaking in. "Paco," I said, "what are my chances of living through this?"

"I wouldn't send you into mortal danger, Raquel," he said. "We will be with you the whole time. But, there is always a chance of the unexpected, so we must prepare for all possibilities. We need a plan that gives us options. That's why I told you to cultivate the relationship with Durman. His romantic feelings are your protection in whatever event."

"Okay! We know that, Paco," said Luis with obvious agitation.

"Sorry, *Luis*, he said, "but it's important."

"I know!" I said, enthusiastically. An idea had just sprung to mind. "I'll keep some of those family photos with me, and Nico will probably figure my uncle would want to see them. So I'll leave them in his car and after he drops me off in Buenos Aires, I bet he'll go straight to Zorrilla, photos in hand."

Paco was pretty impressed with that idea, so we added it to the plan along with a second team. Paco and a colleague would follow us into the cemetery, and another pair from his team would stay just outside the cemetery gates. We agreed that on Thursday I'd keep my plans to walk with the Mothers of the Disappeared in their monthly demonstration. Paco would also take part in the walk, then follow me from the Plaza de Mayo, to the Club Español where I'll meet Nico. His car and driver would be parked nearby and follow us to San Ysidro, the second team would stay behind them. Luis insisted that he be included in one of the cars, but Paco and I were against it. When I explained to him that I had to do a good acting job to encourage Nico's affections, he realized that his presence would be a dangerous distraction to me.

On the drive home, under the blanket again, images of Carmina's scars, and the story she had recounted lurked in my mind. Luis and I hardly said a word. And, though I needed him more than ever, we said good night at the door. I felt so vulnerable that I couldn't take off my clothes to get into bed. I just slipped off my shoes and pulled the covers over me, fully dressed. As I lay there a flashing photomontage played in my head. I saw myself in La Ideal on the first day, just after meeting Alfonso. Then I realized that I hadn't had a full-blown anxiety attack since that first day. I didn't know how I'd accomplished that, but it gave me a sense of pride. I just hoped that having a conscious awareness of the attacks wouldn't bring them on again. Then the memory of our performance at El Beso came strobing through my mind in flashes. Then Luis and I, our beautiful lovemaking. I saw Nico singing Gardel at the Café Tortoni, saw him again beside me at the Arabic restaurant. And finally the images focused on Carmina staring into space narrating her nightmare through the thick haze of cigarette smoke.

I worried about how to tell my family about Tío Mateo; worried that they too would be consumed by the guilt I felt coursing through the blood we shared. For now, I could keep it all to myself, and follow through with what I'd started. I turned on the bedside lamp, got out of bed and brought the letters back with me. I wanted to read the rest before copying them for Paco.

The next letter in chronological order was the one from 1956.

30 julio 1956

Buenos Aires

Felicitaciones Cuñado,

I told you God would bless you with children. You have played your fatherly role as He has declared it. My abuela would be so proud to see a new child named Raquel after her.

Honestly, I am lucky your letter found me. This move to Buenos Aires is, in a way, a promotion. In all the busy details of moving, I forgot to write you. Sorry. But my mail has been sent to me from San Juan, so all is fine in the end.

My new church has a school attached, and an orphanage nearby. I am very busy working in all three places.

I had stopped carrying la pistola for a while. (You know, it became such a part of me that I named it El Señor.) But since Evita died, things have unraveled here. The Perón regime became very, well . . . untrustworthy. I am sure you have read that the Holy Father excommunicated Peron from the Church. One of the problems is that since the end of WWII this country is crawling with Jews. But we have a new government now. I think the military is best, it makes the most reliable government. (We learned that in Spain.) Still, things are

*dangerous now in the capital. So I carry El Señor
with me again. I am, after all, a trained soldier of
the Lord. I do believe Jesus Christ watches over me
at all times, but a little protection on my part just
makes his job easier.*

*Write to me at the address on the envelope. I
receive my mail at the mailbox of another priest so
instead of using my name, address the envelope to
Padre Zorrilla. When he sees your return address,
he will make sure I get it.*

Yours in Christ, Mateo

I'd read this letter just before my first visit to the Diocese, now
it revealed so much more to me. My uncle *had to be* the man Nico referred to as Father. I realized that I hadn't mentioned that to Paco,
and wondered if it was important in the greater scheme of things. I
was dying to read the rest of the letters, but my eyes burned and the
lids were too heavy to keep open. I turned out the light.

The generous morning sun woke me around seven. I felt the
shell-like crust of my clothes against my skin, and when I stretched
my legs the crisp rustle of onionskin reawakened in me the foreboding agenda of the coming days. Sitting up, I found the letters
scattered atop the bedding like early autumn leaves. I decided to
read the rest with my morning coffee.

22 julio, 1960

Buenos Aires

Querido Cuñado,

Thank you for the photos. What a beutiful family. You have made a good husban, as I knew you would. A little too much arroz con pollo, hermano. Time for the gym, heh. I'm not slim anymore either. What can we do, the years add up, and the pounds.

Little Raquel looks so much like Abuela! It is strange to see that face so smooth and innocent on a child, when I remember it as the face of an old woman. And little Marta is a blessing from God. Isabel isn't so young for having children anymore. But the baby looks healthy and so does she. Mamita must be so happy. I am pleased for you, too. I know you wanted to follow me into the priesthood, but it is a lonely life, especially in winter as it is now. Very cold. Praise God, because of the school and the orphenage, I have children in my life. Their young souls keep me strong in my work against the forces of the devil. They are everywhere, Fredo. I cannot let down my guard at all. Thank God I was trained well in Spain for this work, and my heart is strong.

Yours in Christ,

M

I remembered Carmina quoting him in the torture room, talking about the soldiers of God. Here it was, all the rhetoric of a religious man twisted into a Fascist tongue. Still, I never would have imagined him capable of torturing people. I never knew Papa had wanted to be a priest in his youth. He was always a zealous Catholic, too, but his Catholicism was not based on a war against the devil. Of course, Papa had his music and my mother's love, and the love of his children. Mateo, perhaps because of his isolation, became the kind of man who gives religion a bad name.

5 junio, 1966

Mexico, D. F.

Querido Alfredo,

I send you recuerdos from the only vacation I ever had. This is a beautiful city. I am here because students from our local orphanage graduate from university. I arranged their scholarships, so the donors sent me a ticket to see the graduation.

Do you remember how we were, Fredo? Strong brothers! Always together. These boys are nothing like us. They are competitive and spiteful. They hate each other, and I cannot ease the bad feelings in them. Well, maybe I should be glad they are not really my sons.

It is good to be away from Buenos Aires for a few days. I hope you can see this beautiful city some time.

*Thanks God I write you in English. It is the
only practice I get. I am very rusty.*

Forgive me. M

That letter surely marked Nico's graduation from university in
Mexico City. And he did tell me that there was another fellow from
the orphanage with him. I picked up the next letter.

18 octubre, 1973

Buenos Aires

Alfredo

*I got your letter about a trip to visit Buenos Aires.
That would be great to see you. Perón is back. Another
wife. I don't know if his return makes things better or
worse for visitors. Let me know when you are coming. You must come alone. Isabel cannot know that I
am alive after all these years. Also, you can stay in my
house. (No women are allowed, you understand.)*

*You will not know the old neighborhood. Perhaps
you don't remember much from childhood.*

*¡O! to see you again, what a joy. Write before get-
ting tickets to be sure the country is safe.*

En Cristo,

M

15 agosto, 1974

Buenos Aires

Querido Cuñado,

Perón has died. Hold your plans to see what happens next. The wife takes over the government. Another woman! And this wife lacks Evita's charisma and power over the people. There are military men ready to take power, and violent factors are at work. There may be difficult times ahead.

I will write you when it is safe to come.

Yours in Christ, Mateo

22 octubre 1977

Querido Fredo,

Things are bad at the moment. A lot of violence. El Señor is always with me, even under my pillow at night. This brings dark memories of war.

We have a new government, but things are unstable. I have friends among the generals, and they are good Católicos. I'll tell you when it is safe to travel. I can have a guard with you at all times, one of my own Guardia Sagrada. Yes, they are my own soldiers. Some are young priests who I taught from the time they were in the orphanage. Now, they are trained, passionate soldiers of the Lord. We are at war with the devil, Fredo, and these young soldiers multiply the work I can accomplish, especially now that I am aging.

I have a place in the country where you can stay. It's a large stone house, like a fortress. The Guardia live there also. It is very safe. Away from the city. One of my boys can drive you.

Still, do not make plans until you hear from me again.

Cariño, M

There it was. His admission to having friends in the government. 'The generals are good *Catolicos*'? How deeply involved was he by that time, I wondered. And what was I to think of the boys he'd brainwashed for his Sacred Guard?

I realized that there were long periods of time between the letters, and I wondered if some were missing. Whatever the case, these were all I had, and I was glad I'd read them all before tomorrow's visit to the graveyard. The profile was not fractured anymore. There were two sides of the coin, but lamentably, one side of him was simply the painful foundation for the other. I had to accept that I was putting myself into a potentially dangerous position, but, as Paco had reminded me, there were no more prison camps. There was no ESMA, no Club Atlético, nor El Olimpo. Even El Silencio, the Church's infamous house on the river, was shut down. Nevertheless, just thinking about what once existed, frightened me. I couldn't convince myself that age had drained the brutality out of the old man. There was no way to know what a worse case scenario might be. I went into email to distract myself and found something from Marta.

> **Hi Sis,**
>
> **Tía Leti has had some very lucid days after her last dialysis. She remembers that *Abuela* told her how grateful she was to the priest at their church in Buenos Aires. He was the only person who supported little Mateo after the accident. I think Papa was the only friend Tío Mateo ever had. Just look at the photos (attached).**
>
> **If you can find Tío, I bet he's going to love to see these pictures of his youth.**
>
> **One more email coming. Love you and miss you, Marta.**

I was so glad to hear of Tía's improvement, and Marta had put her finger on the key element: The photos. After I see the grave, I thought, Zorrilla will presume that I believe he's dead. I could show the photos to Nico, then 'forget' them in his car, and when he takes the photos to the old man, Paco can follow him straight to Zorrilla. I gave myself a pat on the back for coming up with an excellent plan that would also keep me safe.

When the photos opened across the computer screen, there was my father and Mateo around age eighteen standing in a river in shorts, their hair dripping wet. Two boys roughhousing, as much as Mateo could, I guess. He wore a short-sleeved shirt even there, so his amputation was not visible. "Sacramento, 1930" was handwritten across the front. I loved seeing Papa so alive and happy.

In the second photo they were two young altar boys with their parish priest, probably nine or ten years old. Looking at them, frozen in time, I got a new sense of the value of photography. This photo was not simply a captured moment in the lives of two men, it was also a piece of amber in which my own life lay hidden, folded into the DNA of those bodies. I was the future looking back, the bridge that constituted a biological link making them not just friends, but family.

I forwarded the photos to Luis in an email asking him to make me a couple of good copies, and suggested he keep my sister's email address in case he needed to contact her. The possible necessities were too various and dark to consider, so I just sent it quickly and went on to write to David, attaching the photos from Marta. I wanted him to know those two men as they were in their youth. Then, I said I loved him, without mentioning my upcoming trip to the gravesite, and signed off.

The calm side of me expected to ride out to San Isidro, put some flowers on a grave, ride back to Buenos Aires, fight Nico off at the door, and finish the day by calling Luis from the safety of my apartment. Paco would get the grave dug up, and follow Nico to the old man. End of story. There was no reason to conjecture further.

Besides, Paco would be following us every step of the way.

CHAPTER TWENTY-SIX

Paying the cashier for the letter copies, I asked if he sold large envelopes. He didn't, but offered me a discarded envelope from the trash. It had the word *"Exámenes"* written on the front in big felt tip letters, but it was a perfect size, so I was happy to recycle it. I deposited the copied letters, making a mental note to cross out "Exams" and replace it with "Letters" before passing it along to Paco. Back on the street I called Luis and told him about the photos I'd forwarded to him. I suggested that Jessica bring them to me the next day when I'd be walking with Las Madres in the Plaza de Mayo at three o'clock. She was the only person from his office who knew me.

Luis worried that I was a little too confident about my plan to leave the photos in Nico's car. I disguised my own fears under a jaunty attitude suggesting that he was treating the cemetery visit as if it were a cloak and dagger spy movie. I teased him saying that he wanted to think of me as a woman of intrigue, because it made me seem more seductive.

"I don't need you to seem more seductive," he said, I'm already captivated."

I was grinning like a teenager on the phone with her boyfriend. "Well, you're pretty captivating yourself," I said.

"Hey, let's dance," he said, suddenly.

"Dance?"

"Where are you?"

"I'm just going into the lobby of my building."

"Can you find a place to get out of sight?"

"What for?"

"I want to dance a tango."

The idea of dancing a tango on the phone was delicious. His spontaneity lifted my spirits immediately.

"Go up in the lift," he said, "then push the stop button between floors."

" I could go up to my apartment," I said.

"No, no," he said, "it will be more fun in the elevator. I can just see you dangling there in mid-air, my beautiful little bird suspended in that cage like those birds you love so much at *El Alef.* What tango shall we dance?" he asked.

"Oh, my favorite is *Bahía Blanca.* Does the orchestra know that one?"

"Of course. Are you suspended in your cage?"

"I am."

"Now, hold me close, and press your face to mine."

"You are so warm," I said, "and your arms are so strong."

"All the better to hold you, my dear," he whispered. Then he began to hum Bahia Blanca. We danced like that for maybe a minute or two, and in my mind I pressed my lips against his soft, smooth cheek. Then someone started knocking on the elevator door downstairs, and I could hear people yelling, "*¡Ascensor! ¡Ascensor!*"

"I have to go now," I said, hurriedly resuming my ascent.

"Good bye my little bird," he said. "Be very careful tomorrow. I'd love to see you, but I must trust Paco's guidance. I will be waiting for your call when you return from the cemetery. Call me right away."

"I will, I promise." I said. "I'll talk to you tomorrow evening."

"*Chau, mi amor,*" he said.

"*Chau.*"

The phone was ringing as I entered the apartment. It was Paco calling to go over the plan for the next day. I told him I was sending him copies of the letters via Jessica, who would bring me copies of two new photos in the Plaza de Mayo at 3 o'clock.

"I will be there at three," he said. "It is a fitting time and place. If the mothers knew our plan, they would give you all their blessings, and salute your courage."

"Well, so far I don't feel courageous. I'm hoping to absorb their strength."

He recounted to me the story of how the mothers first began their demonstrations demanding the recovery of their children.

Their demonstration was a singular and courageous act. As a result, some of the mothers disappeared, too. His voice softened as he told me that one of his friends, Azucena Villaflor de Vicenti, who founded The Mothers of the Plaza de Mayo organization was also killed. Frankly, his reminiscence began to make me nervous so I interrupted.

"I have to tell you that I realized that Nico is not just working for my uncle. I think he, Zorrilla, is the priest who found Nico newly born in the rubble of the San Juan earthquake. He practically raised him. He made sure Nico got an education, and then a good job at the Diocese. I've been putting the pieces together, and I feel certain of this."

"This is an important piece of the puzzle," he said. "We tracked Durman's connection to Zorrilla, but never that far back. Good work, Raquel. It means that Durman has an emotional weakness where the old man is concerned. That could make him more dangerous than we thought. Try to turn that to your advantage. If you see that there's a discrepancy between the date on the headstone and that on the death certificate, point it out to him and watch for his response. That will tell you how deeply involved he is in the cover-up."

"Right. I'm going to bring photos Marta sent me of Mateo when he was very young. I'll show them to Nico, and I'm sure he'll want to take them to Zorrilla as soon as he takes me home. Then you can tail him."

I guess he could hear I was nervous because he reassured me

that I was fully capable of carrying through with the plan. And, he reiterated, he and his people would be right behind me. "I will be there," he said. "You will be safe."

"I trust you, Paco," I said, honestly. What scared me most was knowing that my life was really more in my hands than in Paco's.

"I'll see you tomorrow in the Plaza," he said. "*Chau. ¡Suerte!*"

"Good luck to you too, Paco," I said. "See you tomorrow."

CHAPTER TWENTY-SEVEN

"*Habla Alfonso.*"

"*Alfonso*, it's Raquel. I need you."

"How I love to hear those words from the lips of a beautiful woman!"

"It's actually a very serious appointment I have, and I know I can trust you to get me there on time. I have to be at the Plaza de Mayo at 3 o'clock this afternoon. Can you pick me up?"

"Where are you?"

"At my apartment."

"*Perdoname* Raquel, but it is only eleven in the morning. You are dealing with a trained professional. Of course I can get you to Plaza de Mayo by 3 o'clock."

"Well, I'm reserving your taxi for this afternoon."

"I be there at, uh, I am calculating . . . from your apartment, I will be there at two thirty this afternoon."

"Great," I said. "You remember the address?"

"Of course! I am a . . ."

" . . . a trained professional. I know."

"Sounds like an important date."

"Yes, it is important. I'll be in front of the building. Thank you. *Chau.*"

"*Chau, Hermosa.*"

I dressed purposefully: Black slacks, and black high heeled leather boots that made me feel tough, and they'd do well if we had the forecasted rain. My long-sleeved ivory-colored blouse had soft ruffles that fell like one continuous rolling wave down each side of the pearl buttons. It was just a romantic touch, I thought, to suggest to Nico that I had dressed for him. My red all-weather trench coat was perfect for the conditions, and for visibility. Plus, to add a 'flag', I tied a multi-colored scarf around my neck. Instead of using my black purse, I threw everything into my Toulouse Lautrec canvas SFMOMA bag. Visibility would not be a problem.

Leaving the apartment, I stopped at the door for a moment, surveying the cozy scene and anticipating tonight when I'd call Luis. We would order pizza and watch a movie. All the intrigue will be behind me by then, I told myself. It will be so nice to relax.

"*Buen día,*" said Alfonso as I got into the back seat. "Two thirty, right on time."

"*Buen día, Alfonso,*" I said, truly pleased to see him. My breathing was labored and I felt the old anxiety moving in like storm clouds. A tango on the radio helped to ease my mind. "I need to go to the Plaza de Mayo."

"*Señora* Raquel, you told me Plaza de Mayo at eleven this morning. You are very nervous today."

"Yes, am. I'm sure my lack of composure is very evident."

"Do you mind if I make a perception?" he asked.

"A perception? No, perceive away!"

"I notice you do not show your beautiful legs today. Something is wrong? No tango?"

He'd managed to crack the veneer of my anxiety. I had to laugh. "No, I'm hiding my legs today, Alfonso, because I'm going to my uncle's grave."

"Ah, yes? You told me about this grave. Are you sure there is a body in the grave?"

"Frankly, I don't know. But I'm hoping to find out soon."

"This a little dangerous, no?"

"It could be. That's why I wanted your uplifting company on the way." We traveled several blocks in silence, and it seemed he was quiet for the first time since I'd known him. "Why are you so quiet?" I asked.

"I am just thinking," he said. "Where is this grave? It is certainly not near the Plaza de Mayo."

"No. It's in San Isidro."

"San Isidro?"

"Yes. You know where it is?"

"Of course, but that is not inside Buenos Aires city."

"Is it far?"

"Maybe one hour. Who you go with?"

"I'm going with Nico Durman."

"The tango singer?"

"Yes."

He looked at me in the rearview mirror. "You trust him?"

I didn't answer.

"You are frightened. Why you are going, if you are frightened?"

"It's a long story. I'll be fine. Honestly. I'm just tense."

"Why you are going now to Plaza de Mayo?"

"I have some business there."

"*Las Madres caminan esta tarde.*"

"Yes, I know they walk this afternoon. I'm going to walk with them."

At the next stoplight he turned to look at me directly. "Can Alfonso help you?"

I smiled. "You're helping me already. You make me want to take life not so seriously."

He studied my face. "But this business of your uncle is serious, no?"

"The light changed," I said. He turned back to his work. "It's pretty serious. But I won't really be alone. I study at the Academia de Tango *El Alef* and someone from *El Alef* is going to follow us, to insure my safety."

He pulled over at the corner of *Avenida de Mayo* and *Nueve de*

Julio. I went into my wallet for the fare, and when I handed him the money, he clasped my hand. "When do you go?"

"Four o'clock. I have time to walk with Las Madres."

"From here you go?"

"In front of Club Español."

"Why don't you tell him you want to take a cab?"

"Alfonso, isn't San Isidro a little far for a cab?"

"Well, yes."

"I don't think Nico wants to pay a taxi in this situation."

"No. But *Señora* Raquel, you should be very careful with that guy."

"Why do you say that?"

"I know his type. He sings in many places. I think he sells drugs."

"I've heard that. Even if he does, it has nothing to do with this."

"Keep my card with you. You have it? You want another one?"

"I have it," I said, reassuring him, "besides, your number is already in the memory of my phone. I will call you if I'm in trouble."

"Good. I will come to get you, if you need me. Any place. No charge."

"Thank you, Alfonso. It's good to know you're on my team."

"Here." He pulled the photo of Pugliese off the rear view mirror. "*El maestro* Pugliese is good luck. Keep him in your pocket."

"Pugliese is good luck? I never heard that before. I don't want to take him away from you."

"I have another."

"Okay. Thanks. I will take care of your Pugliese," I said, putting it into my pocket.

"No *señora*, he will take care of you."

"Okay. Thank you, Alfonso. *Chau!*" I closed the door solidly.

"*¡Suerte, Hermosa!*" His voice faded into the distance as I turned away hoping Pugliese was a reliable force. Fingering the photo in my pocket evoked the image of Carmina and her rosary, so I let go of it.

On the way to the Plaza I bought a bouquet of flowers with a yellow ribbon from a sidewalk vendor, and deposited them, stems down, into my bag. Their color and fragrance soothed me, and they looked beautiful poking out of the Lautrec design.

When I got to the Plaza, I tried to take a mental snapshot of the scene. This could be one of the most significant days of my life, I thought. Under the canopy of sun and clouds, *porteños* mingled in groups, chatted on benches. Despite the serious nature of the imminent ritual, a quiet and relaxed atmosphere concealed the depth of emotions within the hearts of those assembling. There were a couple of card tables on one side of the plaza attended by elderly women wearing their now famous embroidered kerchiefs. A couple of young people helped them lift cartons of pamphlets. I took a seat hoping to absorb the energy of the place. Looking around, I was reminded of black and white film clips I'd seen of bombings and mêlées. During Peron's time thousands of citizens fought, in hand-to-hand combat, right in this plaza. And just in view, the government watched from the Casa Rosada, Argentina's equivalent of our White House. The political passions of Argentines had been won and lost here for centuries.

It was such a simple thing to do, walk in a circle, yet I felt proud to be there knowing how much courage that simple act had demanded when first accomplished. Now, before a democratic government, this remained a solemn demonstration motivated by a continuing national grief and a determination to remember. Being here had a far greater personal impact than writing a donation check to Amnesty International, the only other act I'd taken against political brutality. Already my pulse was racing, and my breathing had become shallow. I knew I couldn't afford an anxiety attack at this point, so I took a deep breath and walked slowly to the card tables to peruse the publications on sale.

I tried to keep my eyes down at the materials, but the elderly mother on the other side of the table had a magnetism I couldn't resist. In such close proximity I felt a powerful energy emitted from the tiny woman. I didn't want to stare at her, but when she was turned away I read the embroidered name of her loved one on her scarf. Enrique Martinez. Enrique Martinez. She turned toward me and I saw his photo encased in a brooch pinned to her coat. She smiled at me with a nod and a gesture that conveyed the question, 'Do you want to purchase that thing in your hand?' I looked at her blankly, then realized I was holding a stapled booklet with a crude drawing on the cover and the word "Sueños" written freehand at the top.

"*Sí,*" I said.

"*Un peso,*" she said. I wanted to consume her courage, her patience, her dignity. "*Un peso,*" she said again. I let out a grunt and went into my purse for the money. The first bill in my hand was a five-peso note. I handed it to her and she quickly pulled some bills from the change box.

"No," I said. "*No necesito cambio.*" Four pesos was the least I could donate.

"*Muchas gracias,*" she said sweetly.

I took the booklet from her and smiled. I wanted to thank her for the energy that radiated from her. Standing in her presence charged and inspired me. The phrase "the disappeared" had always symbolized a cloud of spirits in my mind, but reading the name as she had stitched it, and seeing the face of her Enrique, brought me eye to eye with the reality of the whole horrifying war. I remembered the shock of the first news footage of their demonstrations in this plaza, under the murderous gaze of the military. Instantly, The Mothers of the Plaza de Mayo became mythic figures, real Amazons in old coats and embroidered headscarves, celebrated and exploited by national and international news media. Now, twenty years later, without a camera in sight, they were still here. Twenty years of furious mourning had engraved canyons and riverbeds of tears into their faces. With no concern for vanity they live every day in that place where justice and deception go head to head.

I turned back toward her. "*Señora,*" I said. She looked up at me curiously. "*Gracias a Uds. por el valor que nos enseñan.*" I wished I could have thanked every one of them individually for the courage they teach, but at least I had managed to thank one of them. Paco had told me that their modest earnings support continued work educating the public, reconnecting families, finding lost grandchildren, and funding their open university. I promised myself that today's four pesos was just my first donation.

When several mothers linked arms and began to walk the customary circular pattern in the center of the plaza, people fell into informal lines behind them. I joined in the pinwheel pattern walking next to a woman about my age. I presumed that the youngsters here had lost parents or grandparents. Looking up at the windows of the Casa Rosada I wondered if anyone there even notices the monthly ritual anymore. The windows seemed shuttered from the inside as if, even in democracy, this government turns its back on the reminders of its tyrants. Then, there in the midst of the scene, I caught a glimpse of Paco. I didn't dare look directly at him, but I was certainly happy to see him. I wondered, for the first time, if he, too, had someone to remember. I'd never asked him directly. I only knew for certain that he had lost his friend, Juan Alvarez.

Someone stepped into the circle to my right. I glanced up into the filtered sunlight and saw that it was Jessica. Her arrival seemed to mark the beginning of my mission and I felt a spasm of nausea run through my stomach.

"*Buenas tardes,*" she said, quietly.

"*Buenas tardes,*" I said.

After we'd walked the circle once, she pulled a manila envelope from a large bag slung over her shoulder. She handed it to me calmly. I tucked it into my bag beside the flowers.

"Don't go," I said quickly. "Stay for another circuit."

"I will," she said, "I often come here to walk with the *abuelas*. My mother used to come every Thursday."

"Did you lose a family member?"

"My grandfather. But mostly I come because our country needs to remember what happened. A nation's memory lives in the hearts and minds of its people. We are each a cell of that memory and the conscience of our country. It's up to us to ensure that our history is written correctly, and its crimes never repeated."

Colorful kerchiefs and scarves fluttered in the cool breeze adding a deceptive sense of celebration to the demonstration, but a storm was clearly approaching as roiling gray clouds overtook their voluminous white counterparts in the sky. When a cold shadow fell across us I took the envelope of letters from my bag and slipped it to Jessica. "Give this to Luis as soon as you arrive back at the office," I said.

She smiled. "Okay."

We walked for another ten minutes in silence, then she said quietly, "Good luck." I watched her step away from the circle and lost sight of her in the busy pedestrian traffic of the plaza. I checked my watch and figured it might take me fifteen minutes to walk to the spot on Irigoyen where I was to meet Nico. I didn't want to arrive breathlessly, or feel ruffled, so I said *adiós* to the lady who'd been on the other side of me and walked away.

It felt good to walk. As the rendezvous time approached,

adrenalin propelled me forward, as if to fend off a deep inner desire to run in the opposite direction. At one point, I stopped and looked back. That circular tide of citizens moving slowly as a weighted waterwheel reminded me again of my mission. By coming to Buenos Aires, I had put myself into position to take part in something that wasn't about me and the tiny world I live in. The fear inside me mattered for the lineage of my family. Acknowledging that, fueled my courage.

CHAPTER TWENTY-EIGHT

In front of the Club Español people were arriving for the *milonga*. It was something I hadn't thought of, and I worried that if I'd forgotten that detail maybe I'd forgotten others, details that could cost me my life. When an aggressive mechanical growl at the curb caught my attention I turned to see Nico waving at me behind the windshield of his deep red Alfa Romeo. He jumped out to greet me looking like a model for The Gap. He wore a white shirt tucked into a pair of dark blue jeans. A pale yellow sweater tied loosely around his neck.

"*Hola tesoro*," he said, kissing me on the cheek.

Every time he said that I wanted to scream 'I'm not your treasure, buddy', but I couldn't break character at this point in the play, so I smiled. "*Buenas tarde*, Nico," I said.

He opened the passenger door, and I nested quickly into the warm leather, and fastened my seat belt. The richly appointed interior created a soothing environment that filled me with an ironic sense of comfort. The fragrance of the flowers wafted from my bag, and I pulled them onto my lap to protect them from getting crushed as I stowed the bag at my feet. The plastic of Pugliese's picture in my pocket jabbed into my thigh and I pulled it out.

"Someone gave me this picture of Pugliese for good luck," I said as Nico adjusted his seatbelt. "I never knew there were such superstitions among tango people."

"Oh sure. Lots of people have those old spiritualistic ideas. Pugliese is supposed to give you luck, and there is another composer who is bad luck."

"Who is supposed to be bad luck?"

He checked his side mirror and pulled into traffic. I'd never seen him chew gum before, but now it appeared to be a significant occupation.

"Who's the bad luck composer?" I repeated.

Still silent, he busied himself with the mirrors and traffic and chewing.

"Nico, why won't you tell me?"

"I just told you, he is bad luck. Now you want me to say his name?"

"You believe the superstition?"

"I don't say I believe in that stuff, but they say even his name can jinx you. So better not to tempt the devil."

I started to laugh and shake my head.

"Keep that Pugliese in your pocket," he said. "It's a good idea."

"Okay. Do you carry one?"

"Can you keep a secret?"

"Of course."

"He is hidden beneath my driver's license."

"Why is it hidden?"

"Well, probably you will never meet my father, but I can't imagine what he would say about his son carrying the picture of a Communist for good luck?"

"Pugliese was a Communist?"

"Yes, very devoted."

"I didn't know that."

"He and Peron had a very public animosity. Pugliese was arrested many times. When the orchestra performed while he was incarcerated, they always put a white carnation on the piano for him."

"I always think of him as the Argentine George Gershwin. His music has such a powerful urban character. But Gershwin wasn't a Communist."

"He was a Jew, no?"

"A Jew? I don't know," I said, "Maybe he was. I never thought about that. Why do you say that?"

"Worse than being a Communist. Communists can see the light, and leave the party. Jews are weasels their whole lives." He laughed.

I just looked at him, nonplussed.

"What?" he asked, still grinning.

"I don't appreciate anti-Semitism," I said.

"Why?" Suddenly he stopped chewing and the grin drained from his face. "You're not a Jew are you?"

"Not in this lifetime," I said. "But I'm a Spaniard, and they say that most of us are at least part Jewish, because of forced conversions during the Inquisition."

"My Father was born in Spain and he is not a Jew. He couldn't live with himself if he were a Jew."

The anti-Semitism in my uncle's letters resounded in my ears. "He'd have to live with it," I said.

"What do you mean?"

"Suicide is a mortal sin for Catholics," I said, "so he'd have to live with a challenging spiritual dilemma. His own religion would compel him to live with self-directed bigotry."

"This is a ridiculous discussion," he grumbled.

We fell silent. My heart was pounding. There was something different about him today. I guessed that the rejection of the other night had stayed with him. Then, a question came out of me, that I had no intention of asking. It was antagonistic, and I didn't want to antagonize him, but once it was out, I had to play the ignorant American.

"Nico, what was it like here, during the junta?"

"What?"

"I was just in the Plaza de Mayo, walking with Las Madres, and I've been wondering, if my uncle disappeared, what happened to him? And why would someone have taken him? Was he wanted for a crime? Or maybe a piece of information? Did people just disappear for no reason?"

"Frankly, I cannot tell you," he said. "I wasn't here."

"You mean you lived in exile during those years?"

"No, I didn't live in *exile!*"

"Then, what?"

"I was working in Mexico City, at a television station."

"Well, that was convenient, uh, good luck, I mean. So, you stayed in Mexico after graduating college? Then when did you return to Buenos Aires?"

"I returned after college. I got that job in seventy-six, and came back here in 1983. Any other questions, Inspector?"

"I don't mean to interrogate you. I'm sorry. I'm just interested."

"You think that makes me a coward or something?" he said defensively.

"I didn't say that."

"Most of it was all a media hype anyway."

"What?"

"You don't think all that stuff really happened, do you?"

I didn't know what to say. I was stunned into silence.

"You really think it happened, don't you?" He said, looking at me sideways. "Of course! The Jew-controlled American news machine manipulates you to think what they want."

"What?"

"Leftists! Especially in California! I spent time in your country, I know how things are. The Jew-controlled mass media is famous for manipulating the news. From Latin America especially. And with the old ladies marching, I can just imagine what they said."

"When did you spend time in The States?"

"I told you, I was engaged for a while to *una americana*, from Texas."

"So you spent time in Texas?"

"Yes. I learned a lot."

"I'm sure you did," I said. It was hard to let it all slide past me without rebuttal.

"Those people," he continued, "those terrorists that called themselves Montoneros, and leftists and Jews, they wanted to take over this country. I wish I *had* been here then."

"Why?"

"So when I tell people what really happened I could have my own experience."

"Whose experience are you speaking from, then?"

He was quiet for a moment. "My father's."

"The priest?"

"Yes, the priest. Why do you say it like that?'"

"Like what? How did I say it?"

"Distrusting. I trust what Father tells me, but I wish it was my own experience."

I watched the traffic thin out as we traveled toward the suburbs. Retail shops became sparse. Industrial businesses and garages dotted the landscape. It looked like the ragged hem of any great city.

"Maybe I can meet your father sometime," I said, "I could ask him what it was like."

"He's not very sociable," he said. "He's old, and he's very ill. He doesn't even live in the city anymore."

"Oh, where does he live?"

"In the countryside, not that far. I see him every few weeks."

I felt proud of myself for steering us calmly away from an intellectual minefield, and I had collected one small piece of information: Zorrilla lived in the countryside. I was formulating another question in my mind when Nico shifted the conversation to geographic points of interest. That kept him talking until we got to the cemetery. As we entered the gates he made the sign of the cross.

"The grave is supposed to be just up this lane," he said. He parked the car, and pulled a parka from the backseat.

Fists of gray clouds threatened overhead, and a crisp wind tumbled gravel and bits of debris across our path. I buttoned my coat and tied the scarf outside the collar around my neck, turning the long tails to flow visibly at my back. Following Nico along the path, I fought the desire to turn and assure myself that Paco had arrived behind us. We walked straight for a ways, then turned left. I carried the flowers away from my body hoping their bright blossoms and yellow ribbon, like the scarf, would make it easy to follow us.

"Who told you where it is?" I asked nonchalantly.

"What?" He bristled defensively.

"Well, no one at the Diocese had even heard of my uncle when I went there. But you found someone who not only knew him, but also knew where he was buried."

"What difference does it make?"

"Nico," I said, "if you met someone who knew my uncle, I'd like to talk to him."

"Oh, sure." He calmed down. "I got the information from some cross references. Someone told me to check the records for this cemetery because a number of priests and nuns from Buenos Aires Diocese are buried here. Then someone in the department knew the cemetery, and gave me an idea of where to find the grave."

"I see." That was a pretty complex tap dance of an explanation, I thought.

"Here," he said, "near this statue." We passed an adult size marble angel holding a dove in her uplifted right hand. In another five feet we came upon a stone that read:

Padre Mateo Vicente López
2-12-12 to 20-9-77
Hermano, Padre, Soldado del Señor
Que En Paz Descanse

I made the sign of the cross and placed the flowers on top of the stone that looked convincingly old. Then I took a deep breath, put my hands together and pretended to pray. The birthdate on the stone was correct, but the death date matched the death certificate, making it unlikely that my uncle was buried here. It seemed almost certain to me that the exhumation would reveal nothing more than an empty coffin, or perhaps the body of an ESMA victim.

"Would you like me to take a photo for you?" said Nico.

I wondered if Paco was nearby.

"Raquel?"

"What?"

"Would you like me to take a photo?"

"A photo?"

"Yes, I thought you wanted to show your family his resting place."

"Oh," I said, "Yes, I'm sorry. This is quite a bit more emotional than I expected it to be, Nico. I'm sorry."

"Well, do you have a camera with you?"

"A camera? Uh, yes. Sure." I plunged my hand past the envelope of photos, past the makeup pouch, and the coin purse. "It'll be at the bottom," I said self-consciously. "Anything you need is always at the bottom." I pulled out the little digital camera and handed it to him. "I'd appreciate it, if you would take a few shots."

"No problem," he said. "Do you want to stand beside the stone?"

"Oh no, I don't think so. Well, maybe one." I stood solemnly beside the stone, my hand on the flowers.

"It's okay," he said, "I know this is an emotional moment for you. I can bring you again if you like."

"No," I said. "No one expects me to look happy here. I'll just stand, and you snap." After the first photo of me next to the stone, I let him snap others without me. In the meantime I pretended to study the nearby gravemarkers while I searched for a sign of Paco.

Then suddenly, I saw him. He was half way across the cemetery, kneeling at a grave with a handful of wildflowers. The sight of him made me smile without thinking.

"What are you smiling at?" asked Nico.

"What? Oh, well, it may seem strange to you," I searched my brain for a creative explanation, "but I was thinking that after all he went through in his painful childhood," I followed the trail of words hoping they'd land me in a believable answer, "and the horrors of the Spanish Civil War, I'm glad my uncle rests in such a peaceful place."

He nodded. "I can see you might like it here. It's away from the city. He had a painful childhood, your uncle?"

The ominous sky cast deep shadows across the geometry of the stones, and a dense ground fog was creeping between trees, statues, and headstones. I realized I had to make something happen. If it started to rain, the moment would be lost. "Nico," I said, "I have a thought. Do you think we could get a photo attached to the stone?"

"A photo?"

"I see that some of these stones have photos of the deceased. I have a couple of photos with me. He left home at a very young age. We could crop one from this larger format and set it into a weather resistant frame." I pulled the envelope from my bag and handed him the photo at the river. This was not in the original plan, but somehow it seemed the right thing to do to provoke him to lead Paco to his Father's whereabouts. Rather than just leaving the photos in the car, now I could see his reaction and we'd know what to expect. "Tío was just a teenager here," I said nonchalantly. "He's with my father." In the photo Mateo's wet hair was slicked back and his scars were prominent. "The next one would be better for the grave, he's in his altar boy robes. We can crop out my dad and the priest." I handed him the second picture. "It's getting awfully dark, but you can see why my uncle didn't take a lot of photos. He was in a terrible accident as a child. Still, I'd like to have his photo on his final resting place."

Nico moved the photos this way and that trying to get a good look in the dimming light. A deep grimace crawled across his handsome features.

"Nico? What's wrong?" There was a look of confusion on his face as he carried the photos to a spot where the light seemed brighter. "Maybe I should have warned you about his scars." He squinted his eyes, then opened them wide and thrust his fingers through his hair.

Shaking his head slowly he said, "This boy, this man, is your uncle?"

"Yes."

"Is this some kind of joke?"

"What do you mean?" He wasn't acting.

"This is *not* your uncle."

"It is, Nico. That's my uncle Mateo. And that's my father beside him."

"Where did you get this photo?" he snarled.

"From my aunt, his sister. My sister scanned it, the quality is . . . ."

"Have you been playing some kind of game all this time?"

Suddenly all the fear dammed up inside me spilled over. "What are you talking about?" I said, raising my voice. "Why are you looking at me like that?"

He grabbed me by the arm. "Is this your idea of a joke?"

"Ouch! Joke? That's my uncle, Mateo Vicente López. You're hurting me."

"We're going to find out what's going on right now," he said. "Come with me." The charm had drained from his voice and demeanor. He stuffed the photos back into my bag and pulled me along by the arm.

"Ouch! Stop it!" I shouted loud enough so that Paco could hear me across the otherwise serene cemetery. "Let go of my arm. Nico! What are you doing?" I struggled to free myself from his grip.

"Shut up!" he barked, tightening his hold as he led me back to the car. Tree branches scratch my face and shoulder.

"Nico!" I yelled. He opened the car door and shoved me in. I scanned the cemetery quickly hoping to see Paco coming toward us, but the fog was so dense that I could barely see beyond the car. Nico jumped in and started the engine. Then I saw my scarf fluttering from a tree branch.

"My scarf!" I said, reaching for the door, but Nico was already in gear, and I was thrust back into the seat as he threw us into reverse. The tires squealed fighting for traction on the gravel path, and suddenly we jerked again.

"You better buckle that seat belt," he said maneuvering the car into position for the exit. I was just about to follow orders when we backed into something with a thud. I braced myself against the dash.

"What was that?" I asked.

"*¡Mierda!*" said Nico, looking into the rear view mirrors. "*¡Mierda! ¡Boludo!*"

I looked in my side mirror and saw a body rolling on the ground behind us.

"My God, you hit someone!" I said, reaching again for the door handle, but Nico grabbed my hand and pulled it toward him.

"*¡Quedate quieta!*" he growled and shifted gears again. The tires squealed again as flying gravel pinged violently off the metal beneath us.

"Let me call for help, Nico. You can't just leave him there!" I was sure he'd hit Paco, but when I looked into the rear side mirror again the victim turned toward me. Luis's bloodied face grimaced with pain and anger. Blood poured from his forehead. I twisted my body to look out the back window, but Nico grabbed the collar of my coat and pushed me back into the seat. Then he gunned the engine and propelled us toward the gates. "Fasten that belt if you want to live," he said, and pulled out of the cemetery, with a high pitched screech that launched us into the unsuspecting traffic of the highway.

My heart was pounding. I latched the seatbelt with trembling fingers. My mind raced with thoughts of Luis. He was not supposed to have been there, and now he was injured. If Paco had to take him to a hospital he couldn't stay on our trail. I didn't dare look back to see if they or the back-up team had followed us out of the cemetery, so I reached into my bag for the cell phone.

"Is 911 the emergency number here?" I asked.

Nico grabbed the phone away from me and threw it into the back seat. "You're not calling anyone," he said, checking the rear view mirror.

"I think that's a mistake Nico, they could have easily memorized your license plate."

"Enough!" he yelled.

I could see it would do me no good to insist. "Why didn't you think that photo was my uncle?" I asked. "And why are you so angry that you'd leave someone injured without calling for help?"

The muscles in his jaw shifted beneath the skin.

"Nico?"

"You know the answers to those questions. Don't pretend."

"I don't. I'm not."

Beads of sweat dripped from his forehead. The storm had broken and the road was slick with early rain. I knew that between the weather and the speed of Nico's driving, following us would be a tricky proposition.

"What's wrong?" I insisted. I honestly couldn't figure out why he was so upset. "At least tell me where you're taking me, for God's sake!" I presumed we were going to Zorrilla, and if Paco or the others hadn't been able to follow us, there was little hope of being rescued, or even found. I felt seeds of a panic attack take root in my chest, so I started counting to slow down my breath. In: two, three, four; Out:

two, three, four. Confessing that I knew Zorrilla was my uncle wasn't going to help me. Nico seemed to be feeling betrayed, but why?

He made a sharp right off the road that threw me to one side then the other. I saw him glancing off and on into the rearview mirror, giving me hope that he saw someone following us. He swiped the glistening sweat from his face with the back of his arm.

"What is wrong?" I demanded again.

"You already know what is wrong," he said, rechecking the mirror.

"I don't."

"How long have you known that your uncle was my father?" he asked.

"My uncle is your father?" He didn't know?

"And who's following us?"

"We're being followed?" Finally, it was my chance to check the rear view. But the vehicle I saw was too far behind to identify beyond a set of headlights.

"Stop playing me as a fool!" he shouted.

"Oh my God! That's why you were so shocked at the photos!" I couldn't abandon my position. "If my uncle is your father, he must be alive. So, who's buried in that grave?"

"That's just one of the things we are going to find out," he said.

It appeared that he really had not known the truth.

"What's your father's name?" I asked. "I mean, you knew I was looking for Mateo Vicente López."

"You already know my father's name. Why don't you tell me?"

"How would I know his name?" I was starting to get very confused about what I was supposed to know from Nico's perspective, so it seemed best to deny everything.

"Those Jews at the *Alef*, I know what kind of people they are. Did you show them that photo of your uncle?"

"What do you mean, what kind of people are they?"

"They are leftists. The husband of that *Maestra*, he was a Jew, and not just a Jew, he was a Communist Jew. Look what he named that school: *El Alef*. What the hell does a Hebrew letter have to do with tango?" He snorted, then checked the rearview again and accelerated.

We were on a busy two-lane highway and there was a lot of traffic coming toward us. The rain had increased, and night was closing in. Between the bright lights, the quick-flipping windshield wipers, and the speed, I felt sure we were headed for a collision. I continued counting breaths to calm my fear, but in this case fear and anxiety were quite appropriate. A big tractor trailer was coming toward us, and behind it a car pulled out into our lane from time to time, as if hoping to pass the truck. The wipers were pushing water at top speed: Flimph flumph, flimph, flumph, perfectly synchronized with my racing heartbeat. I gasped for breath.

"Hang on," said Nico, "we have to make this next left."

"NO!" I screamed.

The tractor trailer was bearing down on us and there was a dense strand of lights behind it.

"Wait 'til this traffic passes, for God's sake."

"You'd love that wouldn't you. Let your guys catch up to us?

Hang on!"

Suddenly he cranked the wheel sharply to the left. The truck headlights flooded the interior, blinding me as we swerved. The horn of the semi was deafening. I threw my hands over my face instinctually, and was thrown forcefully toward Nico, restrained by my belt. With the reverse motion I hit the door violently with my shoulder and my head.

When he straightened our trajectory, we were racing straight into darkness on a road with no light beyond those of our headlights. Nico lifted his foot a bit from the throttle. A cacophonous mix of horns, squealing brakes, tires, and metal crashing against metal came from behind us. No one could have stayed with us after that. I just hoped they had survived whatever conflagration had exploded in our wake.

I rolled down the window for air. "Now I suppose you're going to tell me that you were a race driver, too," I said with a palliative breath. "Was that in Mexico? Or Texas? Or maybe Indianapolis?"

He didn't answer he just looked into the rearview mirror and sneered. I turned back to see the road behind us, but there was none visible, just night and a distant glare of lights and smoke rising from the crash scene.

CHAPTER TWENTY-NINE

The Alfa cut through the night illuminating its path a mere three feet ahead. When I shifted my gaze away from that beam, I realized that a damp darkness had enveloped us. Every now and then the tiny lantern-like warmth of a house set back from the road gave me the vague comfort of knowing that someone was enjoying a peaceful evening. I imagined a woman making dinner for her family, seducing appetites with savory aromas.

Though the road was rough and pocked with holes, Nico seemed determined to maintain highway speed, jostling me brutishly in the seat. He glanced at me every now and then. My tears seemed to give him pleasure. I wanted desperately to dam every emotion within me, but the image of Luis rolling on the ground played over and over in my mind. I wondered if Nico knew who he'd hit.

About half an hour after we'd survived the left turn in front of the truck, we made a right onto a muddy lane that finally slowed us down. He seemed to have decided that no one was following us any longer, at least he'd stopped checking the rearview mirror. I thought about meeting my uncle, well, Zorilla, the man he'd become. It wouldn't be a heart-warming family reunion. No need to pull my camera from its cozy repose at the bottom of my bag.

"Where the hell are we?" I barked.

"You wouldn't know it if I told you," said Nico. I couldn't argue with that.

"I still want to know," I said.

"Why, so you can tell your Jew friends where you went?"

"I can't believe you! You've never said anything like that before."

"I thought there was still hope for you. But now, well, you are quite the surprise package, Raquel."

"I'm a surprise package? I never expected this from you, Nico. Tell me something, that day when I ran into you at La Boca and you took all those pictures, was that really an accident, or were you sent to spy on me?"

"There's no reason not to tell you now," he said. "I was sent to watch you, but I had no idea that Father was. . .was your uncle."

"Well, why did he have you spy on me? And what is his name?"

"It was all for a friend. He was looking out for a friend. But you . . ."

He brought the car to an abrupt halt activating the seat belt, restraining me into what was engineered to be the captivity of safety. A moment later Nico grabbed me by my hair.

"I did not know that my uncle was your father," I said wincing.

"You played me as a fool from the beginning," he said, his left hand squeezed my face like a vice. "You knew I was falling in love with you, and I bet that gave you all a good laugh."

"What? No, it was never like that," I managed the words through my teeth. "I had no idea . . ."

"Did you tell all your Jew friends how you had Nico wrapped around your little finger? Huh? Did you? Did they laugh as they planned to follow us to that cemetery?"

His fingers were tangled deep in my hair, and the fury in his face made me think I might not live to see my uncle.

"Please Nico," I said, " let go. You're hurting me."

"You knew he wasn't dead, didn't you?" He let go my face and grabbed my shoulder.

"The date was wrong," I admitted. "I have a letter from my uncle dated a month after the date on that death certificate. So I knew something was wrong with the document."

"But you didn't tell me that."

"I presumed you were trying to lead me away from the truth. And weren't you?"

"No. I did not create that document. It was given to me."

"By whom? Who gave it to you?"

"A colleague at the Diocese. I thought López was a friend of my father, someone who needed to be protected."

"And the grave?" I asked.

He let go of me finally and looked at the steering wheel.

"You have to know, Raquel, I will do anything to protect him."

"He's a war criminal, Nico. He tortured people."

"So you *do* know who he is!"

I was caught. The Alfa's luxurious interior had snapped shut around me like a hunter's trap. Nico held me in an ominous stare. His breathing quickened and I imagined that he was considering killing me right there, before I could pose any further threat. Instead, he turned the key in the ignition and set us into motion without a word. I was trembling more from fear than from the cold that had quickly settled in around us. As we drove, my mind searched unsuccessfully for convincing lies to save my life.

In about fifteen minutes a house, that had first appeared as another lantern, grew to normal size as we approached. We stopped some twenty yards from dimly lit windows with drawn shades. There would be no mama cooking supper in this house, I thought. The rain had stopped, but a low canopy of dense clouds hung overhead. Nico came around to my side, and opened the door.

"Get out," he demanded.

I unbuckled my seatbelt and pulled my bag over my left shoulder. His fingers squeezed deeply into my right elbow pulling me from the seat. Suddenly blinding light was thrown out from multiple perimeter lamps. Dogs started barking, and two Dobermans launched themselves toward us from the left. I let out a scream just as the animals were stopped by fencing made visible only by raindrops catching light in the delicate pattern of wire squares. The full structure of the two-story house was now revealed, a foreboding stone monolith. I realized that this was probably the house mentioned in Mateo's letters. The whole *Guardia Sagrada* could be in there, I thought, as we trekked through the mud toward the stone steps leading up to the front door.

Nico stopped me on the bottom level. "Stay here," he commanded.

I looked around considering escape, but the darkness beyond the boundary of the perimeter lights seemed impenetrable, the road that brought us here was just a muddy, night black trail. Also, I feared that the fence restraining the dogs might have an automatic gate. Nico climbed to the landing where he stood under the protection of a canvas canopy. Another light went on illuminating him from above as he lifted the metal door-knocker just beneath a small wrought iron covered window. He gave it four strong knocks before the little window opened briefly. Then the door opened slowly. When a figure stepped out into the porch light I felt my mouth drop open. It was a robed and hooded *penitente*. I'd seen them first as a child in *Abuela's* Spanish magazines about Holy Week in Sevilla. With my American upbringing they looked ominously like Ku Klux Klansmen clad in black. Even their photos instilled fear in me as a child, and as one of them stood toe to toe with Nico, fear flashed through me again amplified by the proximity.

Their words dissolved incoherently in the night air, but as the *penitente* talked his breath created a frosty halo that glowed ironically around his peaked head. When they stopped talking, Nico came back to me.

"I cannot take you into the house yet," he said angrily. "Get back in the car."

"What is that person doing there?" I asked, as he pushed me back into the Alfa.

"What person?"

"That *penitente!*"

"Get used to it. You're going to see a lot of them. That one is a sergeant in the *Guardia Sagrada*. They don't allow women in the house. I have to work it out."

"I can stay out here," I said. "I don't need to go into the house. It's not like I could runaway. The only thing I know about this place is how far it is from any form of civilization."

"Don't think of escaping," he said, as if he hadn't heard me. "You are miles away from people. And then, of course, there's the native wildlife."

He slammed the door shut, the jangling keys silenced as he shoved them back into a pocket. I watched him step across the muddy yard and into the house. The guard behind him shut the door with an audible thud. It was cold in the car, but I knew I'd be safer there all night than in that house. When the perimeter lights went off, the world went black. I wondered if Luis and Paco had been able to follow us at least to the turn in front of the truck. And what of the extra team? Had they been behind us? Maybe Luis was in the hospital. Or they could all have been killed in the accident on the highway. I felt sure that no one had any idea where I was. Then I remembered my cell phone. I switched on the overhead interior light and stretched into the back to search for it. Finally I found it by touch, under the driver's seat. I turned off the interior light and turned on my phone. The system roamed and roamed and roamed without any luck. I got out of the car quietly, so as not to set off the dogs, and cautiously tiptoed in the mud around the car hoping to improve my odds of finding a cell signal. Finally, about ten steps from the car, it connected. I dialed Luis knowing that if I managed to make the connection, it might not last long. Just the ring made me feel closer to him. When the message system picked up my heart sank into my gut. The brief sound of his recorded voice was bittersweet and rather than organize my message at the sound of the beep I started babbling.

"Luis! It's me. I am so worried about you. I told you not to come to the cemetery. Nico has driven me into the country. We're on a dirt road. I don't even know if you can hear all of this. There's a big stone house . . ." I thought I heard a sound from the house and clicked off. It started to rain again, and not with a drizzle. It poured down suddenly sending me back into the car for shelter. Instinctively, I locked the doors, though I knew the most menacing predator had the key.

I wondered if my signal could be traced, the way it's done in television detective shows, though I doubted real life could be so simple. I checked my watch. It was eight o'clock. I should have said the time on the phone, I thought. It might at least help them to know how long it had taken to get here. Then I realized that the answering system would have recorded the time.

The lights went on again, and with them the dogs began another furious attack at the fence. Nico came out of the house and
jogged gingerly back to the vehicle. Two *penitentes* stayed under the
overhang. The rain had subsided to a drizzle.

"Get out," he demanded, trying to open the door. "Unlock
this door!"

He reached into his pocket but I unlocked the door before he
could use the key. "You don't have to hurt me," I said, as he yanked
me from the seat.

"Stand up," he said sternly. "I have to put this on you."

"Hey!" I protested and wrestled with him as he pulled a hood
over my head and tied it around my neck. "Nico! What the hell are
you doing?"

"Shut up. You have to wear this. There's no point in fighting me."

"What, no matching handcuffs?"

"They are available I assure you, so shut up." I suddenly had
nothing to say. I was crying, dammit, and I knew if I cried my nose
would run.

"Bring my bag!"

"You can't keep your bag at a time like this."

"It's got the photos in it." It also had my phone, not that it was
too likely I'd get another chance to use it.

"Alright," he said. "Here!" He begrudgingly slung the weighty
bag over my head. "They're just going to take it from you."

My heart was pounding in my chest and ears as Nico guided
me up the steep steps. We stopped when I felt a rough mat beneath

my feet, presumably to clean the mud from my boots. I made a half-hearted attempt at the task, and we crossed the threshold onto what felt like a wooden floor. I knew the guards were there only because I'd seen them. They said nothing. The big door shut behind us. It was immediately warmer, but this warmth lacked comfort. It stunk of frankincense and stale tobacco.

Nico guided me into a left turn, and as we walked I could hear the robes rustling, and heavy rubber-soled shoes squeaked as they pushed off the wooden flooring. I started counting my steps from the first turn hoping to map my position in relation to the front door. It might help in an escape, I thought. At forty steps, we stopped again. "We're getting into an elevator," said Nico. So much for counting steps.

I was cramped into the back corner of a small elevator for a mercifully short but malodorous decent. I felt one *penitente* get out in front of us, then one behind. We walked a few feet, and stalled. I heard keys unlocking what sounded like a big door when it was pulled open. We walked again. Twenty five steps. Metal clanking. Another key in a slot, unlocking . . . a padlock, maybe. The air was as cold as outdoors, but it held the heavy putrid stench of death and decay. Either they are going to kill me now, or hold me here until they do, I thought. Several more steps, until a sharp metallic whine signaled the opening of a gate. It was freezing cold and the smell made me gag under the hood. By reflex I placed my left hand to my nose and scratched myself with the rough cloth. We shuffled forward, stalled again, then another squeal of metal.

Another gate? No. A cell. They were going to leave me locked in this cell, underground.

Nico still had hold of my now-numb arm, and he shoved me another few steps forward.

"*Dejála*," said a husky voice. Nico let go of my arm, and either he or one of the *penitentes* grabbed the strap of my bag and pulled it off over my head.

"My bag!" I cried out as if it were my child. "Please! Don't take it."

"You cannot keep it," said Nico. "I have to leave you here. It's better than being in the car."

"No, it's not," I said quickly. "They've put me in a cell, haven't they?"

"Yes."

"Are they going to lock me in here?"

"Yes."

"But why? Please, Nico, please don't let them do this to me." I was waving my hands in the air desperately reaching for some human contact. I heard muffled footsteps on what was now a dirt floor. Then the lock of the cell.

"Take me back to the car," I begged. "I won't go anywhere, I don't even know where I am. Please." I found the metal ribs of the cell and curled my fingers around them.

"I'm not in charge here, Raquel," he said gruffly. "I'll try to get you a cot, but don't count on it. Women are not allowed in the residence. So this is the only place for you."

"Well, take the hood off, at least. Please. I can hardly breath." I started fumbling with the knot at the nape of my neck.

"Turn around," he commanded. "Lean against the bars."

I felt his delicate fingers untying the knot at the back of my head. When he lifted the hood I squinted to see my surroundings. It was nearly as dark as night. In a faint, quivering gray light, I could make out a stone wall and bars. To the right, metal bars, and bars beyond those bars, more cells than I could count. All empty. I turned my head left, and saw more bars. Only two cells to my left, also empty. In the corner of my cell against the stone wall a bucket was barely visible in the dim light. The toilet, just as Carmina had described it. I turned toward Nico. His shadowed face was stern. Behind him were the two hooded guards. They turned quickly but didn't leave. Tears poured out of me uncontrollably.

"You shouldn't have lied to me," he said coldly.

"*Vamos,*" growled one of the *penitentes*. Nico turned to leave.

"Nico!" I grabbed at his arm, but he wouldn't face me. "Do you think they could at least let me have my bag? I have an asthma inhaler in there. I need it."

He pulled away.

"*Mi bolso,*" I said, as they were leaving. "*¿Puedo quedarme con mi bolso?*"

The taller *penitente* pulled the gate shut, its squawking cry a menacing declaration of my captivity. I heard a metal key turn in the padlock. Then they shuffled out of sight. I heard the wooden door open and shut. Then, silence. The only light was a dull twitching fluorescent fixture at the gate, the rest was metal bars and metal bars, a forest of metal bars.

CHAPTER THIRTY

I mopped the dampness from my face with my coat sleeve, and forced my focus onto my breath. In: two, three, four. Out: two, three, four. In: two, three, four. Out. . .

Over and over, I counted to fend off the swelling fear and anger threatening to drive me into a screaming fit. I had a vision of bashing my head against the stone wall to deprive them of the pleasure of torturing me. "Don't be so melodramatic," I told myself, though looking at my predicament, I wasn't sure melodrama was possible. I was actually locked in a dungeon. I started to count again. "In: two, three, four," I counted aloud, and the words vibrating in my head became an unorthodox, but effective mantra. I repeated it over and over, until my mind relaxed enough to collect information.

My eyes had adjusted so that I could make out shadows, and I studied the organization and structure of the cells. What kind of house has a dungeon in the basement, I wondered. I'd read about *El*

Silencio, the infamous country house owned by the Catholic Church during the junta. I remembered that when an international team of humanitarians came to inspect the rumored prison at the naval school, hundreds of prisoners were moved to *El Silencio.* Of course, that meant that the inspectors found the naval school a clean, innocent facility. From the smell, I determined that even if this house was not that infamous place, some political prisoners had surely been kept here as well.

The smell of death crept inside me. If there'd been any food in my stomach I certainly would have lost it by now. Without the counting, my heart started to pound again. I felt light-headed and dropped to the dusty floor knowing that if I didn't calm myself I'd black out. Stretching back on my knees into a yogic child's pose, I started to count again. "In: two three four. Out: two, three, four." Once I was calm again, I felt the instinct to walk. I put my sleeve up against my nose and took a deep breath, then I pulled myself up using the bars. The first steps were slow and calculated. Struggling to keep balance, I held onto the bars, walking counter clockwise, as in the *milonga.* I tried to lift my posture for *caminada.* "Always proud," I said, voicing *La Maestra's* instruction. The movement brought to mind my tango with Luis in the elevator. I turned to walk backward and imagined first his arms around me, then the warmth of him encircling me. I could smell him. Then I heard him humming in my ear, Bahía Blanca. My left arm rested on his shoulder, my hand touched his collar. I followed him walking backward: *caminada* with *ochos* and *amagues,* then a *molinete.* For a while I even thought I could feel his face against mine. But eventually fatigue overwhelmed me and I leaned against the wall.

"Congratulations," I said, "you've just overcome your first anxiety attack in captivity."

I checked my watch, and realized that doing so was a subversive liberty. I was free to depress that little knob for light whenever I wanted to. Meager as it was, it constituted an act of rebellion as far as I was concerned. I had some power: I knew it was nearly ten o'clock.

I heard voices at the outer door. It opened, and soon there were two guards outside my cell, their figures visible in the flickering strobe of the fluorescent tube. One of them offered a small glass of water through the bars.

"Drink," he said in Spanish-accented English.

Grateful for even this measly sign of hospitality, I drank it quickly, and handed back the glass. But as soon as I let go of it, I was struck with panic and repentance for such thoughtless compliance. The solid metal of the bars hit my forehead, as I fell forward, dizzy and off balance, then sank to the floor, a pile of flesh and fabric. "You drugged. . .me," I remember saying. Really, I feared they'd poisoned me. I fought desperately to remain conscious, but quickly faded into oblivion.

I woke being jostled right and left on the dirt floor. The rough cloth of robes brushed against my skin. Slowly I lifted my heavy eyelids to see two hooded guards looming over me, pushing me from side to side with their feet.

"*Vamos,*" one of them said.

I reached for one of the bars and grabbed hold of it. It was nearly cold as ice and my numb fingers seemed incapable of grasping it. I rolled my weight into a position of leverage, but my head was so heavy, that each time I tried to lift myself, I fell back down.

"*Tome.*"

I was handed a small glass of what looked and smelled like orange juice. The fragrance was bracing and despite my anger and fear, I drank it obediently. In a minute the mental fog cleared and I managed to lift myself and walk as far as the gate holding onto the bars for support. There they stopped me. One put a hood over my head again, but worse than that, the other pulled my arms back and handcuffed me. A shrill terror ran through me.

"Please," I begged them. "*Por favor. Ustedes no necesitan las esposas. ¿Dónde puedo ir? ¡Suéltame!*"

I'd seen people handcuffed in movies and TV cop shows, but the actual experience was beyond frightening. I became completely hysterical. I screamed and threw myself on the ground determined to make it as difficult as possible for them to handle me. But in a moment, one of the guards lifted me off the ground and slapped my face right through the hood. If the other one hadn't been holding onto me, I'm sure I'd have landed against the opposite wall. I struggled to get my footing, but they dragged me painfully by my arms until they threw me into the elevator. I felt it dip with the weight of our bodies.

"*Levantate,*" said one of them.

I managed to stand, staggering as the elevator ascended. My face itched with tears and mucous, and I rubbed it against the wall, finding a strange and unexpected sense of pleasure from the rough sacking of the hood scratching my face. When the elevator stopped they took me out sandwiched between their corpulent bodies, shoving me if I faltered. I'd become a malleable, trembling wad of flesh, not at all the steel-spirited heroine I wanted to be. Their robes brushed against the walls reminding me of the sound of nuns' habits in elementary school. When we stopped, they pushed me through a doorway to my left. Eight steps into a hot, stuffy room that smelled of stale cigar smoke, frankincense, and alcohol – probably whisky or brandy. One of the guards mercifully unlocked the handcuffs and jostled me into a wooden armchair. They stood behind me. I could hear them breathing. I sat erect as a queen hoping to regain my dignity, enshrouded in a cloud of repugnant odors.

The weave of the cloth hood allowed me to see light patterns. I could see that daylight was controlled by shutters adjusted for privacy on two sides of the room, and light poured in from small windows along the ceiling. Daylight was a welcome sight even from behind the hood.

I heard slow, shuffling footsteps approach from the hallway. It was certain to be my uncle, I thought. And behind him, I heard self-assured, graceful footsteps. Nico.

The old man's breathing was audibly labored. Through the hood, his body formed the shape of an enormous elephant seal as he entered. In California I had watched hundreds of them in their annual gathering on a beach where females and cubs were often endangered by rampaging males. I followed his slow progress to a location behind a desk in front of me. A chair creaked with the weight of his obviously decaying body. He smelled like acetone. It was a smell I knew from the clinic where we'd taken Tía Leti. I guessed he suffered from the same inherited kidney condition as she. Marta and I had learned a good deal about diabetes and kidney failure through Mama's illness and by caring for Tía. I was well acquainted with the smell of ketosis. In Mateo's case, I guessed he was suffering from alcoholic ketoacidosis.

"*Sáquele la capucha,*" he barked, startling me. And just as he'd ordered, one of the guards untied and lifted the hood. I kept my eyes closed to adjust gradually to the light, then looked up slowly to gaze upon my corpulent, red-faced uncle dressed in the black costume of a holy man with a purple sash and cap sitting behind a huge, antique desk. In my peripheral vision I saw Nico standing, looking out louvered shutters to my right, though there was another chair there for him.

I just stared at the old man. Having heard so much, it was hard to comprehend the evil accumulated in this malformed specimen of humanity. His head bobbled uncontrollably like one of those dolls made for the back window of a car. The sight and smell of him was nauseating. When our eyes met finally, he raised his eyebrows in surprise.

"*¡Abuela!*" He said.

"*Soy Raquel,*" I said.

"*Sí sí, sos Raquel, pero como te parecés a mi abuela.*" He couldn't stop looking me over, as if I were Madame Tussaud's replica of his grandmother. In photos I had seen that I bore an uncanny resemblance to my namesake, his *abuela*. Now I hoped this fortunate resemblance might save me another night in the dungeon. Or maybe they'd at least bring me a bed, or food.

"I gonna pratice my English with you," he said, as if it were a threat. "*Abuela*, what are you doing in the body of this woman?"

"Why did you drug me?" I demanded.

"To make you sleep," he said. "You don't make trouble when you sleep. Why you make so much troubles? Why you need so badly to see me, *hija*?" He asked. It seemed that a distaste for life had molded the musculature of his face into a permanent expression of disgust. The irregular mustache, noted by Carmina, formed an unruly fringe over the full lips turned down at the corners. Deep grooves cut into the nasolabial folds where fleshy jowls bracketed his scarred mouth.

"Your sister Leticia, is very ill," I said. "I came all this way to find you for her. She'd be very angry to see how you are repaying me for my efforts. I found your letters to my father just a few months ago, and we realized that you didn't die in Spain. He never told anyone. Now Tía Leti hopes to hear your voice, or at least know what happened to you, before she dies."

"Ah Leti, the little one. At least someone in the family cares about poor old Mateo, after all this time. Why your father stop writing to me?"

"He died." I hoped the words would cut into him, as they still cut into me.

"When?"

"December, 1977," I said. "My mother died with him."

He grimaced and dropped his bobbing head.

"You thought he was planning to visit you, remember? You told him to wait."

He looked at me again from under a canopy of flabby flesh. "How do you know this?"

"Your letters." I thought he would have found and read the originals in my bag, but he seemed to have no knowledge of them. "As far as I know, Papa kept your secret. I doubt that he told even Mama that you survived the Spanish Civil War. Not even Mama. Why, Tío?"

His face wobbled with fat as he shook it. "*Tantos años,*" he said.

"Why did you let *Abuelita* die without knowing you had survived? Why would you be so cruel to your own mother?"

He rocked in the chair and scratched his ear. "1977? You find the letters *now?*"

"When we lost them both, everyone was so devastated that we just cleared their house as quickly as possible. This year I found the letters in an old trunk that had been stored in my garage. They're in my bag. I thought you'd have read them by now. Your guards took everything from me."

With a word and a gesture he commanded one of the guards to bring my bag.

The room fell silent, and he daubed at tears, or was it sweat, while we waited for someone to return. I perused the shelves behind him. Among the books and religious statuary I noticed a single framed photo. There was young Nico in his cap and gown, standing with Tío and another young man also in cap and gown. I stood up (somewhat daring, I thought) and leaned forward to see more clearly the face of the other graduate.

"So uncle, I see you have two 'sons'," I said.

"Yes," he said, looking at me. "Nico and Esteban." I was shocked when he indicated the latter touching the arm of the *penitente* now standing to his right. He was one of the two who'd brought me in. I glanced down at the desk and saw the photos Nico had taken at La Boca. "So, one son is a guard, and the other is a spy!" I said, picking up one of the photos.

"Curiosity is not a sin, Raquel," said Nico, finally looking at me. "Lying isn't either, for a just cause. Besides, I told you, he said they were for a friend. I have never known Father as anyone but Sebastián Zorrilla. I'd never heard of Mateo Vicente López."

"*Basta!*" said the old man.

"*Sentate, mujer!*" Esteban commanded. His voice dug into me like a bony finger on my chest pushing me into the chair.

A guard came in with my bag.

"*Qué hay aquí?*" said Zorrilla, pulling things out of my bag.

"*Las fotos están en un sobre.* In the yellow envelope," I said. "There are two photos of you and Papa when you were boys. At my apartment I have more pictures."

He pulled the envelope out with shaky hands. I'd seen many

priests like him, grown alcoholic over the length of a lonely life. Everyone has the parish priest, but the parish priest has no one. The church-ordained solitary confinement of their profession holds all relationships at arms' length, except one. The priest denied a kiss, is allowed a drink. It is a vice without a commandment.

I watched my uncle's swollen fingers fumble to free the photos from their sheath. Holding them to the light, he squinted, then began to tremble with emotion. When tears turned to laughter he fell into spasms of coughing. I shifted my gaze toward the windows keeping him in my peripheral vision while he reddened with the phlegm-fueled fit that climaxed with him spitting into a handkerchief. When I looked back he was wiping spittle from his lips. With the questionable skills of a doctor's wife, I diagnosed possible congestive heart disease.

"*Me acuerdo esa tarde,*" he said, looking at the river picture. "We went, the two *familias,*" he said to Nico, "for fishing and picnic. The river of San Joaquín, in California." He grew quiet then, staring seriously into the photo. "*Ay, Fredo, ¿qué te pasó?* Why did your father stopped writing?" He pierced me with a stare, as if I might have played a role in Papa's disaffection.

"I told you, he died!" I shouted.

"Oh? He died? When?" He coughed and spit into his handkerchief again.

I knew that, no matter what they did with me, my uncle was close to death. His intermittent shifts in consciousness suggested that toxins were overtaking his body and mind. I had to get as many answers as possible, even if they went to the grave with me.

"Tío, why did you change your name?" I asked nicely.

"The church change it."

"Why?"

Esteban laid his hands gently on the old man's shoulders. "*¡No tiene que responder, Padre,*" he said.

"Why are you hiding?" I pressed him. "Why do you live like this, *escondido?*"

"*Padre, Usted no tiene que hablar de eso,*" said Esteban.

The old man began to shake. Nico pushed the *penitente's* hands from his shoulders. "*¿Qué sabés vos?*" he said to Esteban. "*¡Dejalo!*"

"*Yo lo conozco mejor que voz,*" said the *penitente,* "*es mí padre también.*"

In a twist I could never have imagined Nico and Esteban were going head to head to protect their father from me.

"Answer me, Tío? Did you discard our name as you discarded the family?"

Suddenly he had another coughing seizure. Esteban poured him a glass of water, and Nico fed it to the old man gradually.

"*Abuela ¿por qué me traés estos recuerdos?*" said Tío as his throat cleared.

"I am not your *abuela*, Mateo. I am Raquel, your niece, *tu sobrina.*" I said it loudly because his eyes drooped, and he seemed to have nodded off. He didn't respond.

"*Padre,*" said Nico giving him a shake.

The old man's body went limp in the chair. Nico grabbed him under the arms and Esteban grabbed him around the middle. Together they lifted the old man, shaking him and calling his name. Finally, Nico slapped him once. That seemed to rouse him. Esteban went to a side table, and this time poured a glass of orange juice from a pitcher. As Nico held him up Esteban placed the glass between the old man's lips, tilting his head and supporting it while feeding him small sips. Their tenderness was almost touching. When Tío came to, coughing and sputtering, Nico handed him the handkerchief from the desk, and the old man cleared his throat again. He straightened himself in his chair, mopped his forehead with the hanky and looked at me, as if seeing me for the first time. Then he looked down and saw the picture of himself and my father at the river. It startled him.

"Oh," he said, "look at this." Then he looked at Nico, hovering.

"*¿Qué te pasa hijo? ¡Sentate, che!*" he barked. Esteban stayed at his post watching Nico sit down reluctantly, as he'd been commanded. The old man looked at me again, as if I were no relative at all. With a suspicious squint he asked, "What you want here?"

"Maybe I could take your photo back to Tía Leti."

"Leti? La chica? She is too young to remember Mateo."

"She's an old woman, Tío," I said, "and she's dying."

I hoped to touch what was left of his heart, but he seemed to have transferred all familial love to the two orphans. He went into my bag again as if searching for a smuggled weapon. He started pulling things out, manhandling every pouch and object. I could practically feel his fingers rummaging through my soul.

"STOP!" I screamed. "What are you looking for?" Suddenly, I

was on my feet pulling the bag away from him. The guard behind me grabbed my left arm and twisted it sharply until I screamed with pain. "Stop, please," I begged, but he held me in place.

The room fell into a tense silence until the old man signaled my release with the wave of a feeble hand. I fell back into the chair, massaging my already bruised arm and shoulder.

"You want to catch me like the cat and the mouse, no?" Said my uncle. "I think I know you." He shook a scolding finger at me. "You are with the Jews of *El Alef.*"

"*¡La Maestra!*" scoffed Nico. "*Beatriz Pérez-Alvarez.* She has a name, just like everyone."

"That Jew husband of hers was a Communist, and the son, too!" Said the old man. "You will not dance that tango like all the putas. You are not a Jew! Let the Jews go to those *milongas!*" He shouted.

"*Padre,*" said Nico, "calm yourself."

"No time for calm, *hijo,*" he said. "The Montoneros and their leftist *compatriotas* want to take over the government! They are kidnapping and killing generals!"

In his mind he seemed to have fallen two decades back in time. Though my first instinct was to defend the character of Juan Alvarez, I had a much bigger concern. What would become of me? Would Esteban follow an order to kill me? Or would he just kill me of his own volition to protect his Father?

"Tío, it is 2004," I said, "I've come here to find you for Tía Leti. She is dying and she wants to hear your voice, or see you. I have a lot of family photos. I could go home, and bring them to you on another day. Maybe we could call Leti and you could talk to her. I understand, you thought I was some kind of enemy, and that's why you've treated me so badly. But we can forget that. I'll bring the other photos, and we will call Leti."

This sent him into a fit of laughter that provoked more coughing. He took small swallows of the juice until his windpipe cleared. "So, you want me to let you go back to Buenos Aires, *sobrina?*" he said, apparently lucid. "You want to bring me photos?"

"Yes. Obviously, I did not know I would be meeting you, Tío," I said, glaring at Nico, "I thought I was going to your grave."

"Yes, you could return," he feigned pleasantness, "and you can bring your friends. Those peoples from *El Alef?* How about Paco Rosental? You want to bring Paco Rosental for dinner? And some of his friends from CELS? We could invite the director of the Wiesenthal Center, also. And Nico could sing a few tangos, heh Nico?"

Nico sneered in response to the obvious farce.

"Then your old *tío* can learn the tango with you from the Jews *before they take me to jail!*" His voice had built slowly in volume until he blasted me with that final "jail".

"Now you're being ridiculous," I said.

"Ridiculous?" He banged his open hand on the desk. "No, no, my dear, you are the ridiculous one. Why do I want family photos? You think I love those people who sent me away? That father who spit on me every day of my life? Those others who never fought for me? And now you, the last one, who leads those *marranos* to me!"

"No one but *abuelo*. . ."

"*¡QUIETA, mentirosa!*" he shouted, his fist smashing the photos on the desk.

"Oh! You don't want *mentiras* from her," shouted Nico suddenly, "but you didn't mind lying to *me!*" He stood over the only father he'd ever known, red-faced to the tips of his ears. "Why did you use me, *Padre?* Why did you lie to *me?* Why didn't you tell me that all the information you wanted about her was for you, not for some old priest who needed a favor? You didn't trust me? You made a fool of me!"

Esteban took a defensive position behind the old man, and just when I thought Nico was going to lunge for him, he turned away hitting the shutter frame with the heel of his hand. Outside the window I saw trees swaying in a blustery wind. In the blue sky above cumulonimbus clusters rolled past, as if cued to the turbulence of this interior.

"How stupid I was to believe you!" muttered Nico.

"You are too soft of the women," Zorrilla said, dismissing his son's anguish. "She is a beautiful woman. You want her. So *Padre's* secret is a present you make to her, then she will like you. Maybe she will *love* you." After a lifetime of devotion the old man was mocking Nico, transforming his strength, his winning way with women, into his greatest fault and weakness.

"You think I want her?" Nico came at me. "She used me," he said grabbing me suddenly by my hair and nearly lifting me off the seat. I let out a yelp and tried to support myself on the arms of the chair.

"Stop!" I yelled, and he shoved me forcefully back into the seat.

The old man laughed. "Now she won't tell you anything," he said. "*We* will have to get the information without you."

This sounded very bad. "What information?" I asked. "I don't have any information. What can you imagine I know?"

"Who was in that cemetery? Who *followed* you from the cemetery?"

"I don't know, Tío. Honestly, I don't know."

"*Esteban!*" Zorrilla spoke to him under his breath and Esteban went to the door to signal someone in the hall. Two tall hooded guards entered marching toward me. I looked to Nico, but he was staring out the window.

They lifted me by my arms.

"*Llevala al sótano,*" said Zorrilla.

"*¿Sótano?* Not again, no! Please. Terrible things have happened in that basement, I can smell them. Please! Tío!" I tried dragging my feet but it was no use, they easily lifted me and carried me to the doorway where I saw a whole long line of them against the wall, tall ominous creatures in black peaked hoods, headless eyes peering out from behind a cloth wall of anonymity.

"Tío, please, I have no idea where I am. You can drive me back and leave me somewhere in Buenos Aires with a few pesos for cab fare, and this whole thing will be over."

"It is not so easy, my dear," he said. "You know I am alive."

"They already know you're alive," I said, stupidly. The words caught in my teeth.

"Who knows I'm alive?" As the old man came toward me, the

smell of him made me gag. He grabbed my face. "Who knows I am alive?" he demanded.

"I, uh, I don't know." I started to cry.

"*¡La capucha!*" he commanded, and a hood was yanked forcefully over my head from behind.

"Nico!" I tried appealing to the only person who could possibly help me, but my appeal dissolved with no response.

The whining descent of the elevator expressed my waning spirit. I wanted to keep fighting, but I knew I was up against the same force that had destroyed Carmina and thousands like her. Zorrilla wanted to know who had followed us from the cemetery, and he'd use all his power to get the answer.

In the basement, they yanked off the hood and threw me into the cell. With the clang of keys and the shuffle of footsteps I adapted again to the confinement, and the tormenting companionship of that infernal blinking tube. "Well," I said to myself, "you probably won't have to put up with this much longer."

CHAPTER THIRTY-ONE

Thrown again into the cavernous darkness, I knew, at least, that the eleven fifteen illuminated on my wrist was a.m. I closed my eyes and leaned against the stone wall slowly relinquishing my weight to gravity. If I'd had a pencil I might have written and drawn pictures on those stones. I might have left some evidence of this nightmare, of my presence. Maybe one day it would have been uncovered, proof of my demise, by those discovering this savage hole in the innocent earth.

It didn't take long for that desire to take hold of me, and I began feeling frantically for a flat bit of rock face where I could scratch a word or image with my nails or maybe a button. I rubbed my fingertips along the rough stones until I found a smooth section of rock. It wasn't very wide, but as I followed it, I reckoned to have seven or eight inches of space. Then suddenly my fingers stopped. Letters. Letters were already etched into this stone. Of course, I thought, there must have been so many before me, and they had had the same desire to leave their mark. They wanted to be remembered. And here was I to remember them.

The light from my watch was too dull to read the letters, so I tried with my fingertips to read what I quickly named as the Braille of the Forgotten. I expected names and dates, maybe even messages. But as I began to spell them out the letters revealed a strange prayer. "D. E. J. E. M. E." Space "A. M. A. R." Space. "D. E. N. U. E. V. O." There the shelf ended abruptly, and though I felt for more on the surrounding stones, there was no more.

"*Dejeme amar de nuevo.*" "Let me love again."

I let it sink into me. How long had someone sat here on this very spot where fear and bitterness gnaw away at the human heart? Was she alone? Or he. And what had given such hope to imagine a life beyond this place where being is reduced to breathing in and breathing out? The author must have been a saint, I concluded, to rise to such a noble prayer.

The face of Carmina Perraza came to me. Did she love again after her ordeal? She loved Jesus Christ, at least she attached herself so much to him that his body had been worn smooth by her hunger to love and trust him. It seemed to me that though she appeared to have her life back, she was still begging Christ to save her every day.

Dejeme amar de nuevo. It made me realize how bitter I'd become since my divorce. I still loved my aunt, of course, and that love had brought me to Argentina. I loved my family, and certainly my son. But the rest of the world? I certainly was afraid to love Luis.

"Let me love again." As I said it aloud it sounded like a Buddhist koan, a spiritual riddle like, *What is the sound of one hand clapping?* Now, I had my very own koan: *Dejeme amar de nuevo.* Could I learn how to do it, I wondered, and more challenging at the moment, would I ever get back into the world to try. I started to doze off, fatigue exacerbated by my challenging discovery.

My stomach groaned with a vacuous pain and beyond my longing for home, my brain seemed incapable of organized thought. Soon in my head I began to hear tango music. Which one was it? Oh, it was, appropriately, *Mi Dolor*, a tango that overcomes its title with an elegant and hopeful melody. As I listened, it carried me, ascending the nautilus-like chamber of the stairway at La Ideal. Anita greeted me with a kiss on the cheek. "So good to see you," she said. On the way to my seat I smiled at the women posed like flowers competing for the attention of bees. Each one coiffed and blushed, lipsticked, and mascara-ed. Flushed bosoms and smooth fleshy legs shone alluringly between the colorful petals of blouses and skirts. All fluttered seductively in the soft breeze of the fans.

Seated at my own table, I watched the flashy young men whose needy egos out-performed their understanding of the dance. Then I gazed at the refined tangos of the elders, those well-dressed gentlemen cherishing the women in their embrace. In my tango shoes I felt the grace of my body, the balanced alignment of my shoulders and hips, and the elegant extension of my spine. My partner opened his arms and I stepped into the circle of his embrace. We moved in perfect synchronization, the intricate mechanics of our patterns imperceptible even to me. I languished in the reverie of our dance until suddenly the music stopped. I felt my cheek pressed against the cold hard stone. I was back, again, awake in the vacant isolation of this constant night.

I pushed my mind to keep hold of the dream. Who was he, I wondered, that faceless partner whose embrace had given me solace for those few moments? I knew if I could keep a mental hold on him, he might fill this misery with what *La Maestra* would call *tango dharma*. He could be the accumulated energies of the many partners who had taught me the *dharma* in those minutes between dances. "Dancing tango is like polishing silver," I remembered him saying, "each time you dance a tango, it becomes more lustrous. And each day you polish a different part of it. You discover a phrase played by the piano, or a pattern of the *bandoneon*. You dance it in a way that you've never danced it before. So it is always new." If I replaced the word *tango* with *life*, I thought, maybe I could find a way to love every day, even if I didn't have many days left. Even if they killed me, my soul could receive each breath with love. The meditation, led me back to the refrain of *Mi Dolor*. I played it over and over until it led me back to sleep.

I woke with the stench of death in my nostrils. The infernal flickering of that fading fluorescent in the corner teased me with mottled sight. I rubbed my hands together briskly hoping to create some warmth, and the sound echoed strangely throughout the cave. I felt agitated, and wished again for a pencil. Drawing always calmed me. Then I remembered reading about elephants drawing in the dust of their zoo enclosures with the tip of their trunks. So, inspired by pachyderms, I decided to use my fingers as pencils and the whole floor as my canvas.

I started on the side closest to the fluorescent. In that meager light, I used the row of bars for alignment, and started to write my son's name in the dust. I remembered telling Nico that David's heart is my ultimate home. So I wrote it over and over and over, feeling the love that never diminishes. As I wrote, I spoke his name as if it were a mantra of protection: "Davidavidavidavidavidavid." I made a whole border of David's around the cell. Then, inside that, I drew a border of climbing roses, like those on the walls of the patio at *El Alef*. I couldn't see them, of course, but as I drew, I imagined that the thorns could come to life and wound anyone who dared come near me. The roses occupied me for at least an hour, and when I finished them, I sat cross-legged in the center of the space. "This," I declared, "is my sacred space." I etched a circle in the dust and wrote my own name around me with letters that had big thorns. I sat there, cross-legged focusing my breath, and pictured myself perched, like one of *La Maestra's* canaries. I pretended that the bars, like the thorns, were really there to protect me.

Thinking of *El Alef*, I remembered *La Maestra's* lesson about *duende*. Now I had my very own encounter with dark spirits. In my mind I heard her say, "Be tango-hearted, Raquel. Live daringly from the depth of your tigress heart." I knew then that I had to acknowledge my fear and sink into it, in order to transcend it. I could come through to the other side of fear with courage, even to my death.

The rattle of keys sent a hot stroke of fear searing across my belly. Tears patterned like rain on my blouse and coat. I went through my pockets to look for a tissue, and came upon the photo of Osvaldo Pugliese. I knew there was no way that a 1950's tango composer could move the energy of the universe in 2004, but feeling so desperately alone, I said a little prayer asking him for the courage to sustain me. I kissed the picture, then tucked it back into my pocket. Suddenly the thought of Alfonso, made me smile. There, I thought, I needed a friend and Pugliese brought him to me, at least in memory.

The racket of keys got louder as two *penitentes* appeared at my cell. I saw them now as cowards more than evil wizards. Even when they trespassed beyond the inscribed borders of my cell and proved themselves impervious to my thorns, even when they grabbed me again by my bruised arms, and pulled a black hood over my head, I realized that I'd adapted to their routine brutality. "Oh, this again," said a voice within me. This time, though, they had defiled my space and I felt angry. Rebelliously I pushed against them as they threw me onto the bars and pulled my arms behind me cutting into my wrists with sharp metal handcuffs.

"Alright, I'll come with you," I grumbled, "you don't need the *esposas. ¡No se necesita esposas!*" They were unresponsive, and shoved me out of the cell.

Carmina Perraza flashed through my mind, again, and I prayed for her strength, as though she were the muse of survival.

We walked past the gate then, something was different. They didn't take me to the elevator. The change in course was disorienting and I listened for clues, anything to help me adjust. They had unlocked a door I didn't recognize, and we walked down what seemed to be a wide corridor on the basement level. The hood they'd put over my head was thicker than the last one so I could see no shadows or shapes. The floor felt hard and cold, like cement. My heart pounded so loudly that my whole body quivered from its increasing pulse. When we stopped, I heard the guard on the left open a door. They shoved me through it and pushed me down onto a chair. I heard them leave and shut the door. The air reeked of mildew, and it seemed even colder than the dungeon, though I didn't think that was possible. The cold metal structure of the chair told me it wasn't built for human comfort.

Once the guards had gone I could hear my breathing as that of a strangely warm-blooded creature surviving the threatening arctic temperature of the environment. Then, the dogs. I could hear the dogs barking in the distance. I saw them in my mind, lunging viciously toward me as they'd done that first night. That night. I had been free, standing out in the open air, I thought. Yes, I had been free.

Suddenly, the door opened and shut again sharply infusing the air with the aroma of cologne and tobacco. It was Nico, but which Nico? Was it the handsome, gentle man who'd fed me succulent Arabic delicacies, or the furious one who'd grabbed my hair as if to pull it from my scalp? With his hands on my shoulders he lifted me off the chair and turned me away from him. He untied the hood, then, turned me again toward him. A sour vapor of whiskey enveloped me. Slowly he lifted the hood, and I squinted under a harsh fluorescent glare from overhead. I would not look at him.

"How are you?" he asked ominously.

"Oh," I said, "never better."

"I brought you something," he said, and stepped aside. I saw a medical examining table with stirrups and a medical tray table beside it. He picked up one of two white towels from the tray table and brought it to me. I could see it was made of thread bare cotton, and damp.

"I thought you might like to wash off some of the dirt from that dusty cell," he said in an intimate whisper.

"That's a great idea," I said. "Unlock these handcuffs."

"Oh," he said, "you know, they didn't give me the key to those. I can do it for you. I can be gentle."

He swiped the damp towel upward from my neck toward my face, then across my forehead. The fabric was rough, as if it had been starched. Every gesture scratched my skin.

"What a beautiful face you have," he said, dragging the towel across my cheeks. Then he placed it lengthwise behind my neck, and holding onto both sides of it, pulled me into him until our mouths came together. I tried to keep my lips closed, but he pressed the fullness of his mouth into mine and I felt his tongue probe past my lips. Then with his fingers he pried my teeth apart and thrust his tongue into my mouth. His nails cut into the nape of my neck as he grabbed me tightly with his left hand. He tried then to wipe the towel across my chest, pushing inside my coat and blouse. "This will not do," he said. "How can I bathe you with your clothes on?"

"You don't have to bathe me," I said, quickly. "I can do it."

"Tsk, tsk, tsk," he made a clicking noise inside his mouth, then tossed the towel over his arm, and unbuttoned my coat and my blouse, pushing them both down my arms. Despite the cold, I felt sweat drip from my armpits. Reaching in behind me he unclasped my bra and pulled it off my shoulders then thrust his groin into me, letting me feel his arousal. I didn't dare struggle or try to break free fearing any movement might ignite both anger and passion.

"Such beautiful breasts," he said, scraping the towel repeatedly over my nipples.

"I don't know who followed us from the cemetery, Nico," I said.

He stepped around behind me and grasped my neck spreading the fingers of his left hand like a bass fiddle player at my throat. I felt the pressure of his fingers on my larynx. "That is not true, Raquel," he whispered. His mouth nuzzled into my ear as he continued to rubbed harder with the rough towel across my breasts. "Father needs to know who it was," he whispered again. "He's not completely in his right mind, you know. So I thought I would give you one last opportunity to tell me, rather than letting one of the 'professionals' from the *Guardia* work on you."

"Work on me?"

"Oh yes, they are very skilled at getting information," he said, softly. "But they make such a mess."

Tears streamed down my face and onto the back of his hand.

"Oh, look," he said, noticing the dampness on his skin, "tears!"

"What makes you think I know who was following us?"

Suddenly he pulled the towel around my neck and twisted it tightly.

"You think I'm stupid?" he barked into my face. "DO YOU?"

"No, of course not."

"Then do not insult my intelligence!"

He cupped my left breast in his hand. "Such a beautiful body," he cooed, "you don't want to let those barbarians take possession of this body, Raquel. Look at their tools."

With the towel twisted around my neck he shoved me toward the examining table and placed me between the stirrups facing him. Then he lifted the other white cloth off the tray to his immediate right. A menacing assortment of instruments had been laid out: a speculum, scalpels, hemostats, and syringes.

"You don't want those men to use these things on you, do you?" he said. "I'll tell you a secret, they're not medically trained technicians! And most of them hate women." He laughed and pushed against me. Looking into my eyes, he twisted the towel around my throat again. I felt him unbuttoning my slacks.

"You are going to tell me who was following us." He pushed my slacks to the floor. "You're too short," he said angrily. "Sit on the table."

Apparently I didn't move quickly enough because I remember that he yanked up on the towel. I must have blacked out for a moment because the next thing I remember, I was on the table, and his hands were pulling off my panties.

"What beautiful underwear. Raquel, I think this is what you wanted all along. Didn't you?"

I was silent.

"Didn't you?!" His face twisted into a sneer. "Say it, bitch! Tell me, you wanted this all along."

"No," I said.

"You are a tease, then, because I've been getting signals. And I bet you wanted it just like this."

While he was undoing his pants, he started to bite my shoulders, pretending to make love to me. But the bites became stronger and deeper until he actually broke the skin, and I yelped in pain.

"Father was right, you know, I do want you," he said. He was looking into my eyes, his lips brushing against my face as he spoke. "I've wanted you since the first time I saw you. But I thought it would be more fun to charm you than to conquer you by force. But you know what? This is going to be so much more . . . satisfying."

"Please, Nico, how can I tell you what I don't know?"

"Shut up!" he barked, and slapped me hard across the face with his open hand.

Another yelp flew out of me.

"I didn't want to hurt you, you know," he said, "but now you've made me mad. You're making a fool of me in front of Father and the whole *Guardia*. That prig Esteban thinks he knows so much. I bet the fucker has never even been with a woman. You *will* tell me who was in that car because you *do* know who it was."

I worried about Paco and his family, even Carla, and his grandchildren. His whole family could be in danger if I confessed his name. And I couldn't mention Luis. I wouldn't. No matter what they did to me.

"A car came into the cemetery behind us," he said, and without warning he hit me again, this time with the back of his hand. I felt his ring cut my lip as it flew across my mouth. Then, using the twisted towel around my neck he positioned me and thrust into me. I fought to catch my breath, and by pure instinct I struggled against him.

"Please Nico, I can't believe you're doing this," I said. "Stop! You're going to break my arms." They were caught underneath me, the cuffs cutting into my skin. My shoulders felt like they could be pulled right out of the sockets.

He was silent, staring into my eyes and pushing himself deeper into me. Then I saw him pick up something from the tray.

"Please don't do this," I cried.

He spit at me, and held up a scalpel. I closed my eyes.

"Open your eyes," he demanded. "If you don't open your eyes I'm going to cut right into your face. Here, feel the blade."

I felt the sharp steel against my cheek and opened my eyes.

"That's better. I love to look into those big brown eyes," he said, pushing into me again.

But my eyes rolled up toward the ceiling then, and my mind, my whole being, seemed to be tangled in the intricate spider webs woven into the corners of the overhead fluorescent light fixture. I became entranced by the way it had been screwed into the ceiling in nine places, with little bolts and a Phillip's head screwdriver. The towel twisted tighter around my neck and I remember taking tiny breaths. I wanted to stay on the ceiling, woven into those gentle spider webs.

"Tell me, *puta*," he said, "or things are going to get much worse. I can make you my property, you know. That *boludo* Luis won't even want you anymore once you have my initials carved into you."

"Stop it!" I screamed. I watched him place the scalpel onto my breast. He stared into my eyes as though I were the dark abyss of his own soul. His teeth clenched, and sweat trickled down his forehead. As he rolled and pushed into me again I felt the force of the blade on my flesh.

"Who was it?" he demanded. "Was that your Luis? Was he there?"

The blade stung my skin as he drew the first line of what I had to presume would be an N. I bit my lower lip until the taste of blood crossed my tongue. I knew he was right. He or someone else would keep escalating the torture even to the point of killing me. I tried to take courage from the fact that men like Nico and Zorrilla could no longer seek vengeance inconsequentially. The government wasn't behind these people anymore, I told myself. Paco and his family could be protected.

He dug the blade again for the next line, a diagonal. Thank God 'N' was such a concise letter, I thought. But he cut deeper this time and I could feel blood trickling down my breast.

"CELS," I whimpered.

"Rosental?" he demanded with the blade set to cut again.

I didn't say anything.

"WAS IT ROSENTAL?"

"I don't know."

He twisted the towel and turned it toward him like a plumber tightening a wrench around a pipe. I felt the skin on my neck burn and break under the friction of the starched cotton. He pressed down again on the blade.

"WAS IT ROSENTAL?" he demanded.

"Yes," I exhaled the word. "Yes." I began to sob. Choked by his grip, my head throbbed.

"That wasn't so hard, was it?" he said. I feared he would press me next about Paco's sidekick, but he didn't. Instead he followed through with the final cut to complete his mark, his N was branded into my flesh. Whether or not he'd guessed that Luis had been at the cemetery, the punishment seemed to have gained importance over the facts.

"There," he said, "the first letter is enough for now." He threw the scalpel across the room with a grin, and grabbing my hair in his right hand, climbed on top of me. I refused to give him the satisfaction of knowing the pain inflicted by the weight of him. He pushed and pushed again, grunting and groaning with plea-sure. Then he started whispering and murmuring. "Oh, baby, you know just how to do it." "Yeah Baby, fuck me real good." The pretense of my involvement was, I presumed, intended to shame me all the more. It worked.

Finally he shook and quivered and pulled my body tightly into his. I swiped away the tears, mucous, and sweat across his shirt. He pulled back, and looked at the smear on the fabric, then laughed victoriously. "Maybe they can find us a more comfortable place next time. I'm going to want a lot more of you, Raquel."

He pulled up his pants, zipped and buttoned them. Then went into a pocket. "Oh, look what I found," he said. He held up a key for the handcuffs, put his arms around me again and unlocked them. The cuts on my breast were bleeding. I was glad to see they had stained his shirt with my blood. I grimaced, and suddenly he grabbed my whole face in his hand, pinching it in his grip. "What's the matter," he said, "it wasn't good for you? Well, I promise to get better with practice." He pushed me back against the table. "Get your clothes on, *puta*. Or maybe I ought to call in the *Guardia Sagrada* to see you that way." He laughed, tucking in his shirt.

The towel that had been so lethal in his hands lay flaccid around my shoulders as I drew up my underwear and my slacks. I saw that the bloody lacerations around my wrists stained the cuffs of my sleeves. I managed to clasp my bra, tuck the towel over my chest, and button my blouse. Then, I pulled my jacket close around my body, buttoned it to the collar and tightened the belt around my waist.

Just as I thought he was leaving he turned to me again. "Come here," he said, grabbing me by the neck. He pulled me into his chest to cuff my hands behind me again. Then he kissed me as if we'd come home from a date. "Ooh, your lips are a little swollen and bloody," he said, "very sexy! *Chau, Tesoro.*" He slammed the door behind him. "Guardia!" I heard him shout, signaling that he was through with me.

The guards arrived momentarily, as if they could have been nearby, listening. They yanked the hood over my head, and marched me back to my cell. I couldn't understand the banter from beneath their hoods. But as they left me there, mercifully unfettered, their laughter lingered as a final humiliation.

I washed my face with tears, and carefully, I explored the geography of my wounds with my fingertips. There were swollen mounds, cuts, and scabs forming even in places I couldn't reach. Oddly, I felt no pain. Instead, a merciful numbness had set in. I sat there, lost in the wavelike rhythm of my breath. Maybe I slept, because I remember a moment of awakening. I crawled to the perimeter of my cell where it had been so violently trespassed and, though I could hardly see, I rewrote David's name across the threshold. Then I repaired the roses, making the vines stronger and thicker, and the thorns bigger. Crawling back to the center I redrew a circle around myself, then sat there rocking. Amazingly, all my loved ones arrived to surround me. I saw Tía Leti, healthy as she'd been on her sixtieth birthday. David sat beside me, along with Marta and my little goddaughter, Claudia. And there was Luis, La Maestra, Doña Nina, Paco, Carolina, and Alfonso. "I am not alone," I whispered, "I am not alone. Iamnotalone Iamnotalone Iamnotalone Iamnotalone."

CHAPTER THIRTY-TWO

I sat slumped over, cross-legged in the center of the cell, my eyes shut, more from swelling than choice. It may sound ridiculous, but my mind wrestled with plans to outsmart my captors into releasing me. I'd given them what they wanted. Maybe, if I caught my uncle at a good moment, he might summon some compassion if I told him about my son. I couldn't leave David motherless. I couldn't miss his graduation, his wedding, his children. Surely Tío Zorrilla would have compassion for the bond between a mother and her son. I would remind him of his bond with his own mother, hoping he could remember it. Then it came to me and I had just enough hope to ask it, to pray it, *Dejeme amar de nuevo.*

I tried to check the time, but my left eye was nearly swollen shut and the right had little vision. I could see the little light, but if I hadn't seen the numbers before, I wouldn't even know they existed. Trying to focus made me dizzy, so I lay my head on the ground and closed my eyes before the strobe affect of that fucking flickering fluorescent made me puke. Instinctively, I placed my hand to my mouth and discovered again the crusted cuts and swelling bulges. Even licking my lips was painful, and a sudden vanity swept through me as I hoped Luis would not see me like this. Even if they kill me, I thought, I want him to remember me pretty. But then my thoughts turned to worry about his injuries from the cemetery, or worse if he'd been in the car behind us on the highway. Then, the worst thought of all came to me: what if Nico was right? What if I lived through this, and Luis rejected me because of the rape? Would he see that N scarred into my breast and feel the revulsion I felt myself? Tears seeped out of my eyes. The future was too vast a concept to consider. I had to focus on the immediate challenge: survival.

I felt myself growing weaker. I knew that if they didn't feed me soon, or give me water, I could die before my uncle. I was losing my ability to hold a thought. I'd lost the strength to lift myself. Body and spirit, I seemed polluted by the grotesque stench and purpose of my surroundings. Thinking exhausted me. I wanted to pray, but Zorrilla and the *Guardia* had kidnapped God and misappropriated everything holy. Slowly I dissolved into sleep.

Keys. I was sure I'd heard keys. Yes. They were getting closer. The guards were opening my cell. Without lifting my head, I watched their tall ghoulish shapes and the huge shoes that kicked up dust with every step. As the first guard entered the cell, I began to shake uncontrollably. I watched him set down a little stool, and walk out. Another guard came, set down a small table, and left the cell open. What fiendish thing were they up to, I wondered. In a minute a third guard came in with a tray of something steaming.

"*Guiso,*" he said.

The word was muffled by his hood, but it was the sweetest word I'd heard in days, "stew". I lifted my head and saw that there was even a spoon and a napkin on the tray. They locked the cell again, and left.

I crawled to the table and lifted myself slowly. Even in this putrid atmosphere, the aroma of stew was intoxicating. I held my hand over the bowl to test my faculties. My palm grew warm and damp with steam. I wasn't dreaming. I lifted the spoon and dipped it into the broth. It was dense with what appeared to be vegetables and meat. I bolstered myself by pushing the stool against the bars, then propped up my upper body, leaning on the stool. I was dizzy, but managed to open my mouth just wide enough to navigate a spoonful into the narrow space between my lips. I couldn't taste poison or drugs. Actually, no matter what was in it, I had to eat it.

Tears burned slow lines down my face as the warm nourishment sank into me. I placed another spoonful carefully into my mouth, and goose bumps rose up and down my arms. All my life food had been defined by calories and fat grams. I had weighed, calculated, and exercised in a lifetime obsession with body weight. This bowl of stew was the first thing I'd ever eaten that taught me that food is actually about survival. Gratitude didn't even come close to defining my reverence for the meal. I dabbed gingerly with the napkin at the broth and tears dripping from my chin.

Suddenly, I heard voices beyond the wooden door. It was Nico's voice. Was he coming for me? I could throw the hot *guiso* into his face. The wooden door opened and I heard him swearing. I dragged myself to the back corner of my cell, and pretended to be unconscious.

"*¡Boludo!*" he shouted. It sounded like a scuffle. The key went into the gate lock. Nico was talking so fast I could hardly keep up with him. He seemed to be offering a bribe."*¡No me agarres! ¡Hijo de puta!*" He swore.

They were outside my cell. Through the slits of my swollen lids I saw four guards wrestling with Nico. The flickering fluorescent reflected off of his handcuffs. I coughed from the dust set free by their tussle.

"*¡Puta!*" he yelled at me.

They shoved him into the cell next to me with such force that he landed on the ground with a thud. All four stood over him, their arms crossed victoriously.

"*Finalmente, te tengo.*" I recognized Esteban's voice, pleased that he had Nico right where he wanted him.

"*¡Soltame, carajo!*" yelled Nico, trying to lift himself.

It was strange to hear laughter coming from behind the hoods, but Esteban and his compatriots were clearly enjoying the moment. In fact, Esteban lifted that tall hood off his head and despite the lighting and limitations in my vision, I recognized the aged version of the other young man in the graduation photo.

"Leave it to you to abuse this lady," said Esteban. "I knew someday the old man would see you for the psychopath you are."

"You don't give a damn about this one," said Nico, tossing his head in my direction. "You're still pissed about Eugenia. You thought she was so pure." Now Nico was laughing, and in the dim light I could see an expression like thunder come across Esteban's face.

"Shut up!" He yelled.

But Nico kept laughing. "You're still mad that I got to her first! But I can tell you, someone else had been there before me!" His sour laughter echoed off the stones.

"Shut up," yelled Esteban, putting his foot on Nico's chest. But Nico wouldn't quit, and when he started to say the next thing, Esteban kicked him right across the face. Nico was thrown in my direction by the blow, but his body ricocheted off the bars and rolled back and Esteban kicked him again in the torso. Then I heard him say something to the other guards, and one of them took the cuffs off of Nico who immediately tried to stand up. But before he could, I heard the bone to flesh crack of a punch. Then another, and another, with escalating grunts. Without a single word, they kicked Nico back and forth, beating him mercilessly. I lost sight of the prisoner as they surrounded him, but I don't think he got in even a single blow. When the punching and kicking stopped, they dusted themselves off, and locked the cell behind them. Nico lay silent and motionless.

Why did they have to put him next to me, I thought. I stayed in the farthest corner from him where I knew he couldn't reach me. I hoped he was locked up because of what he'd done to me, but that seemed unlikely. I watched him suspiciously, and when I felt certain he was unconscious I brought the bowl of stew back to the corner with me where I could eat it, and keep an eye on him. He didn't move, and after the stew, the pull of gravity overcame me as well. Slumped against the bars and stone, I looked at my watch, but couldn't make out the time. It was simply now.

The rattling keys and shuffling of the *Guardia* awakened me again. This time they dropped a blanket at my feet, and took the empty bowl. One of them brought a pitcher of water and a glass. When they'd gone out of sight I lunged for the blanket. It might have had bugs, I suppose, but it was the most beautiful blanket I'd ever seen. In my head I mused that Zorrilla had had a call from Amnesty International. I didn't think compassion could have survived in this environment, but it was coming from somewhere.

I wrapped the blanket around me, poured some water into the glass and retreated to my safe corner, accepting the possibility that with this water, like the last, I could be drugged again. Nico started groaning, and crawled slowly on his belly toward the bars on my side of his cell.

"Maybe your old uncle isn't such a demon, after all," he mumbled.

I didn't respond.

"Not since he thought I was becoming a Communist have I seen him so angry." He tried to laugh, but it made him cough. He was obviously in pain. "Well, I told him, 'you wanted the information, and you doubted my ability to get it out of her.' I never imagined he'd object to certain *types* of force." He tried to lift himself with the bars but the attempt must have exacerbated his injuries because he fell back down. "You should have heard him," he said, hoarsely. "First, he thought I just hit you; that was okay. But once I told him I'd fucked you, he went berserk. I tried to tell him that you liked it, but he started yelling, then coughing, and spewing spit all over the place." He shifted positions, wincing with every movement. "I said, 'Hey, there's no commandment against rape.' That's when he hit me, for the first time in my life. I didn't think he had it in him." He propped himself up on one elbow, and pulled a crushed pack of cigarettes from his shirt pocket. "He's not going to leave me here. He's just teaching me a lesson." His breathing and speech were labored, but he lit up anyway. "They beat me in the orphanage all the time. Esteban is still pissed off cause I fucked his girlfriend before him." He grinned, and took a painful drag of the cigarette coughing back the smoke. "They'll let me out of here soon," he said. "Very soon. You'll see."

CHAPTER THIRTY-THREE

At least an hour passed before there was another noise at the gate. I heard labored breathing, and the rattling of keys. I recognized the heavy shuffling steps of Zorrilla as he approached.

"*Abuela*," he whispered. "*Abuela.*"

He was at the door of my cell.

"*¡Abuela!*"

I sat up slowly, bringing my face into the flickering gray light.

"*¡Ay, te lastimó, Abuela!*" He exclaimed. I was surprised he could see my wounds. His trembling old hand struggled to fit the key in the lock, and once accomplished he rested a moment hanging on the bars. Then he took one laborious step after another until he slowly came close enough to survey my bruises in the dim light. I would not have imagined him capable of the expression that came across his face. It conveyed genuine contrition.

"*Sí, me lastimó.*" I said playing the grandmother. "He hurt me."

"*Lo siento, Abuela. Perdoname,*" he whispered. He stunk of acetone and alcohol.

"*¿Para qué debo perdonarte?*" I asked. "*¿Qué hiciste, Mateo?*" What
did you do, seemed like the most all-encompassing question to ask.

"*Ay, Abuela,*" he said, "*ese chico, Nicolás, te violó buscando información
para mí.*"

Apparently his two worlds had merged into one. In his
world, Nico had raped his grandmother. He was Mateo again,
not Sebastián.

"*¿Algo más?*" I provoked him to review all the sins that
needed forgiving.

"*¿Más?*"

"*Sí. ¿En España?*"

"*En España yo fui soldado.*" His role as a soldier seemed to make
him proud.

"*Y mataste a mucha gente.*"

He was quiet. His mind wasn't good for much anymore, but I
felt certain that the indelible memory of brutality was in his body.
Perhaps it was the body's remorse that had plunged him into the
alcoholic ailment soon to take his life.

"*¿Te acuerdas esa mañana en Río Olvidado?*" I persisted, trying to take
him to the exact place where he'd killed Nina's father with the bayonet.

"*¿Río Olvidado?*"

"*Cerca de Jaen.*" I had to paint a vivid picture. "You were saying
mass, and you saw people in the back of your church."

"*¡Hijos del Diablo!*" he yelled hoarsely.

"Tell me what you did, Mateo!"

"I stop the mass, and tell the peoples the devils are in the back of the church. The mens chase them. I grab my rifle, but the bayonet comes off in my hand, so I pick it up and I run out. We catch them and we kill them. In the name of Our Lord we killed those heretics." He made the sign of the cross, as if the memory filled him with honor.

"You killed with your bayonet?"

"Yes! With the swift hand of God, I killed with the bayonet." He thrust his right fist into the air, stabbing it over and over. "*Soy soldado de Jesús, y de la patria. Maté a mucha gente.¡A la Gloria!*"

"*¿Y aquí en Argentina?*"

His expression changed. He squinted. Nico stirred in his cell. I hoped he wouldn't come to and shake the old man out of his current identity.

"*Qué hiciste aquí. Conozco a una mujer que se llama Carmina Perraza.*"

"*¡Esa mujer! Sí, me acuerdo, era hermana de un Montonero, pero no era judia,*" he said, shaking his head. His memory was impressive, he remembered that Carmina was not Jewish, but he persisted in thinking that she was the sister of a Montonero.

"*¿Y tuviste qué torturarla para obtener información?*" I needed to know, did he remember torturing her?

"*Sí, por supuesto,*" he said, nodding matter-of-factly. "We try to take the devil from her."

I'd known what he'd done, so why did this confession matter to me?

"*Y me acuerdo que tenía una hija,*" he said, recalling the details.

"Yes, she had a daughter," I said, "four years old."

"*Tuve que torturala tambien, enfrente de su madre, eso sí, me dolió.*"

Carmina hadn't told us that he'd forced her to watch as he had tortured her little girl. I shook my head regretting that I had wanted to prove his innocence when his brutality had been even worse than I thought.

"How many did you torture, Mateo?"

"*Habían muchos,*" he said. "and some were not even Jews. Please, forgive me, *Abuela.*"

"*No te puedo perdonar,*" I said, as loudly as possible. My voice echoed through the hollow chamber of the cave. "*No.*" Weakness gripped me but I leaned against the bars for support and stood up. The old man was a swaying blur, but I didn't know if I was moving or he was. Nico stirred in the cell.

"*Abuela,*" said Mateo, falling to his knees. "*Tuve que torturarlos.*" He started sobbing. He repeated himself over and over, one moment in tears, the next in a calm explanatory tone. "*Tenía que encontrar los judíos,* find the Jews, kill the Jews, and *los Comunistas, los anarquistas.* They are hidden, *escondieron su identidad,* I have to torture *para saber la verdad.* It's the work of the Lord, *del Señor, el trabajo de La Inquisición.*"

Was it possible that a man living in 2004 could believe that The Inquisition continues to do God's work?

"Stop crying!" I scolded. "Why did you change your name?"

"To save my life, *Abuela,*" he said. "Many Spaniards want

to kill me. I have always a guard, many threats. General Sánchez-Trujillo arrange my transfer. He also change my name, and Mateo disappears."

I took a deep breath. I was finally getting the answers I needed. The philosophy and brutality of the Inquisitors and the Nazis had slithered into Argentina hidden under my uncle's vestments, and under his skin. Now, all that was left of him was the rhetoric and zeal of Anti-Semites and warmongers.

"*Padre*," said Nico, weakly.

"Shut up, Nico!" I shouted.

"What are you trying to do to him?" His voice was fading.

"*¿Como te puedo perdonar, Mateo?*" I said, ignoring Nico. "I cannot pardon you."

"*Padre*," said Nico, barely audible. "*Padre*, do not confess."

"*¿Abuela?*" The old man whined like a child who couldn't believe he'd be held accountable for his actions.

"Leave him alone," whispered Nico. "He's old and sick."

"He's been sick his whole life," I said.

"*Padre . . . .*"

"Shut up, Nico!" Adrenalin pumped through me, numbing my body and making me stronger than I'd imagined I could be.

"Who taught you this hatred?" I asked the old man. "*¿Quién te enseñó ese ódio?*"

"Stop . . ." said Nico, gasping for breath.

"*Padre Paolino y los padres, Abuela. Me enseñaron que los judíos mataron a Jesucristo.*" Bigotry had been engrained in him throughout his formation. Knowing he'd been taught such vile beliefs helped me see that his evil violence was not in our blood. If only my *abuela* had known that the old priest, *Padre* Paulino, was training him to hate, she could have saved him and all the victims who died by his hand.

"How can you say that all your killing has been God's work?" I said. "*No te puedo perdonar. Solamente El Señor te puede perdonar.* Only the Lord can forgive you. *Solamente El Señor, Mateo.*"

His old body slumped to the ground before me, cornering me against the cold stone and bars. Though I wanted to feel compassion for the boy he once was, revulsion overpowered sympathy. Tears ran from my eyes, though I had no sensation of weeping. I did the only thing I was free to do, I turned my back to him.

His weeping grew softer, and he became very quiet. "*¿El Señor me puede perdonar?*" He said. "*El Señor, sí, claro. El Señor.*"

I thought he was going to pray, so I turned toward him again, expecting to witness his contrition. "*Por supuesto, El Señor, Mateo,*" I began to say, but the next moments exploded so quickly, that to this day I cannot replay the correct sequence of events in my head. I remember the shape of him moving as he raised himself off the ground, and his right arm toward his head.

"*Señor,*" he said, "*perdóneme si he hecho algo malo.*"

"No!" yelped Nico in a painful howl that turned all my attention toward him. Then suddenly a deafening gunshot exploded and reverberated throughout the cavernous space. The body in front of me fell over like a big sack of potatoes.

I felt splattered with something that stung my face as it hit. Displaced dust billowed into my nostrils and throat. I covered my ears coughing and gagging, while the impact of the ricocheted gunshot echoed on and on and on.

"Tío?" I called out. He didn't respond. The smell of burning gunpowder overcame the stench of decay. I pushed against the ribs of the cell for support and dropped slowly to my knees pulling the blanket in front of my face for a protected breath.

The echo had not yet subsided when a thunderous rumble preceded a throng of guards flooding into the cavern. I pulled down the blanket just enough to see them arrive, flashlights ablaze, some guards without hoods. All at once they let out an enormous spontaneous gasp, as they discovered the body of their *Padre*. Then there were curses and epithets and cries of grief. I was paralyzed with fear. One of them cried out, "El Señor"! Suddenly I realized that he'd shot himself with the gun he'd been carrying since the Spanish Civil War. Who would have guessed that he still carried it with him? 'Only El Señor can forgive you,' I had said. In his delirium, Mateo might have thought I meant the gun.

I cowered absolutely still, afraid that one of them would shoot me in revenge. But they were busy crying and moaning. I opened the blanket just enough to survey the blurry scene. All hoods had been removed and with the increased light the frightening soldiers were revealed. Some of them were only boys. Esteban knelt over Zorrilla's body, and made the sign of the cross in the air. The rest all dropped to their knees. Together they created a single reverberating voice reciting The Our Father in Latin. Another guard rushed in with something in his hands. He pushed his way to the front and handed it to Esteban. I realized he was going to administer the last rites, Extreme Unction. Did this mean they thought I had shot him? I knew that any suggestion of suicide would have destroyed his standing in the Church, and condemned him to hell for eternity. Even if they didn't think I had shot him, it was likely that they would make it look like I did. Then, they'd just shoot me and no one would be the wiser. All I could do was stay frozen in place beneath the blanket.

Suddenly there was commotion upstairs. I heard scuffling, then a gunshot, and another. In another moment armed policemen stormed the scene nearly blinding me with their powerful flashlights. The shocked mourners froze like statues in a tableau.

Quickly the police took them one by one, shoving them against the walls, and handcuffing them. I released the blanket slowly and stood up so that the police would know I was there. I looked to Nico and saw him still sprawled on the floor, motionless.

"Raquel?" I heard Luis's voice.

"I'm here!" I scanned the commotion, trying to locate him.

Someone must have found a light switch because suddenly the place was flooded with harsh fluorescent light. I lowered my swollen, twitching eyes, covering them until they adapted to the brightness, and as I opened them, the first sight was the grim form of my uncle sprawled out before me. Blood pooled around his head like a dirty red halo. Luis rushed in and stepped over the body to reach me.

"You don't have to see anymore, my love," he said, sheltering me in his embrace. "You're safe. Safe."

"You cannot arrest us," yelled Esteban, "we're on our own property."

"*Boludo!*" Said a dusty-voiced cop, "it is not legal to run your own prison."

"The Church will protect us, you'll see," he said as they dragged him up the stairs.

CHAPTER THIRTY-FOUR

Two policemen went over to Nico's cell.

"That man needs medical attention," I said. "The keys should be there somewhere . . . . near my . . . uh . . . Zorrilla, near this body."

"Raquel, don't worry about all that, they'll take care of him," said Luis.

The jangle of the keys triggered a fear reflex and I felt my body go rigid.

"Don't worry, my darling," said Luis, "it's over."

"*Está muerto, señora,*" said a cop in Nico's cell.

"Dead? Nico is dead?" I asked.

Luis placed a delicate kiss at the center of my forehead. "I don't know what he did to get locked up," he said, "but he certainly didn't protect you. Look what they've done to you." He pulled out a handkerchief and wiped away the debris from my cheeks and forehead.

"*Señora*, do you know the name of this man?" Asked the cop.

"Durman," I said. "Nicolás Durman." In my mind I pictured Nico the first time he'd told me his name on the dance floor at Gricel.

"She needs medical care," said Luis, "you can get those details later."

"The medical team is right upstairs, sir," said the cop. I could hear their voices clearly, but the swelling had left my vision so foggy that I saw everything in a haze. I clung to Luis as he steered me around the corpse and blood on the ground. In that commanding voice he'd used with the copy machine problem he demanded that the cops bring a gurney or a chair for me.

"No," I said, "let me walk freely into the elevator and out the front door." I wanted to exit this place on my own two feet, with dignity.

"Are you okay to walk?" asked Luis as we moved uncertainly toward the elevator.

"Raquel! My God, they beat you!" Said Paco, approaching. "I'm so sorry." I felt the warmth of his hand on the top of my head. "*¡Ay, Dios!*"

"Don't cry, Paco, it's not your fault," I said. "Not your fault."

A stranger in a white shirt or jacket approached me and tried to separate me from Luis. "Stop," I barked. "Don't touch me."

"You need medical care, *señora*. We want to help you," he said.

"Don't touch me!" I screamed. "Luis, stay with me."

"I won't leave you," he said.

"I want to walk," I said, though my legs quivered like young tree limbs in a storm.

Luis and Paco had replaced the brutal guards that had dragged me along that route, and now each step was a victory. Past the gate. Through the big wooden door. Then, into the elevator, and we ascended. At the front door I stopped, startled to see the night sky. "Oh, it's night!" I breathed in the fresh free air. Then my body started to shake uncontrollably, and tears poured out of me. "I don't feel sad," I said, "I am just crying. My body is crying." I let the EMT carefully place an oxygen mask on my face, and they lowered me slowly onto a stretcher. I remember that Luis held my hand. I saw an ambulance. Maybe they put me in it. I don't remember.

The ceiling fan overhead captivated my attention with its circular motion until I slowly recognized my surroundings. I was back in my apartment, in my own bed, and through the skylight, I could see my own little patch of blue sky. I started to smile, but smiling hurt my face, and I wanted to retreat back into sleep. I covered my head and wrapped the bedding tightly around me, like a swaddled newborn, comforted by the cocoon-like embrace of the linens.

"Are you awake?" Luis whispered from the foot of the bed. Slowly, I lowered the sheet just enough to reveal my eyes.

"Is it morning?" I asked.

"It is for you."

"And for everyone else?"

"It is three in the afternoon."

"How long did I sleep?"

"14 hours. But you can sleep more if you like. You need to heal."

"No. Don't let me sleep. I want to stay awake. I want to savor my freedom." Tears oozed from my eyes. "How many days have I been free, Luis?"

Quickly he was by my side, stroking my hair with his warm fingers. "*Querida*, you've only been home since yesterday. And before that the two days in the hospital, do you remember them?"

"Four days? I've been free four days? I want to remember every minute," I said.

"Thank God, Paco knew the right people to search for you, people who know the terrain and the old buildings around there," he said. "I was so frustrated, and I was so useless."

"How *did* they find me?"

"Well, first your phone message helped us determine the time it took from the accident site to the arrival point. Then also there was a reference to Zorrilla's stone house in the letters," he said. "The problem was, we didn't know we had the letters."

"But I told Jessica to give them directly to you."

"Well, I wasn't in the office when she returned, so she put them on my desk.

But the envelope was marked "*Exámenes*", not "Letters", so we couldn't find them. I had laid out a blueprint on top of them. It wasn't until I picked up that blue print that I realized I'd had the letters all along. Why did you write *Exámenes*?"

"Oh, that was the envelope I got from the *locutorio* when I made the copies. I intended to cross it out at home and write *Letters* on the front. Obviously, I forgot to do that. Almost a fatal mistake."

"Well, once we found them we had a whole team of people reading through them, searching for clues. When we got that mention of a country house, we put it together with the length of time it took you to get to the place where you called. Paco's researchers went to work looking up all the properties owned by the church within the radius of where we lost you on the highway. Your phone call was a big help, I only wish I could have talked to you. Oh, and then there was the cab driver."

"Cab driver?"

"Yes, a cab driver came to *El Alef* with the license number of Nico's car!"

"Alfonso!"

"He said he knew you, and that you had told him the tango singer was going to pick you up in front of Club Español."

"Oh my God. He must have been watching us."

"It turned out to be a good clue because the cops sent out a bulletin for a red Alfa Romeo with that license, and by the morning of the day we found you, we had focused on a geographic sector on the map. When a cop spotted that Alfa outside that house, we knew we'd found you."

"Alfonso." All I could do was say his name and shake my head in amazement.

"I had his card in my bag. My bag! What happened to my bag?" Fear flushed through me.

"It's downstairs," said Luis, quickly, "don't worry."

"It should be against the Geneva Convention to imprison a woman without her purse," I said.

He broke out in a hearty laugh. I loved to hear it, and I loved to have caused it, even though I was deadly serious. "It's true! You have no idea what a violation it is to have your purse taken."

Wrapping himself carefully around me, we lay like spoons in the kitchen drawer. "I will have to tell you what happened to me, Luis," I said.

"Tell me whatever you want, whenever you are ready," he said.

"I want you to know it all, even though you may want to leave me."

"Leave you? I never want to let you out of my sight again."

"But you don't know the whole story. I wasn't just beaten."

"Raquel, I thought I might have lost you. Now, that I have you with me, I will never let go."

Over the following days I got the courage to relate the complete events of the stone house. Well, I didn't go into unnecessary details, and I did not reveal the cuts still bandaged over my breast. Luis listened compassionately, he even cried with me. And when he knew the whole story, he let me know that none of it had changed his mind or heart.

"I love you, Raquel," he said. "After Mari's death, I thought I'd never love another woman. But when you were lost, I realized how lucky I was that love had come to me a second time. I swore that if you came back to me, I would never risk losing you again."

I liked the sound of that determination, though deep within I knew it wouldn't be easy. I hadn't seen the scar myself, but I knew that it could pose a challenge, for me as well as for Luis. That's when I remembered the message carved into the stone. "Let me love again." Even though I wanted nothing more passionately, it would take time.

"I have to return to California eventually, you know. I hope you have a lot of frequent flyer miles," I said.

"Plenty," he said.

Hearing Marta's voice was an indescribable pleasure. I told her simply that I had been with Tío Mateo when he died, in a remote location. She guessed that there was more than what I was revealing, but she'd wait to hear it all in person. Tía Leti, unfortunately, had retreated into her own world of distorted perceptions. She recognized Marta occasionally, but Mateo had sunk into the quicksand of her dementia. She'd been moved into a hospice facility, giving Marta a much-needed rest. Of course, she expected me to be coming home since my task had been completed. I couldn't tell her that I wasn't yet physically or emotionally strong enough to make such a long trip, so I lied and said I'd broken a bone in my foot, and the trip would be too difficult. I had to wait for a doctor's clearance.

When I was finally able to get David on the phone he was uncharacteristically talkative. On and on he went, acquainting me with his renewed love of soccer and the friendships he'd made since we'd last talked. I guessed there was a girlfriend, too, though he didn't name her. When I said I'd buy his ticket so that he could come to Buenos Aires for Christmas, he explained that he'd promised to go to his father's for the holiday. They had the new baby, a little brother, so he couldn't disappoint Dad. He'd see me at spring break, whether I came back to California or he came south. I had to agree.

CHAPTER THIRTY-FIVE

The gruff voice of *Doña Nina* was an auditory welcome mat to *El Alef.* On my way through the patio I stopped to stand in the presence of the canaries that I had previously thought of as serene monks in their cells. Today I saw the bars of their cages as if I were sitting inside them. Perhaps the demeanor I'd read as serenity was actually a despondent acceptance of captivity, I thought.

"Raquel," said Luis from the residence door. I turned to see him standing just where he'd stood on the first morning he brought me there. When I came up next to him I realized that I was completely different from the woman I had been only weeks ago.

"Do you remember the first time you opened this door for me?" I asked.

"Of course. I thought you were one beautiful pain in the ass," he said

"Really! And now?"

"Now, I . . ."

"Luis? Raquel? I thought I heard your voices." Paco welcomed me back with a gentle embrace. His expression reminded me that my face was still a suggestion of my ordeal. He took me by the arm and walked me into the salon with an affectionate, "Watch your step."

La Maestra and her beloved Juan had created a school and a philosophy that inspired the application of tango elements to all aspects of life. They emphasized harmony and respect for Earth and humans, yet the rotting hearts of my uncle and his followers had cast a long toxic shadow across their accomplishments.

"Seems like I've been gone a very long time," I said.

"Well, you spent four days and nights in hell, plus two days in the hospital, and several more just recuperating."

"Paco, I thought about Carmina so many times," I said. "I didn't suffer as she did, but I understand her so much better." Tears seeped from the corners of my eyes. "I don't know how to stop crying," I said in frustration. "I absorbed so much violence. What can I do, Paco? How can I make the tears subside?"

Gingerly, he took my face into his hands. "There are people who can help you, Raquel," he said softly. "Therapists and specialists who work with those who've been imprisoned as you were. Believe me, Argentina has trained many therapists with such a specialty. We will find you someone."

"Thank you."

"Just remember that you are not alone," he said. "I am here,

Luis is by your side, and *La Maestra* and Nina will support you, too."

"Where is *La Maestra?*"

"I am right here."

I turned to see her coming toward me from the kitchen. Though elegance and grace could never fail her, *La Maestra* walked more slowly than usual and was supported by a cane. She was pale, and thinner.

"*Maestra*," I said, embracing her.

"Welcome home, Persephone," she said, stroking my hair and gazing into my face. "We were so worried about you."

"What did you call me, *Maestra?*"

"You are our Persephone, my dear. Taken from us into the underworld and later released. I might have mentioned her in class."

The allusion was haunting. "Yes, *Maestra*," I said, "but I have to give credit where it is due; I was not released, but rescued. I looked first at Luis, then at Paco. "My confinement gave me time to think about *duende, Maestra*," I said. "I don't think I need to work on that anymore. I do feel like Persephone, except that as I recall, she had to return to the underworld every year. For me, thank God, I may only return in my mind, and even that is painful."

"Well, as Paco says, we are all here to love you. It is so good to see you," she said, wrapping me in her twig-like arms.

"But you are so thin, *Maestra*."

"Looks like Nina needs to fatten us both, heh?" she said, holding me at arms' length.

"I still have some bruises, and this swelling, as you see. But I'm much better than I was when Paco and Luis found me in that filthy cell. My face was crusted with dirt and blood. Tears were all I had to wash myself."

She put her arms around me again and held me for a long minute. "I am so sorry," she said, "I brought such violence into *your* life."

"No, *Maestra*, I brought that man back into your life. I hope this dark episode has not robbed you of your energy and health."

"No, my dear," she said. "Not all the villains of this world walk on two legs. I am fighting with a villain of my own. His name is Leukemia."

"*Maestra!*"

"The doctors say my prognosis is good, for my age. I am under treatment, but sometimes the treatment makes me sicker than I'd be without it."

A deep hollow ache bore into my gut. "I don't know what to say, *Maestra*."

"There is nothing to say, *hija*. Along with treatment, I can have transfusions. I am tougher than I look. I have at least several more productive years in me. Plus, I have a secret weapon."

"What's that?"

"I have tango! Dancing tango is healing to the body and the mind. It releases endorphins. So, with tango as medicine, and Paco as my partner, I know I will last longer than those doctors expect."

The kitchen door swung open and Nina came in carrying a tray of tempting delights. She set it down on the coffee table, then ambled over to me. We embraced without a word. She smelled of saffron and freshly ground black pepper. Tears traveled the crevices and ravines of her old face as she kissed me on one cheek, then the other. Then she squeezed my shoulders.

"You too skinny," she scolded. "Nina will make you *una paella* for coming home dinner. Today, *coma*, eat *tortilla española, aceitunas, pan, y queso*." She started to guide me over to the sofa. "Beatriz," she said, turning back to *La Maestra*, "*tu también. Coma tortilla.*"

We gathered round the coffee table and shared Nina's repast over talk of the *Alef* community, and stories about the *milonga* scene as if I'd been away for months. But I knew we had to address a topic still unmentioned.

"I know you are wary of bringing up the subject, so let me begin," I said. "My uncle was a man who rotted from the inside out. I could see that the accident that took part of his body in childhood, also tore away part of his humanity. He never recovered from it, probably because it was only the first of many events that continued to poison him."

"You're not trying to make excuses for him again, are you?" *La Maestra* asked.

"No, but it was too easy to hate him, *Maestra*. I had to look deeper into him. I could see that brutality had built up in him over time. Violence ate away at his mind and body. His alcoholism, kidney problems, and probably heart disease and diabetes literally poisoned him with his own venom." She and Nina sat quietly. "He was a very sick man," I continued. "I want you to know, *Maestra*, that he didn't seem to have had anything to do with the disappearance of your loved ones, though he believed they were leftists who wanted to take over the country."

La Maestra nodded, and pressed her lips together. "Nina and I have worried that we pushed you too hard to find Zorrilla," she said. "We thought he would never harm his own flesh and blood. Then, when you were lost, we feared he might harm you just because of your connection to us."

"Finding my uncle was a big part of why I came to Buenos Aires. Who could have guessed, when Carolina introduced me to you, that the man I was looking for had been haunting you for decades. Of course, he did *not* want to be found, and apparently once he learned I was looking for him, and that I was studying at *El Alef*, well, I became a suspicious character despite my lineage. He had no idea, of course, that his 'victory' at Rio Olvidado had any connection to you. I hate to say it, but he remembered it with pride. Anyway, Nico became his spy without knowing of his father's connection to me."

"I feel so responsible," said *La Maestra*.

"*Maestra*, you didn't put him in my family."

"By the way," said Paco, "a report came in this morning about the death of Nicolás Durman. Apparently, he suffered several broken ribs and a lacerated spleen as the result of a beating. One of those ribs punctured a lung. He died of internal bleeding."

Hearing Nico's medical report brought back the cadaverous stench of the dungeon, and a shiver rippled through me. I went over to sit on the arm of Luis's chair knowing that the fragrance of his cologne could serve as aromatherapy.

"Are you okay?" he asked.

"Yes," I said, "but let me squeeze in with you."

"Can I ask you, Raquel," said Paco, "why was Nico in a cell?"

"Oh, it's an unpleasant story," I said, "He was responsible for my wounds"

"So Zorrilla punished him?"

"Well, I can only say that Nico's death was another violent twist in a long chain of events. For all my uncle's hatred and racism, he loved Nico as his own son. It would have broken his gangrenous old heart to know that Nico died beside him."

"You know," said Paco, "the police had just surrounded the house when we heard that gunshot. Fortunately, they didn't waste any time getting in there. If that Guardia had not been in a state of shock and chaos, there could have been many injuries and perhaps worse. The sergeant told me they discovered a storeroom full of guns and rifles."

"No one threatened me with a gun," I said. "Of course, I was hooded so much of the time that if they had a gun, the threat was lost on me. I never saw any of the Guardia without their hoods until the very end. Those hoods made them threatening *without* weapons."

"I should have known that the stakes were too high to get you involved," he said. "I knew Zorrilla had been a part of a pro-Nazi clergy. I never should have put you in that situation."

"Are you saying that my uncle's anti-Semitism was not an isolated factor?"

"Not at all. Those who disappeared during "*El Proceso*" were disproportionately Jewish. In fact, . . ."

"*Basta!*" said *Doña Nina*, getting everyone's attention. "We talk of something new. Beatriz, tell Raquel *nuestra decisión.*"

"*Sí, sí, Nina,*" said *La Maestra*. "Raquel, we were so sorry to send you into such danger, that Nina and I decided that the past has no place in our lives anymore. History will vibrate in the memory of these bodies, but we will not paint every new day with a black brush."

"My family," said *Doña Nina*, tapping her heart, "at peace inside now."

"I'm very glad," I said. "You know we've all been players in a story that began over ninety years ago."

"Your uncle's story began in 1492, with the Reconquista of Spain!" scoffed *La Maestra*.

"You're right, *Maestra*," I said, "the Inquisition was still vibrating in his bones."

CHAPTER THIRTY-SIX

For several days I did nothing but savor the phenomenon of freedom. Before my misadventure in the stone house, I presumed that freedom was a birthright. As an American, my freedom is insured by the U. S. Constitution. Outside of the obvious social and systemic inequities of being a woman and a person of color, I never questioned my basic right to live freely anywhere in the world. But in captivity, I relished even the tiniest opportunity to exercise my free will. Checking the time became a subversive act. So when Luis and I went back to *El Alef* for Nina's *paella* dinner, I took *La Maestra* out into the patio to visit the canaries. "*Maestra*," I said, "if you will just open their cage door, they can choose to stay inside or leave."

"I'm not sure that canaries are the same as people, Raquel," she said. "I worry that they will not know how to survive in the wild, or how to return home safely. I promise to think about this and give you my answer when I have one. Is that acceptable?"

"Since they are so well cared for, *Maestra*," I said, "yes. I trust you to ponder it."

Lingering at the dinner table after the sumptuous meal, we came to a quiet lull in the conversation. "Raquel," said *La Maestra*, "I have something important to say."

She hadn't had time to think about the canaries, so the announcement piqued my curiosity.

"Sounds important, *Maestra*, I can't wait to hear."

"I am tough enough to fight this leukemia for years, but my energy drains away at times, and I cannot keep up all the demands of *El Alef*. So, I want you to assist me."

"*Maestra!*" I said.

"Before you can do that you must attend more classes, of course, and I want you to read Juan's essays and journals. I have never allowed another person to see his work."

"His journals?" I was almost speechless.

"Yes. I even have a few journals from his school days. I think I told you, he and Gardel went to the same school in Almagro. Juan was younger, but there was a great *amistad* between them always. Once, when Carlos was singing in Paris he sent Juan a post card of the Eiffel Tower. Juan kept it in a box of mementos with a map where he marked Gardel's travels. In fact, it was Gardel's death that sent Juan on his spiritual journey."

Suddenly I had a deeper sense of Juan Alvarez's place in tango history. And I have to admit that the image of Nico singing Gardel on the stage of Café Tortoni flashed through my mind.

"I told Paco," she continued, "it's time to plan the future of the school, beyond my own lifetime. No one has walked through fire as you have. You are a remarkable woman, and I think you can guide *El Alef* into the future."

I was stunned. "I don't know what to say." I looked at Luis. "Did you know about this?"

"No," he said. "But it's wonderful."

"I have to admit," she said, "when I first saw that you and Luis had fallen in love, I began to think about this possibility, but I wasn't sure the relationship would endure, and I didn't know you enough. Now, I know that Juan would share my opinion of you."

"I am so honored, *Maestra*," I said. "I can't express how I feel."

"Think about it, of course," she said. "First, you need time to heal from your recent trauma, and I know you have a life in California to consider. You wouldn't have to be in Buenos Aires all the time. Your son may need you, but we don't have classes in January anyway, so you could spend part of the year in California."

"You've had more time to think about my future than I have," I said. "In fact, just a few days ago, I didn't know if I'd have a future. I'm very flattered by your proposal, but I'm glad you realize that I need to think about it."

"Of course, my dear," she said. "Take your time."

The encounter with my uncle had destroyed all surviving shreds of my Roman Catholicism, and in the weeks after my rescue, I wondered how Carmina Perraza could cling to her rosary. I remembered the worn crucifix clutched in that trembling hand, the body of Jesus worn smooth under the constant grasp of her fingers. Was she punishing him, I wondered, or trying to assure herself that he'd never leave her again? More than ever, I wanted to believe in something. I missed the God of my childhood, the omnipotent He with mysterious reasons for everything, and the protector who sent guardian angels to keep me safe. Without that Him or someone to take his place, I feared that my battered psyche would never heal. Christmas found me, as it did the year my parents died, caught in an impenetrable mourning.

Without David or Marta near me, I stayed in my apartment listening to tangos, and studying their lyrics. Paco invited me to a Hannukah celebration, but I declined. Luis begged me to join him at his daughter's house for Christmas Eve, but I didn't want to cast a shadow on their festive celebration. Instead, my spirit paced the apartment, heavy with distrust for the world. I knew I couldn't seriously consider *La Maestra's* offer to teach at *El Alef* until some part of me could stand in sunlight without suspicion. I envied children at the shopping mall still believing in Santa Claus, the baby Jesus, wise men, and stars. Wonderment itself was a vexation.

I thought again and again of the message left in the dungeon as if it had been left there just for me. Perhaps, I thought, *déjeme amar de nuevo* doesn't just refer to romantic love, or even human relationships exclusively. It seemed my greatest challenge was to love the world again, and whether I ascribed my relationship to one with God or not, loving the world would be a way of loving God. I couldn't live in a world in which my uncle or anyone could kidnap God. If anything God was held for ransom in my uncle's life. He'd been manipulated and misled from childhood. He was, in the end, the saddest person I'd ever known.

I thought about Genesis and the very beginning of everything: In the beginning was the Word and the Word was God. I remembered that in other translations the Word was equivalent to breath. In the beginning was the breath.

I took a deep breath. "In two, three. Out two three," I said. "Oh."

Suddenly I realized that my breathing, that practice I turned to when everything got hardest, was a way of praying. Could that be possible, I wondered. Yes, I decided, it could.

On the first Tuesday after Christmas, Luis arrived with a mandate: "Get your purse and a sweater," he said.

"Why? Where are we going?" Like all people who've abandoned hope, I didn't want to be cheered up.

"We're going to the museum, and the air conditioning can get chilly," he said. "And put on some lipstick and blush, you look ghostly."

"I don't want to go to the museum," I said. "I was just going to make tea."

"We can have tea at the museum," he said, nudging me out of my chair.

"What museum are you taking me to?"

"MALBA."

"What kind of art is that?"

"The art of the living and the dead," he said emphatically.

Finally, I relented and made myself presentable. On the way to the car, my heartbeat quickened, and I felt suddenly off balance.

"Wait!" I said, grabbing Luis's arm.

"What's wrong? Did you forget something?"

I couldn't speak. I just looked at the ground, breathing with all my might.

"Look at me," he commanded. He took my face in his hands, and brought me eye to eye with him. "You are feeling anxiety again, I presume." I couldn't find my voice, and my vision became a liquid blur, so I nodded.

"You are a *free* person," he said. "The sky is up, and the earth is down, and gravity holds everything in place. If you have to believe in something, you can believe in that until something better comes along. Now, take one deep breath." I followed his instruction. "That old man died in that cellar, Raquel," he continued. "He didn't take you with him, and I'm not letting him take you now. I love you. Do you hear me?"

My breathing restored, I finally found words. "I hear you," I said, "but I have to ask you something."

"What?"

"Carla. Do you still see Carla?" Poisonous fantasies had haunted my mind for weeks and I'd grown fearful of being near him, suspicious that Carla had made herself an alluring and compassionate companion again.

"Raquel, I will only say this one more time. It wouldn't matter if I saw her every day. I do not love Carla. I don't lust after Carla. Yes, when you were gone, she tried to console me. So I made it clear to her that I love *you*, and your *safe* return was the only consolation that would help me." He looked at me directly, "I need you to believe that, so we can leave it all behind us. All of it, Raquel: Zorrilla, Carla, Nico, the dungeon, the whole thing!"

I looked into his eyes. My vision cleared. "I believe you," I said, and suddenly I realized that I did believe him. I knew I could choose to keep wading in the dark ocean of memories, or I could stop here. He wasn't hiding anything from me, he was begging me to come back into the world with him. All I had to do was take his hand.

"I've been afraid to love you, Luis. Afraid because of her, and also because I've become suspicious of life. I'm sorry to be so difficult. You know there was something in the dungeon that I didn't mention to you. I found some words carved into one of the stones. It said, *Dejeme amar de nuevo.* Now I know that if you will hold onto me, I can do that. Your love will give me that strength."

"I need you to do that, *querida*. I don't care if you believe in God, I just need you to believe in me." He pulled me to him and kissed me.

The tall light-filled galleries of the museum lifted my spirit. I felt like a child, as if experiencing for the first time a building dedicated to the creative spirit. It made me realize that I still carried the dark enclosure of the cell inside me. I had let it darken the world around and within me. But as I studied the colorful paintings of accomplished Latin American artists whose names and work I'd never known, I realized that there was still a lot of life – a lot of light - to be discovered. If I could push against the darkness that had inhabited me, I could do more than survive. I could create every day spontaneously, just as I would create a work of art.

Gallery after gallery I consciously breathed in the vivacity of the work and the energy of the people engaged in lively discussions, sharing observations. Luis's words echoed in my mind, "I just need you to believe in me." The warmth of him beside me fueled my determination. He understood me. He knew the most likely environment to resuscitate my flagging spirit: "The art of the living and the dead". There it was, all around me: The human drive to flourish in color, line, composition, texture, and shapes, constantly reformed by imagination and invention. I suddenly remembered that creativity had been my weapon in the cell, too. Though inadequate to the force of my captors, my sharp-thorned roses were the weapons of my creativity, like the names and images of loved ones, they rose up in my defense and my instinct to survive.

"I believe in Art," I said, feeling triumphant.

"Of course you do. You always did," he said. "You just lost touch with yourself."

"And I wish I knew the name of whatever brought you into my life."

"Tango brought me into your life," he said.

"Yes. So it did. Then I believe in Tango, too."

ABOUT THE AUTHOR

Adriana Díaz is a writer, artist, educator, and life coach. A bilingual native Californian, she is the grandchild of Spanish immigrants. Adriana began studying Argentine Tango in 1994 in both California and Buenos Aires, and in 2000 she won the first American Salon Tango Championship. Her first book, Freeing the Creative Spirit, a non-fiction guide to creativity as a fulfilling personal and spiritual experience, was published by HarperSan Francisco in 1992. Her essays and poetry have been published in anthologies and magazines. She has a Master's Degree in Culture and Spirituality, and a long history as a teacher, and an exhibiting painter.

www.adrianadiaz.com